WOMEN, WORK,

AND FAMILY

IN THE SOVIET UNION

WOMEN, WORK, AND FAMILY

IN THE SOVIET UNION

Edited with an introduction by
Gail Warshofsky Lapidus

M.E. Sharpe, Inc.
Armonk, New York
London

Copyright © 1982 by M. E. Sharpe, Inc.
80 Business Park Drive, Armonk, New York 10504

Russian texts are translated by arrangement with VAAP, the USSR Copyright Agency.

Translated by Vladimir Talmy.

Library of Congress Cataloging in Publication Data

Main entry under title:

Women, work, and family in the Soviet Union.

    Translated from the Russian.
    "Published simultaneously as vol. XXIV. no. 5-7 of Problems of Economics"—T.p. verso.
    Bibliography: p.
    1. Women—Soviet union—Addresses, essays, lectures.
2. Women—Employment—Soviet Union—Addresses, essays, lectures.
3. Family—Soviet Union—Addresses, essays, lectures. I. Lapidus, Gail Warshofsky.
HQ1662.W63   305.4'0947   81-9281
ISBN 0-87332-181-2   AACR2

Printed in the United States of America

Table of Contents

Preface

In the course of the past fifteen years, questions of female
employment and its impact on family structure and demographic trends have come to the forefront of both scholarly research and public controversy in the USSR. These questions
have already provoked a series of major new policy initiatives,
most notably those announced at the Twenty-sixth Party Congress in 1981, and they will continue to pose policy dilemmas
for the Soviet political agenda throughout the 1980s and beyond.

This volume is designed to offer an overview of current
Soviet concerns by presenting a selection of the best recent
Soviet writings on these subjects in English translation. The
materials have been selected with three objectives in mind:
to illuminate the problems which stand at the center of current
discussions, to present the findings of some of the more recent
Soviet research on female employment and demographic
trends, and to offer a glimpse of current policy debates by including articles which express diverse points of view. The
duplication of previously translated materials has deliberately
been kept to a minimum; where appropriate, the reader's attention will be drawn to such studies in the notes. For the
benefit of readers who wish to pursue these issues further, a
selected bibliography of both Russian and English-language
books and articles is included.

Acknowledgments

I would like to express my appreciation to the Institute for International Studies at the University of California at Berkeley for its research support, to Murray Feshbach of the Foreign Demographic Analysis Division of the U.S. Department of Commerce for his generous assistance and advice, and to the Rockefeller Foundation for the opportunity to complete this project in the lovely setting of the Villa Serbelloni. John Litwack, Barry Jordan, and Bob Weinberg deserve recognition for their assistance in the painstaking task of revising and polishing the translation.

I would also like to thank Joseph Hollander of M. E. Sharpe, who provided the mixture of initiative, support, and patience needed to launch this undertaking, and my son Alex, who provided the mixture of encouragement and impatience needed to bring it to completion.

G.W.L.

Introduction
Women, Work, and Family:
New Soviet Perspectives

Gail W. Lapidus

In the industrial societies of Europe and the United States,
as in the developing countries of the Third World, the relationship between changes in women's economic roles and changes
in the structure and functions of the family has attracted growing attention from social scientists and policy-makers alike.
The scope and pattern of female employment, it is increasingly
recognized, exert a critical influence on many other aspects
of economic and social behavior, and most importantly on
fertility.

In virtually all industrial societies, rising levels of female
labor force participation have been accompanied by rising divorce rates and declining birthrates, provoking widespread
anxiety among many observers that the family itself is threat-
ened by current trends. Throughout Western Europe, and now
in the United States as well, a whole array of economic and
social programs is being reassessed with a view to their impact on family stability and size. For policy analysts concerned with the Third World, on the other hand, these linkages
present an opportunity rather than a problem: they hold out the
prospect that development strategies which enhance the educa-

tional and employment opportunities of women will not only
increase national income but also contribute significantly to
efforts at population control.

In the social sciences and in policy studies, prompted in
large measure by recent feminist scholarship, these issues
have stimulated fresh research in a number of intellectual
disciplines. Demography, social and family history, the new
"social economics," and industrial and family sociology have
all been enriched by a growing body of research and writings
addressed to the interdependence of women's work and family
roles.

Impinging as it does on all these concerns, the Soviet experience deserves the close attention of social scientists and
policy analysts alike. An extensive reliance on female labor
has been a central feature of the Soviet pattern of industrialization over several decades, with important consequences for
virtually every aspect of economic and social life. The highest
female labor force participation rates of any industrial society
are to be found in the USSR — over 51% of all workers and
employees are women — at the same time that sharply declining birthrates have already made the single-child family the
norm in the urban regions of the European USSR. Moreover,
important regional and ethnic variations, linked to sociocultural as well as economic differences, make the Soviet Union
a fascinating universe for comparative analysis. The economic
and demographic patterns characteristic of the European regions of the country contrast sharply, for example, with those
which prevail in the largely agricultural Moslem republics of
Soviet Central Asia.

While these economic and demographic trends deserve
closer study in their own right, Soviet reactions to them are
also of considerable interest. Widely differing assessments of
the causes of current developments, and of their implications
for larger economic, social, and military priorities, regularly
appear in Soviet publications. Closer analysis of these discussions reveals much about the scope and limits of public debate in contemporary Soviet society and about the role of so-

cial scientists in the formation of public policy.

Until the mid-1960s high levels of female labor force participation in the modern sector of the economy were viewed as
unambiguous evidence that socialism and sexual equality went
hand in hand. Soviet policy, official sources claimed, had created optimal conditions for the harmonious combination of female work and family roles. If no feminist movement had
emerged within the USSR, it was because these questions had
been happily resolved.[1]

Beginning in the mid-1960s, however, in specialized publications designed for internal audiences, ritual self-congratula-
tion began to give way to serious discussions of "shortcomings" and ultimately of "contradictions" in Soviet everyday
life. A growing array of scholarly studies, to which female
economists, sociologists, and demographers were important
contributors, began to document in some detail the low level
of skill, mobility, and income of women workers, the heavy and
conflicting demands of their dual roles, and the harmful effects of poor working conditions and inadequate social services
on the health and well-being of working mothers and their
families.[2] Rising divorce rates and declining birthrates provoked particular concern, challenging as they did the comfortable assumption that under "developed socialism," economic
progress and social stability went hand in hand. As a dis-
tinguished family sociologist ruefully put it:

> While growing prosperity since the end of World War II
> has strengthened the family, the positive influence is not
> as direct as had been expected. Life shows that improved
> conditions and equal rights for both sexes do not auto-
> matically strengthen the institution of marriage.[3]

These anxieties were not confined to the scholarly literature
alone. Trade union and party meetings as well as scholarly
conferences began to devote themselves to discussions of female labor and everyday life. The Twenty-fourth Party Congress officially proclaimed the need for a comprehensive na-

tional demographic policy, while the Twenty-sixth Party Congress explicitly inaugurated one. And Brezhnev himself, addressing the Trade Union Congress in 1977, admitted: "We men... have thus far done far from all we could to ease the dual burden that [women] bear both at home and in production."[4]

With growing awareness that effective economic planning demanded greater attention to the social requisites and social consequences of economic policies, the work of labor economists was increasingly supplemented by a growing body of sociological and demographic surveys in a carefully circumscribed but officially sanctioned rebirth of social science research.[5] Social planning was now explicitly incorporated into the Soviet policy agenda.

Official public discussion formed only the tip of a far larger iceberg of private dissatisfaction. Natalia Baranskaia's evocation of "A Week Like Any Other" in the harried life of a young scientific worker, wife, and mother gave fictional expression to the stresses and conflicts faced by millions of her counterparts in daily life.[6] Two decades later the samizdat publication of the first Soviet feminist journal, with its implicit repudiation of the official view that the "woman question" had been solved in the USSR, would be greeted by the expulsion from the USSR of its four founding editors — a dramatic revelation of the extent of official sensitivity and the limits to public discussion.

The reassessment of earlier assumptions and policies which began in the mid-1960s was prompted by the emergence of two serious and interrelated problems. First and foremost was the declining birthrate. Its ominous implications for future political and military power, for the supply of labor resources, for the balance between the productive and the dependent age cohorts in the total population, and above all for the ethnic structure of the USSR brought demographic problems to the forefront of political concern. At the same time, the virtual exhaustion of the vast labor reserves which had traditionally fed the expanding Soviet economy compelled a shift from an extensive to an intensive strategy of economic development. Future economic growth was now heavily dependent on increased labor productivity and the optimal utilization of all available labor resources. Given the irreplaceable contribution of women to both production and reproduction, the conflicting requirements of these two overarching priorities created profound policy dilemmas and established the framework for subsequent debates.

Soviet discussions of these issues turn on five distinct but interrelated questions which this essay will explore in turn. First and foremost, what is the optimal level of female labor force participation for the Soviet economy, a level consistent with demographic and social needs? Second, how could female labor be better distributed among different economic sectors and occupations? Third, what changes need to be made in the elaboration and enforcement of protective labor measures to improve the working conditions of the female labor force? A fourth set of issues involves the impact of female labor force participation on family structure and fertility. Finally, what changes in present policies are needed to achieve an optimal balance between female work and family roles?

Female Labor Force Participation: Levels and Determinants

The causes as well as the consequences of high rates of female labor force participation in the modern sector of the Soviet economy are a subject of sharp controversy among Soviet authors. The heavy reliance on female labor which has characterized the Soviet pattern of industrialization had as its rationale the ideological conviction, originating in Marxist-Leninist theory, that the full entry of women into social production held the key to genuine equality. However, it was the inauguration of the First Five-Year Plan which provided its real impetus. Female employment outside agriculture was further accelerated in subsequent decades by the interaction of economic, demographic, and social pressures created by Soviet policy, and above all by the enormous deficit of males. The cumulative

effects of war and civil war, of collectivization, purges, de-
portations, and then of World War II transformed wives and
widows into heads of households and deprived a large proportion of Soviet women of any opportunity to marry. In 1946
there were only 59 men for every 100 women in the 35 to 59
age group.

Although World War II made especially heavy demands on
female labor, female participation rates have not declined in
recent years but have actually risen further, now in response
to deliberate efforts to alleviate the growing labor shortage.
A campaign launched in the early 1960s, and accompanied by
increases in minimum wages and in pension benefits, raised
the cost of not being employed and brought an additional 25
million women into the labor force by the mid-1970s (see Table 1). The average length of female employment increased
from 28.7 to 33.5 years, and the number of nonworking years
fell from 12.3 to 3.6.[7] Today almost 90% of able-bodied adult
women are employed or engaged in study, virtually all full time.

The only remaining major untapped reserves of female labor
are found in the Central Asian and Transcaucasian republics,
where female participation rates outside agriculture — particularly among the local nationalities — remain much lower
than the national average (see Figure 1). In Turkmenistan, for
example, of the total of 516,300 workers and employees in 1973,
only 63,000, or 12%, were women of the local nationality, and
only 14,000 of them were employed in industry or construction.[8] The recruitment of native women into industry has encountered great difficulties in these regions, for reasons that
are examined in the selection by R. A. Ubaidullaeva. A high
proportion of women workers and employees in Central Asia
continue to be Russian and Ukrainian.

Urgent efforts are still under way to locate and utilize every
potential source of additional labor. A special questionnaire
was administered in conjunction with the 1979 Census to establish how many persons of working age were engaged only
in housework or private agriculture and to ascertain under
what conditions (i.e., the availability of day-care or boarding

Introduction

Table 1

Average Annual Number and Percentage of Female Workers and Employees, 1922-80

Year	Total of workers and employees (in thousands)	Number of female workers and employees (in thousands)	Women as % of total
1922	6,200	1,560	25
1926	9,900	2,265	23
1928	11,400	2,795	24
1940	33,900	13,190	39
1945	28,600	15,920	56
1950	40,400	19,180	47
1955	50,300	23,040	46
1960	62,000	29,250	47
1965	76,900	37,680	49
1970	90,200	45,800	51
1973	97,500	49,959	51
1976	104,235	53,632	51
1979	110,592	56,678	51
1980	112,480	57,700	51

Note that women constituted 55% of the total population in 1959 and 63.4% of the age cohort 35 and over.

Sources: Tsentral'noe statisticheskoe upravlenie pri Sovete Ministrov SSSR, Narodnoe khoziaistvo SSSR; 1922-1972 (Moscow, 1972), pp. 345 and 348; idem., Zhenshchiny SSSR (Moscow, 1975), pp. 28-29; idem., Narodnoe khoziaistvo SSSR za 60 let (Moscow, 1977), p. 470; "Zhenshchiny v SSSR," Vestnik statistiki, 1980, no. 1, p. 70; Tsentral'noe statisticheskoe upravlenie pri Sovete Ministrov SSSR, SSSR v tsifrakh v 1978 godu: kratkii statisticheskii sbornik (Moscow, 1979), pp. 178-79; idem., Narodnoe khoziaistvo SSSR v 1979 godu (Moscow, 1980), pp. 387-88, 391; idem., SSSR v tsifrakh v 1980 godu: kratkii statisticheskii sbornik (Moscow, 1981), p. 160.

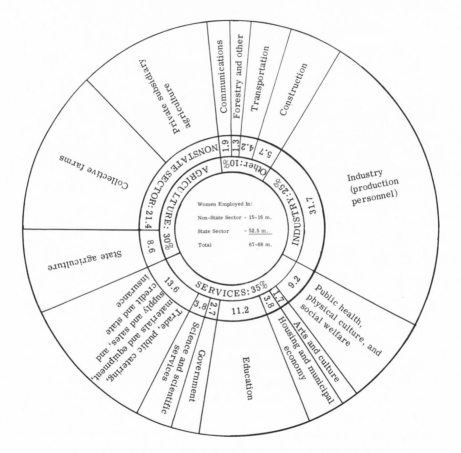

Women Employed In:

Non-State Sector - 15-16 m.

State Sector   - 52.5 m.

Total   67-68 m.

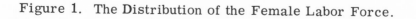

Figure 1.   The Distribution of the Female Labor Force.

school, of part-time work, of work at home or in a particular specialty) such persons would be willing to accept employment.

While no Soviet analysts would publicly challenge the view that high levels of female employment in the modern sector are a progressive phenomenon, and indeed a major achievement of socialism, not all see current participation rates as either natural or desirable. Taking issue with the view that current patterns reflect positive and irreversible changes in the social position of women, some authors, Kotliar and Turchaninova among them, argue that present levels are abnormal and excessive, the result of extraordinary but temporary economic and demographic conditions. Challenging conventional orthodoxies, they insist that

> In and of itself a high level of female employment cannot serve as a criterion of the rational use of female labor resources if it is not associated with the socially necessary level of fertility and rate of population growth.[9]

Their view is shared, as we shall see, by a number of demographers who argue that long-term demographic needs are being sacrificed to short-term economic priorities, and who advocate measures to reduce the level and intensity of female employment in regions where it is especially high.

Surveys which have been conducted to ascertain the attitudes of women themselves have been marshaled in support of both points of view. According to Soviet sociologists the overwhelming majority of women interviewed attached great importance to the contribution of work to economic independence, social status, and personal satisfaction; relatively few indicated they would withdraw from the labor force even if that were to become economically feasible. At the same time, economic need was repeatedly cited as a more central motivation in employment than "broadening of horizons" or "civic satisfaction."[10] A number of Soviet analysts therefore conclude that the "participation of women in social production is, under the conditions of socialism, dictated to a significant extent by economic necessity."[11] As a team of labor economists recently put it:

> The supply of female labor is more elastic [than that of
> males]. It depends to a greater degree on the extent to
> which a family's requirements are satisfied by the earn-
> ings of the head of the family [the male] and by income
> from public consumption funds. The lower the level at
> which these requirements are being satisfied, the more
> the family needs earnings from its women.[12]

The policy implications of this perspective are clear: to the
extent that the Soviet leadership encourages further rises in incomes and in public consumption funds, it will facilitate a slight
reduction in what these analysts view as an excessively high
level of female employment.

However, the fact that participation rates have risen sharply despite the palpable economic improvements of the past twenty years
suggests that other forces are also at work. "Economic need" is
relative; if rising aspirations outrun rising incomes, a second income may still appear essential. Moreover, rising wages increase
the opportunity cost of not being employed, encouraging women to
prefer employment to either larger families or more leisure. In
addition, rising education and professionalism further strengthen
labor force attachment. For all these reasons it is unlikely that female participation rates will undergo a substantial decline in the
years ahead in the absence of far-reaching governmental measures
with a pronatalist thrust. However, the intensity of female participation may be diminished slightly if part-time work and more flexible work schedules are actively encouraged. Indeed, advocates
of such measures can point to much evidence that they would
be especially warmly welcomed by working mothers.

The Distribution of the Female Labor Force

The distribution of the female labor force, both horizontally
across different economic sectors and occupations and vertically
within a given enterprise or occupation, raises a second set of issues for Soviet analysts. As a number of selections translated here

point out, women are heavily concentrated in certain types of economic activity and significantly underrepresented in others. They account for three fourths or more of the labor force in the service sector, public health and social welfare, and education and culture, and only one fourth of the labor force in construction and transportation (see Figure 1 and Table 2). In industry, where women represent almost half of all production personnel, they constitute over 80% of food and textile workers and over 90% of garment workers. Shifting from economic sectors to occupations, women predominate in the lower and middle levels of white-collar employment and the paraprofessions: virtually all nurses, librarians, typists, and stenographers are female, as well as a high proportion of technicians; but women are underrepresented in supervisory and managerial positions.

Moreover, within any given occupation or workplace, women are concentrated at lower levels of the job pyramid. In agriculture, as Fedorova's essay points out, the overwhelming proportion are engaged in heavy manual labor, while men move into the newly mechanized jobs. A similar situation prevails in industry, where women predominate in low-skilled, non-mechanized, and poorly paid positions. The findings of Kotliar and Turchaninova's study of machine-building enterprises parallel those reported for a typical industrial city: 4% of the women workers were in high-skill job classifications, 30% were of average skill, and 66% were low-skilled, compared to 31%, 50%, and 19% respectively for their male counterparts.[13]

This situation cannot be attributed to the predominance of an older generation of women with limited education and few skills; the educational attainments of the female labor force now match and even exceed those of males. Moreover, a recent study of industrial enterprises in Taganrog yielded the interesting fact that 40% of all female workers with higher or secondary specialized education occupied low-skill industrial positions, compared to only 6% of males with comparably high educational attainments.[14] Most striking of all was the fact that the distribution of the male labor force as a whole, without respect to education, was more favorable with respect to high-skill positions than the distribution of this highly educated female contingent. Although Soviet

Table 2

Distribution of Women Workers and Employees and
Average Monthly Earnings, by Economic Sector

Economic sector	Number of women workers and employees	Women as % of labor force	Average monthly earnings (rubles)
Construction	3,002,000	28	196.6
Transport	2,211,000	24	192.8
Industry (production personnel)	1,662,000	49	180.4*
Science and scientific services	2,015,000	50	173.6
Nationwide average	52,539,000	51	163.3
Credit and state insurance	423,000	82	151.5
Apparatus of government and economic administration	1,457,000	65	147.8
Agriculture	4,530,000	44	146.0**
Communications	1,042,000	68	142.6
Education	5,904,000	73	133.3
Trade, public catering, materials and equipment, supply and sales	6,763,000	76	128.8
Housing and municipal economy, everyday services	2,010,000	53	126.7
Arts	207,000	47	124.1
Public health, physical culture, social welfare	4,851,000	84	119.1
Culture	747,000	73	104.7

Sources: Figures on female labor are for 1975, calculated from Tsentral'noe statisticheskoe upravlenie, Narodnoe khoziaistvo SSSR v 1975 g. (Moscow, 1976), pp. 542-43; 546-47; wage data are for 1979, as reported in Tsentral'noe statisticheskoe upravlenie, Narodnoe khoziaistvo SSSR v 1979 godu (Moscow, 1980), pp. 394-95.

*Within industry the average wage of workers was 180.3 rubles, of engineering and technical personnel 208.9, and of the largely female white-collar category 142.9.

**Within agriculture the average wage of workers was 144.9, of engineering-technical personnel 186, and of the largely female white-collar category 123.

analysts differ on this question, at least one specialist on female employment concluded that the available evidence does not demonstrate there has been any appreciable growth in recent years in the proportion of highly skilled and highly paid women workers. Rising levels of educational attainment and labor force participation by Soviet women do not appear to have diminished occupational segregation by sex.

The tendency for the proportion of women to decline as the level of skill, responsibility, and pay rises is as characteristic of the professions as it is of industry. As Table 3 indicates, women have moved upward into technical and specialist positions but not into supervisory roles in the proportions one might expect on the basis of their training and work experience, even in professions, such as teaching and medicine, in which women predominate. When we bear in mind that women constitute almost two thirds of the key administrative age cohort, their absence in managerial roles is especially striking. Rising levels of educational attainment and labor force participation do not appear to have diminished the scope of horizontal and vertical occupational segregation by sex.

As a consequence of this situation, women's earnings in the Soviet Union are considerably lower than those of males. While there are no published national wage data which would permit precise comparisons of male and female earnings, the evidence of fragmentary local samples compiled in Table 4 suggests that average female earnings are about 65-70% of those of males, a figure slightly higher than that calculated for the United States but lower than the 73% prevailing in Scandinavia. A figure in this range is also supported by a detailed study of family budgets conducted among Soviet emigrés in Israel. Comparing basic wages only, female earnings averaged 68% of those of males. When additional sources of income were added, the differential widened from 32 to 41%.[15]

While numerous Soviet studies document the disparities in male and female earnings, they flatly rule out direct wage discrimination as a possible explanation. Even an author highly critical of many aspects of Soviet occupational

Table 3

Proportion of Women in High-Level Positions in
Selected Fields and Institutions

Enterprise management	1959	1970
Enterprise directors (including state farms)	12	13
Heads of shops, sections, departments, and foremen	15	15
Heads of production-technical departments, sectors, groups, offices	20	24
Scholarly research and teaching	1970	1979
Academician, corresponding member, professor	9.9	10.7
Senior research associate	25.1	22.5
Junior research associate and assistant	49.8	47.7
Scientific personnel	38.8	40.0
candidate in science	27.0	28.0
doctorate in science	13.0	14.0
Education	1960/61	1979/80
Directors of secondary schools	20	32
Directors of 8-year schools	23	37
Deputy directors of secondary schools	53	67
Directors of primary schools	69	80
Teachers	70	80
Medicine	1959	1975
Chief physicians	54	53
Physicians	79	74
Midwives and feldshers	84	83
Nurses and pharmacists	99	99

Communist Party	1976	1981
Politburo	0	0
Central Committee: full members	2.8	2.5
candidates	4.3	6.0
Urban and district party secretaries	4 (1973)	n.a.
Party membership	24	25

Executive Committee of a Leningrad district soviet	1962	1966
Chairman, his deputies and secretary of executive council	24.9	24.9
Directors and deputy directors of divisions, directors of sectors	63.1	40.0
Specialists (instructors, inspectors, etc.)	87.2	92.9
Clerical personnel	100.0	100.0

Sources:

Enterprise management: Tsentral'noe statisticheskoe upravlenie, Itogi vsesoiuznoi perepisi naseleniia 1970 goda, vol. 6 (Moscow, 1973), p. 167. According to figures for 1973, women were 9% of all directors of industrial enterprises; Tsentral'noe statisticheskoe upravlenie, Zhenshchiny v SSSR (Moscow, 1975), p. 80.

Scientific work: Tsentral'noe statisticheskoe upravlenie, Narodnoe khoziaistvo SSSR za 60 let (Moscow, 1977), p. 141; Narodnoe khoziaistvo SSSR v 1979 g. (Moscow, 1980), p. 107; "Zhenshchiny v SSSR," Vestnik statistiki, 1981, no. 1, p. 15.

Education: Tsentral'noe statisticheskoe upravlenie, Zhenshchiny i deti v SSSR (Moscow, 1963), p. 127; Vestnik statistiki, 1981, no. 1, p. 73.

Medicine: Tsentra l'noe statisticheskoe upravlenie, Itogi vsesoiuznoi perepisi naseleniia 1970 goda, vol. 6, table 18.

Communist Party: Partiinaia zhizn', 1977, no. 21, p. 32; V. A. Kadeikan et al., eds., Voprosy vnutripartiinoi zhizni i rukovodiashchei deiatel'nosti KPSS na sovremennom etape (Moscow, 1974), pp. 192-93; Pravda, March 6, 1976, p. 2; Radio Liberty Report 171/81, April 28, 1981, p. 6.

Leningrad District Soviet: V. G. Lebin and M. N. Perfilev, Kadry apparata upravleniia v SSSR (Leningrad, 1970), p. 176.

segregation routinely insists that women receive equal pay for equal work.

> ... [working women] as a whole still earn less than their husbands. This is in accordance with the demands of the law of distribution according to labor and in no way signifies [the existence of] any sort of discrimination.[16]

Starting from the premise that wage differentials are essential to the efficient allocation of labor resources, and that existing differentials reflect objective differences in the quantity and quality of labor, Soviet writings tend to focus on the reasons why women choose particular kinds of jobs rather than questioning the prevailing structure of wages or the low value placed on "women's work."

Soviet discussions of occupational segregation begin with the assumption that sex-linked differences in abilities and preferences, largely rooted in biology, shape prevailing patterns of employment; the effects of differential socialization receive relatively little attention. Although the rationale for particular classifications may be questioned, there is widespread acceptance of the distinction in principle between "men's work" and "women's work." Labor economists write routinely about the need to create conditions which correspond to the "anatomical-physiological peculiarities of the female organism and likewise to the moral-ethical temperament of women." They take for granted that "the psycho-physiological makeup of women permits them to carry out certain kinds of work more successfully than men, as, for example, work demanding assiduity, attention, accuracy, and precision."[17] Consistent with these assumptions, each of the 1,100 occupations for which training is offered at Soviet technical-vocational institutions is explicitly designated for males, females, or both sexes, and only 714 are accessible to women.[18]

The central concern in Soviet discussions of occupational segregation is to encourage the transfer of women out of unsuitable jobs and into more appropriately feminine positions.

Only rarely will a Soviet author argue, "Women have no need of 'light work' but of qualified work commensurate with their professional preparation and training, their education, and their talents."[19]

Soviet discussions of why women tend to be heavily concentrated in unskilled and low-paid occupations have recently begun to focus on social as well as biological constraints. They reveal increasing recognition that both the system of formal education and the heavy reliance on continuing education through combining work with study act to limit the occupational mobility of women. Family responsibilities, which, as we shall see, fall heavily on the shoulders of women, aggravate the problem still further. A vicious circle is thus created: women have lower expectations of occupational mobility than their male counterparts; they gravitate toward jobs which are most compatible with their domestic responsibilities; they have less time available for study and are not able to improve their qualifications as rapidly as men; they tend to become stuck in less rewarding and stimulating jobs with few incentives or opportunities for upward mobility; and they are viewed by enterprise managers as less promising and productive, which reduces their leverage and opportunities still further.

Soviet writings have also begun to take note of the subtle but widespread prejudices which further limit women's access to positions of responsibility. One recent study argued that women are widely, though erroneously, believed to have less initiative and creativity than men and to be less suited to managerial positions.[20] Another study demonstrated that even among highly educated scientific personnel, both men and women express a strong preference for males in supervisory roles.[21] After a comprehensive discussion of the recruitment and training of industrial executives in the pages of The Literary Gazette, it took a letter from an irate female reader to point out that "for some reason it seems taken for granted that an executive is a man."[22]

This problem has not gone unrecognized in political circles. Complaints that insufficient attention is paid to recruiting

Table 4

Male-Female Earnings Differentials

	Monthly earnings in rubles		Female earnings as % of male
	males	females	
1. Leningrad and Rostov, 1960s industrial enterprises			69
2. Industrial Center, 1960s	131	84	64.5
3. Leningrad, 1970: workers in machine-building plants,			
unmarried	132.6	98.6	74
married	149.1	108.1	73
4. Kiev workers in light industrial enterprises			83-90
5. Kiev, 1970 20,000 newlyweds	116	84	72
6. Erevan, 1963 3,600 families	114	74	65
7. Latvia, 1967 women who married in 1959	120.8	76	62.9
8. Moldavia, 1965-70 industrial employees	145-55	90-100	58-69
9. Tatar Republic, rural enterprises, 1967:			
manual workers under 35	69	47	68
manual workers 35 and older	60	37	62
nonmanual personnel under 35	109	76	70
nonmanual personnel 35 and older	104	80	74

10. Soviet Jewish emigrés, 1973: 2,100 workers and employees, European Russia			
basic wage	153.6	104.6	68
all earnings	208.5	123.8	59

Sources:

1. E. Z. Danilova, Sotsial'nye problemy truda zhenshchiny-rabotnitsy (Moscow: 1968), p. 23; A. L. Pimenova, "Sem'ia i perspektivy razvitiia obshchestvennogo truda zhenshchin pri sotsializme," Nauchnye doklady Vysshei shkoly: Filosofskie nauki, 1966, no. 3, p. 40.

2. L. A. Gordon and E. V. Klopov, Urbanizatsiia i rabochii klass v usloviiakh nauchno-tekhnicheskoi revoliutsii (Moscow, 1970), pp. 105-6.

3. E. K. Vasil'eva, Sem'ia i ee funktsii (Moscow, 1975), pp. 124-25.

4. N. A. Sakharova, Optimal'nye vozmozhnosti ispol'zovaniia zhenskogo truda v sfere obshchestvennogo proizvodstva, pp. 28-31.

5. L. V. Chuiko, Braki i razvody (Moscow, 1975), p. 87.

6. S. A. Karpetian, "Modelirovanie semeinykh dokhodov po materialam perepisi naseleniia" (unpublished dissertation; Rostov, 1968), as cited in M. Swafford, "Sex Differences in Soviet Earnings," American Sociological Review, October 1978.

7. Sh. Shlindman and P. Zvidrin'sh, Izuchenie rozhdaemosti (Moscow, 1973), pp. 54, 61.

8. N. M. Shishkan, Trud zhenshchin v usloviiakh razvitogo sotsializma (Kishinev, 1976), p. 54.

9. Iu. V. Arutiunian, ed., Sotsial'noe i natsional'noe (Moscow: Nauka), pp. 168, 189, 323-24. Figures refer to Russians only.

10. G. Ofer and A. Vinokur, "Earnings Differentials by Sex in the Soviet Union: A First Look," Research Report no. 120, The Hebrew University of Jerusalem (June 1979), p. 22. The distribution of wages recorded for this sample indicates that 40% of the women but only 10% of the men earned 100 rubles or less, while 7% of the women and 62% of the men earned over 200 rubles.

women to responsible positions occur with monotonous regularity in official pronouncements. At a recent meeting of the Ivanovo Oblast Party Committee, the underrepresentation of women was explicitly attributed to the presence of "a certain psychological barrier": "On the one hand, a number of leaders are afraid to entrust women with responsible positions, and on the other, women themselves demonstrate timidity, doubting their strength and refusing, under various pretexts, a promotion to leadership positions."[23] Dubious of the value of mere exhortation and impatient with the slow pace of change, one labor specialist recommended a more radical solution: the adoption of sexual quotas, with the number of women in managerial positions to be proportional to the number of women working under their jurisdiction.[24]

Working Conditions and Protective Labor Measures

One subject on which virtually all Soviet authors agree is the need for substantial improvements in the working conditions of the female labor force, and particularly its blue-collar contingent. Despite the elaborate provisions contained in Soviet labor legislation for the protection of female labor, complaints abound that existing regulations are inadequate and their requirements widely violated.

The catalogue of violations most frequently reported in Soviet publications includes charges that large numbers of women are employed in unhealthy and unsafe jobs, including some which are specifically proscribed; that they are obliged to work overtime, on night shifts, and on scheduled days of rest; that illegal dismissals are a frequent occurrence, even of pregnant women or women with infants under one year of age, an act specifically forbidden by Soviet law; and that requests by pregnant and nursing women for transfer to lighter work are refused.

The failure of enterprise management to observe these regulations is repeatedly criticized in scholarly publications. The

selections by Sheptulina and by Novikova and Kutyrev point out
that although many managers show little concern for observing
protective legislation concerning female workers, they are
rarely punished severely for their negligence. The authors
note that managers often prefer to "compensate" for bad working conditions with additional pay instead of attempting to improve the conditions.

Trade union organizations and local factory committees
share in the responsibility for violations because of their failure to protest them, as the recently published study by T. E.
Chumakova, Women's Work and Daily Life, makes clear.[25]
In this exceptionally comprehensive and frank account, for
which translation rights were refused by Soviet authorities,
Chumakova attributes the lax enforcement to a combination of
factors, including the heavy emphasis on production; lack of
knowledge of existing regulations by enterprise administration
because of a more general failure to give female labor protection sufficient attention at all levels of the system; and above
all, the failure of local factory committees to defend workers'
rights. Taking issue with unnamed opponents, Chumakova insists that factory committees have both the right and the responsibility to ensure the observance of protective regulations
and to hold factory management accountable for any violations.
Citing innumerable decrees which assign various rights and
responsibilities for labor protection to unions, management, and
legal and administrative bodies at different levels, she takes
them all to task for failing to exercise their right of control.

If the need for better enforcement of existing protective measures is widely recognized, the rationale for some of these
measures has been questioned. Some regulations ostensibly
designed for the protection of female labor serve in fact to re-
move women from the most highly rewarded jobs. As one labor
economist observed after interviewing women working in the
largely male construction industry:

A significant proportion of women are still not interested
in restrictions on the use of their labor, since heavy and

harmful job slots usually pay better. In the majority of
them annual holidays are longer, the retirement age is
lower, and nutritious foods are provided. The absence
of night shifts in construction and the provision of ac-
commodation for a substantial proportion of the labor force
are potent factors explaining female employment in this
sector.[26]

Moreover, it is not always clear whether sophisticated medical research or administrative fiat explains the classification
of many highly paid occupations as hazardous or unsafe for
women. In response to widespread criticism that the list of
occupations considered strenuous or harmful and therefore
closed to women, first drawn up in 1932, was obsolete, a revised and expanded version was issued on July 25, 1978. New
regulations which came into effect in January 1980 banned
women from some 460 occupations. However, a number of
authors have pointed out that unsafe and unhealthy conditions
abound in industries and occupations considered especially
suitable for women. The textile industry is a case in point;
obsolete equipment, poor medical and sanitary facilities, and
strenuous work, often involving night shifts, all contribute to
high rates of fatigue and illness. A recent study of health and
living conditions among female textile workers, for example,
found the incidence of illness and of health-related absenteeism
to be significantly higher among spinners and weavers than
among white-collar workers of comparable age in the same enterprises.[27] Rising infant mortality rates, which may also reflect
the increasing exposure of women to hazardous working conditions, are a legitimate cause for heightened concern. But in the
absence of sophisticated medical research in this entire area,
protective measures are more likely to reflect traditional
stereotypes about "male" and "female" work than a scientifically grounded recognition of occupational hazards engendered
by new technologies.
    One way to reduce the discriminatory effects of protective
measures on women, widely advocated in the West, is to ex-

tend their coverage to men; but this suggestion has not been taken up in Soviet writings. Soviet authors, however, have given more emphasis to the need to adapt new technologies and even work norms to the special physiological and psychological characteristics of women. In 1970-71, as part of an effort to increase the proportion of women tractor drivers, their output norms were reduced by 10%. This precedent is often cited by advocates of more far-reaching measures along these lines. Urging a preferential work regime for women workers, the authors of a pioneering study argue:

> Equal rights presuppose essentially unequal rights for various social groups in the society. In order to eliminate the disproportion in the development of the personality of men and women, women must enjoy additional opportunities relative to men.... This signifies the creation of "privileges" for women.[28]

Recent Soviet discussions have devoted particular attention to the needs of working mothers. In addition to urging that part-time work be expanded and more flexible work schedules introduced, some specialists advocate the creation of a preferential work regime for mothers of young children to allow more time for family responsibilities. They propose that mothers be given one or two additional free days each month, that they be freed completely from overtime and night work as well as work on free days or vacations, that paid maternity leaves be increased in length, and that vacation schedules be arranged to coincide with school holidays. Moreover, some even advocate a shortened workday with no loss of pay for working mothers. Insisting that the definition of women's working time ought to include not only the workplace but the socially valuable work performed in the domestic economy as well, they argue that because the development of everyday services has failed to keep pace with the expansion of female employment, working mothers should be compensated for the "double shift" they perform.

The advocates of a shortened workday with no loss of pay appeal to more traditional forms of legitimation as well. The principle that working conditions should be adapted to the special physiological and psychological needs of women has a venerable history in Soviet theory, if not always in practice; Lenin himself can be cited in defense of the principle that the intensity of female employment need not be identical to that of male. Whether or not this line of argumentation will prove successful, it illustrates the way in which conventional formulas can be used on behalf of new and socially progressive purposes. By refusing to exclude women's domestic chores from the definition of work, and by arguing that women have a right to be compensated for the failure to provide sufficiently supportive conditions for their employment, the advocates of such measures are not only insisting that socially valued work be adequately rewarded; they are also holding policy-makers accountable for existing shortcomings.

The Impact of Women's Work on the Family

The impact of women's employment on the family has become a major subject of controversy in recent years. Until the mid-1960s Soviet writings routinely assumed that the increased participation of women in economic and political life would have a direct and favorable impact on their role within the family. In a striking parallel to Western sociological and feminist writings, the conventional Soviet wisdom assumed that rising educational and occupational attainments among women would lead to greater sexual equality within the family, a more democratic pattern of family relationships, and a higher degree of family stability.

In recent years, however, rising levels of female education and labor force participation in the urban and industrial regions of the USSR have been accompanied by lower rates of marriage, later marriage age, rising rates of divorce, and declining birthrates. These trends have become the focus of anxious discussion, challenging as they do the expectation that in a socialist society sexual equality and family stability went hand in hand. For the first time since the 1920s, Soviet writers are compelled to confront the prospect that female liberation and family stability may prove to be "at odds," to draw on the title of a recent American work.[29]

Soviet discussions of the impact of female employment on the family focus on three broad areas: its effects on patterns of marriage and divorce, on fertility, and on the sexual division of labor. Looking first at patterns of marriage and divorce, current Soviet trends appear to support the view that female education and employment are inversely associated with family stability. With 3.5 divorces per thousand population, the Soviet divorce rate is exceeded only by that of the United States. Regional differences, however, remain pronounced. In Central Asia divorce rates are only one third as high as in the RSFSR, while in major cities like Moscow and Leningrad they reach 5.1 and 5.6 respectively.[30] Thus, if patterns of marriage and divorce found in the highly industrialized and urbanized republics with high rates of female labor force participation are compared with those prevailing in predominantly agricultural regions with low female participation rates outside agriculture, the proportion of married women is lower, the mean age at marriage higher, and divorce rates considerably higher in the former than in the latter.[31]

High divorce rates are also associated with the growing tendency for women to initiate divorce actions. While Soviet studies of the causes of divorce are beset by methodological problems, as the selection by Kharchev and Matskovskii indicates, the fact that women are less willing than formerly to hold together a marriage at any price, or to marry irrespective of the cost, is evidence of the wider range of options which economic independence has created.

A second way in which female employment affects the family is through its influence on childbearing. Declining birthrates in the urban and industrial regions of the USSR are directly

attributed by many Soviet authors to excessively high levels
of female employment. An inverse relationship between female employment and fertility in the USSR was first established
by Strumilin in the 1930s; he found that housewives bore twice
as many children as working women.[32] More recent studies
have been adduced to show that while the gap has narrowed,
nonworking women have 20 to 25% more children than do their
working counterparts, and the latter have 2.5 times as many
abortions.[33] Deploring the fact that the one-child family has
become the norm in the urban regions of the European USSR,
a number of Soviet authors call for reducing the level of female
labor force participation and even restricting abortions in
order to increase birthrates to a socially optimal level.[34]

Other writers, however, have challenged the assumptions
that underlie such recommendations. Articles such as
Kiseleva's emphasize the broader changes in economic organization and social values that have transformed the structure and role of the family and that are responsible for declining family size. While recognizing the need for slightly higher
birthrates, they point out that a decline in the quantity of children is associated with greater investments in their quality,
and that future economic growth depends less on large additions to the labor force than on higher skills and productivity.
Rejecting proposals for the legal or administrative regulation
of family size, they call instead for the adoption of a comprehensive demographic policy that corresponds to the specific
circumstances and needs of different social and ethnic groups,
that provides more substantial social and economic support to
families, and that is congruent with broader economic and
social priorities.

Yet a third way in which female employment affects the
family is through its impact on the sexual division of labor.
A broad array of Soviet writings insists that women's entry into
the labor force has resulted in greater female authority within
the family, a more democratic pattern of family decision-making, and above all, a more equal sharing of family responsibilities. Yet these conclusions are not fully corroborated by the

voluminous body of Soviet time-budget investigations.[35] According to Soviet data, men and women devote equal time to paid employment, but women devote an additional 28 hours per week to
housework, compared to 12 hours for men. Men, as a consequence,
enjoy 50% more leisure than women. Although the share of women's
time devoted to housework has diminished over several decades, and is lower among women with higher levels of education, this trend is less the result of greater male sharing of
chores than of the availability of new technologies, household
appliances, and services that higher incomes make possible.

While Soviet authors routinely decry the "double burden"
which working women continue to bear and enjoin men to
assume a greater share of the responsibility for domestic
chores, few directly confront the fundamental sources of the
problem. The household continues to be viewed as preemi-
nently a female domain, and the family as a female responsibility. The fundamental assumption of Soviet economic and
family policy — that women, and women alone, have dual roles
— is a continuing barrier to fundamental improvements in
women's position.

Optimizing the Balance of Work and Family Roles

At the heart of current Soviet discussions of women's work
and family roles lies a central controversy and a major policy
issue for the 1980s: how to achieve an optimal balance between
women's work and family roles. The irreplaceable contribution of women to both production and reproduction militates
against measures which would seriously circumscribe their
roles in either domain. At the same time, there is widespread
agreement among Soviet authors that the present situation
gives rise to profound "contradictions" between women's roles
as workers and their roles as wives and mothers, contradictions which bear a very high economic, social, and demographic cost. They adversely affect women's health and welfare, as well as their opportunities for professional and per-

sonal development; they engender "tensions and conflicts in internal family relations"; they lead to a "weakening of control over the conduct of children and a deterioration of their up-bringing"; and finally, they are one of the basic causes of the declining birthrate.[36]

Although Soviet analysts share a common alarm over current trends and agree that new policy departures are essential, they diverge both in their assessments of the causes of current problems and in the policy recommendations which flow from their divergent diagnoses. Three distinct orientations can be discerned in current Soviet writings.

A first orientation, which might be termed social feminist, is relatively orthodox in its assumptions and moderately reformist in its policy recommendations. Typified by the work of Zoia Iankova, a leading family sociologist, it views the present balance of work and family roles as optimal and focuses on reducing the tension between the two by expanding the availability of consumer goods and services — from super-markets and laundromats to day care — and by modest reforms in the conditions of female employment. It proposes an agenda for slow but incremental reforms in the expectation that the combination of technological progress and socioeconomic reform will obviate the need for more far-reaching changes in the structure of family or work.

A second orientation, which is strongly pronatalist, reflects a sharper concern about current demographic trends. Critical of policies which, in their view, subordinate women's primary roles as wives and mothers to short-run economic needs, a number of Soviet scholars and journalists, including Urlanis and Perevedentsev, advocate an all-out effort to increase the social status and material rewards of motherhood. They urge the Soviet leadership to assign highest priority to a comprehensive population policy designed to achieve higher birth-rates "regardless of any considerations that may be advanced from an economic, ecological, sociological, or any other point of view."[37] The central and most controversial aspect of this pronatalist position is its proposal to transform maternity into

paid social labor, using substantial financial subsidies based
on foregone wages to induce women to withdraw from the labor
force in order to have children. The short-term costs of such
a program, in the view of its supporters, would be more than
offset by its long-term contribution to labor supply and by more
immediate savings generated by a cutback in nursery facilities.

A third orientation, which echoes Western radical feminist
concerns, opposes such a diminution of women's role in production and considers any such reversion to traditional maternal and home-making roles a "step backward." Emphasiz-
ing both the critical importance of female labor to the national
economy, and the equally critical importance of economic participation to women's social status and personal development,
its advocates — typified by M. Ia. Sonin — call for an extension
of women's roles in economic and political life and a reduction
in the family burdens that inhibit it. The solution, in this view,
lies in a fundamental redefinition of male-female relationships,
a more equal sharing by men and women of functions, responsibilities, and rewards.

For some who share this orientation, the problems of working
mothers with young children could better be solved by an expansion of part-time work rather than by extended maternity
leaves. Part-time employment, in this view, would have two
benefits: it would create employment opportunities for women
who are currently at home because family responsibilities prevent them from taking full-time jobs (as well as for students
and pensioners), and it would permit working mothers to reduce
their workday to create more time for childcare, for personal
and professional development, and for leisure. By enabling
women to maintain continuity of employment with reduced
strain during the years of family formation, part-time work
would prevent the loss of skills and promotion opportunities
which would result from extended maternity leaves.

However, the introduction of part-time work on a large scale
would have high costs of its own. As a number of authors have
pointed out, it is far more feasible in routine white-collar and
service occupations than in skilled technical or supervisory

positions. In industry it would require the creation of special sections and assembly lines that would segregate part-time workers from the regular labor force. It would, in all likelihood, increase the concentration of women in low-skilled and poorly remunerated jobs. And, if recent experiments like those described by Porokhniuk and Shepeleva are any indication, it is also likely to impede a more equal division of domestic responsibilities between males and females.[38]

The sense of urgency in all these controversies is clearly shared by the Soviet leadership itself. The economic and demographic issues which surround questions of female employment have come to occupy an increasingly important place on the Soviet political agenda of the 1980s. A number of specific measures "to improve the conditions of labor and everyday life of working women" were included in the Tenth Five-Year Plan outlined at the Twenty-fifth Party Congress in March 1976, and an extension of paid maternity leave was promised in the new Constitution of 1977. The State Committee on Labor and Wages was reorganized and renamed the State Committee on Labor and Social Questions, with a new mandate to address precisely these issues. In October 1976 new standing commissions were created in both chambers of the Supreme Soviet and in the soviets of all republics to address the special problems of women workers and mothers. And in an address to the Trade Union Congress in 1977, Brezhnev not only explicitly acknowledged the problems but committed himself to further initiatives.

It is still too soon to ascertain what direction Soviet policy will ultimately take, and what resources will be committed to sustain it. Nonetheless the Eleventh Five-Year Plan, announced at the Twenty-sixth Party Congress in 1981, and the decree of January 22, 1981, "On Measures to Strengthen State Assistance to Families with Children," indicate that a decision has clearly been made to commit additional resources to the implementation of pronatalist measures. The new decree has two key provisions. (For an excerpt from the decree, see Appendix D.) The first is the introduction of partially paid maternity leave initially promised in 1976. Working mothers are scheduled to

receive 35 rubles a month for a full year after the birth of a
child, and 50 rubles a month if they reside in Siberia, the Soviet Far East, or certain northern regions of the USSR. (These
payments, it should be noted, are to be introduced in stages,
with their scope and timing left unspecified.) Women may also
choose to take an additional half-year of unpaid leave, and this
leave will eventually be extended to a full year.

The second major feature of the new decree is the inauguration of what is in essence a regionally differentiated population
policy in the form of new child allowances that pay 50 rubles
on the birth of a first child and 100 rubles for the second and
third child, with no further payments for subsequent children.
This new plan will be superimposed on the existing system of
state benefits, so that the resources now flowing to the large
families which predominate in Soviet Central Asia will not be
reduced; but the clear intent of the new payments is to encourage the single-child couples in the urban regions of the European USSR to have second and third children. Whether the size
of the payments offers sufficient incentive to offset the existing
impediments, however, remains open to question. The new decree also includes several additional provisions to lighten the
burdens of working mothers: an increase in the monthly benefits paid to single mothers from 5 to 20 rubles; an increase in
the number of days of paid leave granted to mothers to care
for ill children from a maximum of 7 to a maximum of 14 con-
secutive days; a general encouragement of part-time and full-
time work arrangements; and the promise of further assistance
to newlyweds.

Taken by themselves, these measures are too limited to have
a substantial impact on current patterns of female employment
or reproductive behavior. They are significant, rather, as indications of the high priority which the Soviet leadership has
begun to attach to demographic and family policy, of the pronatalist direction which future measures are likely to take,
and of the growing role of social science in the formation of
public policy. The irreplaceable role of Soviet women in both
production and reproduction makes it virtually certain that the

Introduction

questions of women's work and family roles will remain central issues on the Soviet political agenda in the years ahead.

Notes

1. A typical example of this genre, intended for foreign as well as domestic audiences, is Vera Bilshai's Reshenie zhenskogo voprosa v SSSR (Moscow, 1956). An English version was issued in 1957: The Status of Women in the Soviet Union (Moscow, 1957).

2. The initial contribution to this reassessment came from labor economists. Four pioneering studies of female labor in the USSR, all by female authors, were published between 1964 and 1970: N. I. Tatarinova, Stroitel'stvo kommunizma i trud zhenshchin (Moscow, 1964); V. I. Tolkunova, Pravo zhenshchin na trud i ego garantii (Moscow, 1967); E. Z. Danilova, Sotsial'nye problemy truda zhenshchiny-rabotnitsy (Moscow, 1968); and V. B. Mikhailiuk, Ispol'zovanie zhenskogo truda v narodnom khoziaistve (Moscow, 1970). The fine study by A. G. Zdravomyslov, V. P. Rozhin, and V. A. Iadov, Chelovek i ego rabota (Moscow, 1967), includes some important findings on male-female differences in work orientation and job satisfaction; translated into English as Man and His Work (White Plains, 1970).

3. A. G. Kharchev, Zhurnalist, 1972, no. 11, pp. 58-61.

4. Pravda, March 22, 1977, p. 2.

5. The earliest sociological studies focusing on female roles and the family include A. G. Kharchev, Brak i sem'ia v SSSR (Moscow, 1964), unpublished research by S. I. Golod, and A. L. Pimenova's "Sem'ia i perspektivy razvitiia obshchestvennogo truda zhenshchin pri sotsializme," Nauchnye doklady Vysshei shkoly: filosofskie nauki, 1966, no. 3, pp. 35-44. A joint Polish-Soviet research project examining the interdependence of female work and family roles laid the foundation for a whole series of further Soviet studies: G. V. Osipov and Jan Szczepański, eds., Sotsial'nye problemy truda i proizvodstva: Sovetsko-pol'-skoe sravnitel'noe issledovanie (Moscow, 1969). A. G. Kharchev and S. I. Golod's Professional'naia rabota zhenshchin i sem'ia (Leningrad, 1971) is the most comprehensive of such undertakings; excerpts have been translated in Soviet Sociology. The large number of time budget surveys carried out during these years yield useful information about the sexual division of labor.

6. Natalia Baranskaia, "Nedelia kak nedelia," Novy mir, November 1969, no. 11, pp. 23-55.

7. A. E. Kotliar and S. Ia. Turchaninova, Zaniatost' zhenshchin v proizvodstve (Moscow, 1975), pp. 106-7.

8. Tsentral'noe statisticheskoe upravlenie pri Sovete Ministrov Turkmenskoi SSR, Zhenshchiny sovetskogo Turkmenistana (Ashkhabad, 1976), pp. 70, 78, 79, 81. For a more extensive treatment of this issue, see Nancy Lubin, "Women in Soviet Central Asia: Progress and Contradictions," Soviet Studies, April 1981, pp. 182-203.

9. Kotliar and Turchaninova, p. 8.

Introduction

10. Between 75 and 80% of respondents reported they would continue to work even if their income were no longer vital, with the proportion higher among white-collar than blue-collar workers. See Mikhailiuk, p. 24; Z. A. Iankova, "Razvitie lichnosti zhenshchiny v sovetskom obshchestve," Sotsiologicheskoe issledovanie, 1975, no. 4, p. 43; Pimenova, pp. 36-39; Osipov and Szczepański, pp. 444-46; Kharchev and Golod, pp. 38-69.

11. Mikhailiuk, p. 24.

12. G. Guseinov and V. Korchagin, "Voprosy trudovykh resursov," Voprosy ekonomiki, 1971, no. 2, p. 49.

13. M. Ia. Sonin, "Aktual'nye sotsial'no-ekonomicheskie problemy zaniatosti zhenshchin," in A. Z. Maikov, ed., Problemy ratsional'nogo ispol'zovaniia tru-dovykh resursov (Moscow, 1973), pp. 362-63.

14. E. B. Gruzdeva, "Osobennosti obraza zhizni intelligentnykh rabochikh," Rabochii klass i sovremennyi mir, 1975, no. 2, p. 94. The discrepancy between the educational attainments of workers and the content of the jobs they perform has been a serious general concern in recent years. The authors of Chelovek i ego rabota report a typical statement by a woman worker: "In the shop no one looks to see who has an education, but they put you where they think best." The authors comment: "It is obvious how abnormal the situation is in which a female worker with secondary education stands on the assembly line..." (pp. 280-81).

15. Gur Ofer and Aaron Vinokur, "Earnings Differentials by Sex in the Soviet Union: A First Look," Research Report No. 120, The Hebrew University of Jerusalem (June 1979), p. 22.

16. N. M. Shishkan, Trud zhenshchin v usloviiakh razvitogo sotsializma (Kishinev, 1976), p. 55.

17. A. Kotliar and A. Shlemin, "Problemy ratsional'noi zaniatosti zhenshchin," Sotsialisticheskii trud, 1974, no. 7, p. 111.

18. E. L. Manevich, ed., Osnovnye problemy ratsional'nogo ispol'zovaniia trudovykh resursov v SSSR (Moscow, 1971), pp. 168, 39.

19. Berezovskaia, Literaturnaia gazeta, June 28, 1975, p. 12.

20. M. Pavlova, Literaturnaia gazeta, September 22, 1971.

21. V. N. Shubkin and G. M. Kochetov, "Rukovoditel', kollega, podchinennyi," Sotsial'nye issledovaniia, 1968, no. 2, pp. 143-55.

22. Literaturnaia gazeta, September 15, 1976, p. 10.

23. Partiinaia zhizn', 1975, no. 16, p. 44.

24. Tolkunova, p. 103.

25. T. E. Chumakova, Trud i byt zhenshchin (Minsk, 1978). See also Kazakh-stanskaia pravda, October 23, 1973, p. 3.

26. Shishkan, p. 116.

27. N. V. Dogle, Usloviia zhizni i zdorov'e tekstil'shchits (Moscow, 1977), pp. 77-93.

28. Zdravomyslov et al., p. 267. See also G. A. Slesarev, Metodologiia sotsiologicheskogo issledovaniia problem narodonaseleniia SSSR (Moscow, 1965), p. 136.

29. Carl Degler, At Odds: Women and the Family in America from the Revolution to the Present (New York: Oxford Press, 1980).

30. Iu. A. Korolev, Brak i razvod (Moscow, 1978), pp. 136-37.

31. Based on figures given in Tsentral'noe statisticheskogo upravlenie pri Sovete Ministrov SSSR, Itogi vsesoiuznoi perepisi naseleniia 1970 goda, vol. 2 (Moscow: Statistika, 1972), pp. 263-68.

32. S. G. Strumilin, Izbrannye proizvedeniia, vol. 3 (Moscow: Nauka, 1964), p. 140.

33. Sh. Shlindman and P. Zvidrin'sh, Izuchenie rozhdaemosti (Moscow: Statistika, 1973), p. 74. A smaller difference is reported by V. Nemchenko, "Mezhotraslevoe dvizhenie trudovykh resursov," in Narodonaselenie, edited by D. E. Valentei et al. (Moscow: Statistika, 1973), pp. 35-36. For abortions, see I. M. Musatov, Sotsial'no-ekonomicheskie problemy trudovykh resursov v SSSR (Novosibirsk: Mysl', 1968), p. 321.

34. One recent example is Boris Urlanis in Nedelia, December 1-7, 1981, p. 16.

35. A detailed examination of these studies can be found in chap. 7 of the author's Women in Soviet Society.

36. A. G. Kharchev, "Byt i sem'ia," in N. Solov'ev et al., Problemy byta, p. 19. See also Shishkan, Trud zhenshchin, p. 38.

37. Boris Urlanis, Problemy dinamiki naseleniia SSSR (Moscow: Nauka, 1974), p. 283.

38. For a more comprehensive treatment of this issue, see Joel Moses, "Women and the Politics of Alternative Work Schedules in the Soviet Union and in the United States," Monograph series, Institute of International Studies, University of California at Berkeley, 1981.

Selected Bibliography

In Russian:

Belova, V. A., and Darskii, L. E. Statistika mnenii v izuchenii rozhdaemosti. Moscow, 1972.

_____; Bondarskaia, G. A.; Vishnevskii, A. G.; et al. Skol'ko detei budet v sovetskoi sem'e. Moscow, 1977.

Chuiko, L. V. Braki i razvody. Moscow, 1975.

Chumakova, T. E. Trud i byt zhenshchin. Minsk, 1978.

Danilova, E. Z. Sotsial'nye problemy truda zhenshchiny-rabotnitsy. Moscow, 1968.

Dogle, N. V. Usloviia zhizni i zdorov'e tekstil'shchits. Moscow, 1977.

Ekonomika i organizatsiia promyshlennogo proizvodstva, "Trud i byt zhenshchin," May-June 1978, no. 3.

Fedorova, M. "Ispol'zovanie zhenskogo truda v sel'skom khoziaistve," Voprosy ekonomiki, 1975, no. 12, pp. 55-64.

Gordon, L. A., and Klopov, E. V. Chelovek posle raboty: sotsial'nye problemy byta i vnerabochego vremeni. Moscow, 1972.

_____, and Onikov, L. A. Cherty sotsialisticheskogo obraza zhizni: byt rabochikh vchera, segodnia, zavtra. Moscow, 1977.

Gruzdeva, E. G. "Osobennosti obraza zhizni intelligentnykh rabochikh," Rabochii klass i sovremennyi mir, March-April 1975, no. 2, pp. 91-99.

_____; and Chertikhina. "Zhenshchiny v obshchestvennom proizvodstve razvitogo sotsializma," Rabochii klass i sovremennyi mir, November-December 1975, no. 6, pp. 133-47.

Iankova, Z. A. "O semeino-bytovykh roliakh rabotaiushchei zhenshchiny," Sotsial'nye issledovaniia, 1970, no. 4, pp. 76-87.

_____. "Razvitie lichnosti zhenshchiny v sovetskom obshchestve," Sotsiologicheskie issledovaniia, 1975, no. 4, pp. 42-51.

_____. "Struktura gorodskoi sem'i v sotsialisticheskom

obshchestve," Sotsiologicheskie issledovaniia, 1974, no. 1, pp. 100-10.

_____, and Iazykova, V. S., XX vek i problemy sem'i. Moscow, 1974.

Iuk, Z. M. Trud zhenshchiny i sem'ia. Minsk, 1975.

Iurkevich, N. G. Sovetskaia sem'ia: Funktsii i usloviia stabil'nosti. Minsk, 1970.

Kharchev, A. G. Brak i sem'ia v SSSR. Moscow, 1964.

_____, ed. Izmenenie polozheniia zhenshchiny i sem'ia. Moscow, 1968.

_____, and Golod, S. I. Professional'naia rabota zhenshchin i sem'ia. Leningrad, 1971.

_____, and Matskovskii, M. S. Sovremennaia sem'ia i ee problemy. Moscow, 1978.

Korchagin, V. P. Trudovye resursy v usloviakh nauchno-tekhnicheskoi revoliutsii. Moscow, 1974.

Kostakov, V. G., ed. Trudovye resursy: Sotsial'no-ekonomicheskii analiz. Moscow, 1976.

Kotliar, A. E., and Kirpa, I. "Demograficheskie aspekty zaniatosti v gorodakh raznymi promyshlennymi strukturami," Vestnik statistiki, 1972, no. 7, pp. 12-18.

_____, and Shlemin. "Problemy ratsional'noi zaniatosti zhenshchin," Sotsialisticheskii trud, 1974, no. 7, pp. 110-19.

_____, and Turchaninova, S. Ia. Zaniatost' zhenshchin v proizvodstve. Moscow, 1975.

Maikov, A. Z., ed. Problemy ratsional'nogo ispol'zovaniia trudovykh resursov. Moscow, 1973.

Mikhailiuk, V. B. Ispol'zovanie zhenskogo truda v narodnom khoziaistve. Moscow, 1970.

Novikova, E. E.; Iazykova, V. S.; and Iankova, Z. A. Zhenshchina, trud, sem'ia. Moscow, 1978.

Osipov, G. V., and Szczepański, J. Sotsial'nye problemy truda i proizvodstva: Sovetsko-pol'skoe sravnitel'noe issledovanie. Moscow, 1969.

Sakharova, N. A. Optimal'nye vozmozhnosti ispol'zovaniia zhenskogo truda v sfere obshchestvennogo proizvodstva. Kiev, 1973.

Solov'ev, N.; Lazauskas, Iu.; and Iankova, Z. A., eds. Problemy byta, braka i sem'i. Vilnius, 1970.

Sonin, M. Ia. Razvitie narodonaseleniia. Moscow, 1980.

"Sotsial'no-filosofskie problemy demografii," Voprosy isto-
rii, 1974, no. 9, pp. 84-97; 1974, no. 11, pp. 83-96; 1975,
no. 1, pp. 57-78.

Tatarinova, N. I. "Nauchno-tekhnicheskii progress i trud
zhenshchin," Voprosy ekonomiki, 1973, no. 11, pp. 57-64.

_____. Stroitel'stvo kommunizma i trud zhenshchin. Mos-
cow, 1964.

_____. "Trud zhenshchin v SSSR," Sotsialisticheskii trud,
1975, no. 9, pp. 7-16.

Tolkunova, V. I. "K voprosu o ravenstve zhenshchin v trude i
bytu pri sotsializme," Sovetskoe gosudarstvo i pravo, 1969,
no. 10.

_____. Pravo zhenshchin na trud i ego garantii. Moscow,
1967.

_____. Trud zhenshchin. Moscow, 1973.

Tomskii, I. E. Sotsial'no-ekonomicheskie problemy zhenskogo
truda (na materialakh Iakutskoi ASSR). Novosibirsk, 1979.

Valentei, D. I., et al. Zhenshchiny na rabote i doma. Moscow
1978.

Volkov, A. G., ed. Demograficheskoe razvitie sem'i. Moscow,
1979.

In English:

Atkinson, D.; Dallin, A.; and Lapidus, G., eds. Women in Russia. Stanford, 1977.

Besemeres, John F. Socialist Population Politics. White
Plains, New York, 1980.

Lapidus, Gail Warshofsky. Women in Soviet Society. Berkeley,
1978.

McAuley, Alastair. Women's Work and Wages in the Soviet
Union. London, 1981.

Moses, Joel. The Politics of Female Labor in the Soviet Union.
Ithaca, New York, 1978.

_____. Women and the Politics of Alternative Work Schedules in the Soviet Union and the United States. Institute of International Studies Monograph Series. Berkeley, California, 1981.

Ofer, Gur, and Vinokur, Aron. "Earnings Differentials by Sex in the Soviet Union: A First Look," Research Report No. 120, The Hebrew University of Jerusalem. June 1979.

Sacks, Michael Paul. Women's Work in Soviet Russia. New York, 1976.

Swafford, Michael. "Sex Differences in Soviet Earnings," American Sociological Review, October 1978.

The following journals of translations should also be consulted:

Current Digest of the Soviet Press
Problems of Economics
Soviet Sociology

PART ONE
LEVELS AND PATTERNS
OF FEMALE EMPLOYMENT

1

Current Problems of Female Labor in the USSR

L. Rzhanitsyna

International Women's Day, March 8, was celebrated in 1979 for the sixty-ninth time. The decision to celebrate it was made in 1910 by the International Congress of Women Socialists in Copenhagen, Denmark, in order to unite women of all countries and peoples in the struggle for their rights. International Women's Day was first celebrated in Russia in 1913, when a "Scholarly Morning on the Women's Question" was held in St. Petersburg, under police surveillance. When it was over, several of the women speakers were arrested for attempting to discuss the hard lot of the working woman and the absence of elementary rights and political freedoms for her in Russia. Thus began the conscious association with revolution of representatives of the women's movement, whose significance was given high marks by V. I. Lenin.

March 8 is now a national holiday in our country. It is an expression of the active participation of women in the struggle for socialism, for its consolidation and development. At the same time, it remains a day of international solidarity for women of all countries to unite to secure general equality, defend the interests of children, and assure peace on earth.

Russian text © 1979 by "Pravda" Publishers. "Aktual'nye problemy zhenskogo truda v SSSR," *Sotsialisticheskii trud*, 1979, no. 3, pp. 58-67.

3

L. Rzhanitsyna

Socialism has shown the whole world how the "woman's question" should be solved. It provided the basic conditions for equality: elimination of all forms of exploitation and oppression and the involvement of women in social production and sociopolitical life. Simultaneously, a special system of socioeconomic guarantees has been set up for women as workers and as mothers. These vitally important rights are confirmed in the Constitution of the USSR. Article 35 states, "Women and men in the USSR have equal rights.

"The exercise of these rights is ensured by providing women with opportunities equal to those of men in receiving an education and vocational training, in labor, remuneration, and promotion, and in social, political, and cultural activity, as well as by special measures to protect women's labor and health; by the creation of conditions enabling women to combine labor and motherhood; by legal protection and material and moral support for mother and child, including the granting of paid leave and other benefits to pregnant women and mothers; and by the gradual reduction of working time for women with small children."

L. I. Brezhnev spoke vividly of the constant and special concern for women in socialist society at the Twenty-fifth CPSU Congress: "The Party considers its duty to be to show constant concern for woman and to improve her position as a participant in the labor process, as a mother, counsellor of children, and housewife."

All these basic directions in improving living conditions for working women in our country are supported by an appropriate system of measures.

*   *   *

The firm foundation of equality and the achievements of our country in changing the social position of women provide a basis for the new measures currently being taken to create ever more favorable conditions for women's work, daily life, rest, and recreation. The laws of developed socialism and the

4

dynamic and proportional development of social production create ever greater opportunities for satisfying the needs and promoting the comprehensive development of the personality of all Soviet people, including women. In view of the role of women in bearing and bringing up children, one could say that concern for them is at the same time concern for future generations of builders of communism. These considerations are fully taken into account in the program of socioeconomic measures approved at the Twenty-fifth CPSU Congress and in subsequent party and government decisions currently being implemented in the USSR.

The economic base for carrying out this program is provided by our country's increased production potential. Its implementation is linked with the needs of further social development and the continued growth of the people's well-being. From 1966 to 1978 the country's capital funds almost trebled, and the national income more than doubled. Industrial output increased 2.5 times, and agricultural output rose by 40%. All this made for an 84% increase in per capita real income and a rise in average wages per worker and employee to 160 rubles, as against 97 rubles in 1965. Income from public consumption funds per inhabitant increased correspondingly from 182 to 400 rubles per year. Purchases of goods increased 2.3 times, and the volume of public services expanded approximately fivefold. Over these years the rate of development of culture and education accelerated. The number of students increased by more than one third, and today eight out of every ten persons working in the national economy have a higher or secondary (complete or incomplete) education.

At present the program for improving the position of working women in the USSR has several specific features.

First of all, it is being carried out under conditions of greater labor participation by women. Thus the proportion of women workers and employees is 51% of all workers at state-owned enterprises. The proportion of women among those working on collective farms is 48%. Today more than 62 million women are employed in the national economy. More than 40 million

5

of them participate in the socialist emulation movement, including 25 million who take part in the communist work movement. Lately women's councils have become more active, special committees for work among women have been set up in
the country's legislative bodies, and women are playing a
greater part in government management and administration
and in the party and trade unions (see Table 1).

It is important to emphasize that the growth shown in the
public activity of women was accompanied by positive processes
in the family and domestic sphere of life. They included a general rise in the people's well-being, improvement in the sex
ratio (whereas in 1959 there were 45% men and 55% women,
in 1978 there were 47% men and 53% women, while in the age
groups up to 30, since the late '60s the number of men has been
greater than the number of women), reduction in the marriage
age, and a stabilization and some increase in the birthrate
(17.3 births per 1,000 inhabitants in 1967, 18.1 in 1977).

Another important feature of the measures for the general
improvement of women's living conditions is that over the last
few years, these measures have been increasingly incorporated
in plans of economic and social development both on a national
economic scale and at the level of industries and enterprises.
The idea of drawing up an integrated plan of social development
of a large production collective and the first experience in carrying it out appeared a little over ten years ago in the Leningrad production association "Svetlana." Today it is common
practice for thousands and thousands of enterprises. With the
endorsement of the USSR State Planning Committee's single
method for drawing up integrated plans of economic and social
development of enterprises, it is possible, in our view, to speak
of the creation of a comprehensive system of social planning
in the USSR. The enterprise plans make it possible to supplement extensive government measures with daily detailed work
in every labor collective. This makes it urgent to expand the
volume and improve the quality of scientific information, and
to supplement general and averaged indicators in the area of
working conditions, rest, everyday life and recreation of women

Table 1*

Forms of public activity of women	Year	Number of women, in thousands	Share, in %	Year	Number of women, in thousands	Share, in %
Deputies of the Supreme Soviet of the USSR, union, and autonomous republics	1966-67	3.4	33	1974-75	3.9	36
Deputies of local soviets (oblast, krai, raion, urban, and rural)	1967	875	43	1977	1,093	49
Members of committees of trade union locals and trade union organizers	1965	1,833	53	1975	2,464	61
Communist Party members	1965	2,372	20	1975	3,646	24
Komsomol members	1965	10,506	48	1975	17,597	52

*Zhenshchiny SSSR, Moscow, "Statistika" Publishers, 1975, pp. 45-51; Zhenshchiny i deti v SSSR, Moscow, "Statistika" Publishers, 1969, pp. 89, 93; Vestnik statistiki, 1978, no. 1, pp. 85-86.

7

with data gleaned from mass statistical and sociological studies, which makes it possible to take fuller account of women's characteristics and to comprehensively evaluate the consequences of measures taken to improve working and living conditions, with mothers principally in mind.

Participation of Women in Social Labor

Economists estimate that more than 90% of all women of working age are now either working or studying (in 1959 this index was lower: 73%). If we consider that women account for the majority of people of retirement age who continue to work, it seems natural to assume that in many parts of the country the possibility of drawing women from the household and private subsidiary holdings into social production is virtually exhausted, and a high level of employment has been achieved.

We know that high levels of female employment in developed machine production are an objective law. Noting this, Klara Zetkin wrote at the turn of the century that to oppose the employment of female labor in industry and seek to get women back into the home is as senseless and self-defeating as the efforts of the English workers who thought that by destroying factories they could eliminate the competition created by machines. Those who would eliminate or restrict female labor (except when it is absolutely harmful to the health of a woman or her progeny) have no understanding of the essence of the economic and social processes of our time.

Under the conditions of socialism, which have fostered a new attitude toward work, and even more so in the period of the transition to communism, when the creative character of labor is increasing, women see work not only as a basis for economic independence but also as a source of self-affirmation and personal development, as well as a prime civic duty. This confronts socialist society with new and ever more complex tasks of improving their working conditions in the broadest sense of the word. It involves, as is noted in the Constitution, providing work according to ability, making it more meaningful, creating conditions for improving skills and qualifications, eliminating harmful effects of the production environment on the organism, making work itself easier, introducing rational work schedules, and reducing working hours, mainly for mothers of small children.

People's expectations of working conditions rise together with their well-being and culture. Lenin wrote that "The difference between the 'formulas' of genuine communism and solemn rhetoric is precisely that they reduce everything to the conditions of labor."[1]

The basic principles of women's employment are by now firmly rooted in socialist society. They include: correspondence of the content, organization, and conditions of work to the specific features of the female organism; due account of the special role of the working woman as a mother and housewife; the introduction of a system of additional measures to facilitate the growth of their professional skills and advance at work; and enforcement of the principle of equal pay for equal work. It is important at the present stage and in the long run that these general principles of social policy are consistently carried out at all levels.

Of prime importance among the basic ways to improve working conditions are mechanization and automation of production. The introduction of the achievements of technological progress in industry has made it possible to increase the number of women engaged in mechanized and automated work. This process is continuing. In the Tenth Five-Year Plan period, it is planned to reduce the number of workers not operating machines and mechanisms by 15 to 20%. This involves a substantial segment of the working women. It is especially important to accelerate the reconstruction and modernization of auxiliary production, where mechanization is lagging and many women perform manual labor.

In addition to these general measures that have been planned and are being carried out to raise the level of mechanization and improve working conditions for all working people, the

9

plans of economic and social development of industries and enterprises provide for special indicators characterizing the improvement of working conditions for women.

Concern for alleviating and improving working conditions for women is reflected in the decree "On Additional Measures for Improving Working Conditions of Women Employed in the National Economy," passed by the USSR Council of Ministers and the All-Union Council of Trade Unions (AUCTU) on April 25, 1978.

The State Committee of the USSR on Labor and Wages, jointly with the AUCTU and with the endorsement of the USSR Ministry of Health, approved a new List of Industries, Trades, and Jobs with Arduous or Harmful Working Conditions, at which female employment is prohibited.

The new list became operative on the day it was approved. It means that factory managers can no longer employ women on jobs and in types of production and trades covered by the list. Since 1978 the State Committee of the USSR for Vocational and Technical Education and ministries and departments with training programs for personnel in the national economy have been prohibited from training women in the trades on the list.

Women who lose their jobs must (with their consent) be offered jobs according to their trades (specializations), or if this is impossible, they must be offered opportunities (also with their consent) for training in new trades. During the training period the women retain their average monthly wage, as well as continuity of work record for social security benefits, for calculation of supplementary benefits to state pensions, and for bonuses or seniority raises, annual premiums, and other benefits.

Of course, arduous and harmful jobs are detrimental to any organism, female as well as male, and therefore the prime objective aimed at making work for women easier and less hazardous to health should not be the replacement of women by men but the complete elimination of such jobs and types of production, especially their restructuring and the radical improvement of working conditions. A great deal can be done by

enterprises themselves in this respect. More and more measures, such as the installation of ventilation, antivibration, and
other systems, should be included in the integrated plans of
economic and social development of collectives.

The removal of women from arduous and harmful jobs is a
complex socioeconomic and organizational undertaking. The
logic of life is such that, in view of the high wages and other
important benefits offered by such jobs, the process cannot be
smooth or effortless. Women are certainly not indifferent to
where and how they will work after being transferred, or how
much they will earn. Women must be offered timely retraining
opportunities, retention of their former wage level, as well as
such incentives as better shift schedules, etc., on their new
jobs. For women who have worked for a long time under such
conditions, it would be expedient to let them continue until retirement age, improving working conditions by reducing the
working day.

Our Constitution regards a reduction in the workday of working mothers as one of the decisive factors for improving their
working and living conditions. It would seem that for women
employed in harder or more hazardous jobs, the question of
reducing working hours and improving schedules should be resolved faster than for other categories of women workers. As
for nighttime employment, the enterprises themselves have
many opportunities to deal with this problem. Thus the plans
of industrial enterprises provide for removing 335,000 women
from night shifts in the course of the Tenth Five-Year Plan
period.

Greater consideration is now being given to female characteristics in designing new machines and technologies for
equipping workplaces. With regard to rate-setting for women
employed in arduous jobs, female workers' traits are taken
into account only for women machine operators in agriculture,
whose output norms are 10% lower than for men. This is only natural because the jobs require considerable physical exertion, and
the application of identical norms places women at a disadvantage
in comparison with men. We feel that in the future, the differen-

11

tiation of norms by sex (as well as by age) should be substantiated scientifically and verified in practical experience more
extensively.

The growth of mechanization, the changing character of work,
and the improvement of working conditions lend greater urgency
to the problem of advanced training for women. Today everyone
agrees that the natural interruptions in work entailed in motherhood, as well as the lag in the development of child-care institutions and the service sphere, result in the loss, in the course
of the careers of many women, of the educational advantages
they had when they started work. Studies carried out over the
last few years give an idea of the extent of that lag (see Table 2).

Table 2*

Branch of industry	Average wage category	
	men	women
Baking	4.5	3.9
Meat and dairy	4.0	3.1
Textile	3.8	3.7
Machine building	3.5	2.1

*A. E. Kotliar and S. Ia. Turchaninova, Zaniatost' zhenshchin
v proizvodstve, Moscow, "Statistika" Publishers, 1975, p. 67.

Today a number of enterprises, in addition to the general
forms of industrial and advanced training for all working people, try to reduce existing qualificational differences through
a system of on-the-job advanced training for women. In this
way the A. A. Zhdanov Shipbuilding Works in Leningrad and
other enterprises have trained many skilled workers.

In all efforts aimed at the occupational advancement of
women, it is important for the management and factory committees of all enterprises to pay greater attention to the growth

of female personnel, encourage those who study, and support those who try to master new trades and specialities. At present, for example, at the Kaunas radio factory in Lithuania, the Kurako metallurgical works in Gurev, the Novokuznetsk cement plant in Kemerovo Region, and other enterprises, people taking training courses are paid higher year-end bonuses. Why not offer special bonuses for women who study?

Woman, Family, and Children

The process of involving women in social production in our country was, as we know, accompanied by the implementation of a variety of measures for organizing state protection of motherhood and childhood and increasing government assistance to the family in raising new generations. Soviet women constantly feel these real gains and advantages of socialism. Public expenditures in this sphere are rising steadily, and the system of guarantees and benefits is expanding. Thus from 1966 to 1976 government budget outlays for child benefits, services, and education increased 70%, with 37% of the increase covering the years 1971-76.[2] During this period important public assistance measures for working mothers were implemented.

In the Eighth Five-Year Plan period (1966-70), overtime and business trips for women with small children were banned; unpaid leave for looking after a child was increased, for those who desired, to one year without detriment to work record or job; the minimum wage at which a grant is provided on the birth of a child was raised; allowances were introduced for people disabled since childhood; social security, allowances for looking after a sick child, and other benefits were extended to collective farm women; budgeting was increased for meals in preschool children's institutions, etc.

In the Ninth Five-Year Plan period (1971-75), payment for pregnancy and maternity leave was increased to 100% of the wage regardless of length of service; paid leave for looking after a sick child was increased from three to seven days; payment for temporary disability leave for families with three or more children was increased to 100%; allowances were introduced for children in low-income families, etc.

In the Tenth Five-Year Plan period (1976-80), expenditures have been increased for food and drug supplies in children's hospitals and maternity homes; budget rates of children's homes and boarding schools have been raised; material help has been improved for pupils of vocational-technical schools. Plans provide for introducing partially paid leave for looking after a child up to one year of age, raising allowances for invalids and people disabled since childhood, introducing new pension benefits for mothers of large families, and so on.

The number of places in preschool children's institutions increased from 7.7 million in 1965 to 13.2 million in 1978, that is, by 70%. Between 1966 and 1977 new schools with places for more than 19 million pupils were built. In the 1977/78 school year there were more than 40 million pupils in general education schools. In 1978 some 11.5 million children, 4 million more than in 1965, went to trade-union sponsored Young Pioneer camps. At present more than 13 million people are studying in vocational-technical schools, specialized secondary, and higher educational institutions. We should note that the upkeep of a child in a preschool institution costs 400 to 500 rubles a year and that the state annually spends 180 rubles on every pupil, 650 rubles on every technicum student, and more than 1,000 rubles on every university or college student.[3] In 1976 grants and allowances for children (for pregnancy and maternity, mothers of large families, unmarried mothers, baby care and nursing items, children in low-income families) totaled 3.1 billion rubles, or almost 2.5 times more than in 1970.[4] We estimate that another 800 million rubles were paid in allowances for looking after sick children. The system of price discounts for children's wares also makes it possible for families to save some 800 million rubles a year. Income tax discounts for dependents run roughly 200 million rubles a year, and so on. Taking into account expenditures of enterprises from their own

funds to improve services for children of their employees, we
estimate that total funds spent on bringing up the younger generation and preparing them for work amount to approximately
30 to 32% of the social consumption funds, or in 1979, 33 to 35
billion rubles.

It is gratifying to cite these figures in 1979, which the United
Nations declared International Year of the Child. It is something to take pride in in a country where only sixty years ago
"two million barely kindled infant lives were snuffed out every
year by the ignorance of oppressed and downtrodden people, by
the backwardness and indifference of the class state. Every
year two million suffering mothers shed bitter tears on Russian
soil as, with calloused hands, they filled the early graves of
senselessly doomed innocent victims of a vile state system."[5]

Today the accomplishments of a country in which the very
first decrees of the new government were permeated with an
impassioned desire and readiness to do everything for its children and future generations are acknowledged universally. The
state system of aiding the family in bringing up children is con-
tinually developing and improving. Today, relying on our
achievements and on all our rich experience, we must continue
to advance. New tasks are the order of the day: further expansion of public forms of child raising (kindergartens, nurseries), improvement of the work of schools and after-school
groups, the creation of conditions for working shorter hours
or at home, increasing free time for mothers of large families,
and further encouragement of natality.

One of the most important tasks in this sphere is the expansion and improvement of the work of children's preschool institutions. They now service 41% of all children up to the age
of seven. However, as indicated by the waiting lists for placing
children in preschool institutions in some regions and cities,
as well as some cases of crowding in kindergartens and nurseries, the demand has not yet been fully met.

In spite of the shortage of placement opportunities for children of working women, the plan for building preschools was
not entirely fulfilled during the Ninth Five-Year-Plan period

and the first three years of the Tenth Five-Year Plan. The overwhelming majority are built at the end of the year, to the detriment of the quality of the decor, interior design, finish, and equipment of kindergartens and nurseries. It is evidently time to increase the financial accountability of construction organizations for the timely completion of high-quality children's institutions and to strengthen measures of public control.

Constant attention has been paid to improving the operation of existing preschool institutions. Improvement of social education and services in preschool institutions was discussed at a meeting of the All-Union Council of Trade Unions committee on work among women held in December 1978. Kindergartens and nurseries of the Novomoskovsk automobile repair plant, the Primor'e production association "Bor," the Karaganda metallurgical works, and many other enterprises were cited as examples. At the Gorky automobile plant, for example, a special administrative division has been set up: the Administration for Preschools, which in collaboration with the factory trade union committee, the district health department, and the district public education department, has drawn up a comprehensive plan for improving children's services. Special groups have been organized for handicapped children. The best experience in the work of pedagogical and medical personnel of the children's establishments of the association is being studied and adopted, socialist competition between them has been organized, and a system of moral and material incentives for best achievements has been introduced. The results of these measures were, of course, soon apparent: the rate of illness is half the mean national level, and indices of children's development have improved.

However, the public upbringing of children has not always been shown the concern such a noble and rewarding cause deserves. There are inadequacies in the material and technical maintenance of kindergartens and nurseries and in providing medical services.

Experience shows that the more thoroughly shortcomings are

16

analyzed, the more readily and quickly they are overcome. Much in this respect can be done by enterprises and local organizations. The point is, in the first place, to increase the responsibility of administrative personnel at all levels and of builders for completing preschools on schedule and for uninterrupted supplies of the best food products, furniture, equipment, and toys. It is important to encourage and spread the experience of using enterprise funds for financing the construction of children's institutions; this can also be done on a share basis. Enterprises should provide greater aid to kindergartens and nurseries.

The trade union committee for work among women receives numerous proposals for improving the organization of work and remuneration. In particular, it has been suggested that workers at preschools be awarded bonuses for improving the quality of services (for example, for reducing the rate of illness among children) and supplementary pay be granted for combining educational work with other duties in looking after the children. In view of the fact that the work load of children's doctors is high and the growth in the numbers of pediatricians still lags behind other specialties, they could be helped by teams of medical college senior students capable of professionally carrying out doctors' orders. To provide greater control over the activity of preschool establishments, it has been suggested that the staffs of district and city health departments include the position of physician-inspector for preschool children's institutions.

Reports from enterprises unfortunately still offer few examples of providing part-time jobs for women, even though the decisions of the Twenty-fifth CPSU Congress are very specific on this point: "To create extensive opportunities for women with children to work a partial workday or partial workweek or to work at home." Literature on the subject still continues to cite the examples of the same organizations successfully applying such work schedules: garment, knitwear, and textile enterprises in Estonia, Georgia, Moldavia, and Moscow.

It seems that enterprises are still not very interested in or-

17

ganizing work on a part-time basis, although the economic effectiveness of such work and its effect on stabilizing personnel
and bringing up children have been amply demonstrated.

Woman, Home, Household

In their concern for the comprehensive development of women
and the harmonious blending of labor activity with the duties of
mother and housewife, party decisions and our plans provide
for a system of measures aimed at reducing time spent on household work. Well-known estimates by Soviet economists indicate
that at present, 100 to 150 billion man-hours, which is the equivalent of the ordinary work load of 40 to 60 million workers a
year, are spent annually on household duties. Even more striking figures are cited about time spent on household work in
France, where, if we trust the estimates of French experts,
more time is spent on it than on all gainful employment.

Since the overwhelming share of household duties is borne
by women, Lenin rightly regarded elimination of the burdens
of running the household as "the real emancipation of women,
real communism."[6]

In capitalist countries the easing of living conditions for
women in the home is the private affair of the family. Even
though the women's movement is, of course, concerned with
solving the problem, it cannot influence it adequately because
"the trade unions do not wage this kind of struggle, insofar as
a large part of the excess work load is not generated at the
workplace. It does not interest the labor inspectorate or concern the political parties."[7]

In our society, under the conditions of developed socialism,
the task of reducing women's time and labor spent in household
chores is tackled on a national scale and has been incorporated
into the social program of the Communist Party. The major
aim in this respect is the development of public forms of serving the domestic needs of the family and the transformation of
ever more types of domestic work into specialized and mech-

anized branches of the economy, into an organized, industrial service.

Public services have been developing at an accelerated rate over the last 15 or 20 years. Between 1961 and 1977 the number of public service enterprises doubled. Seating space in public dining establishments numbered 15.1 million in 1977, compared to 4.5 million in 1960. Thirty-eight million apartments were built, and communal services have improved, which has rid women of a variety of laborious household jobs. Fulfillment of the targets of the Tenth Five-Year Plan will make it possible to provide half again as many public services and greater opportunities for more useful and interesting utilization of nonworking time for all working people.

Today, along with expanding the volume of services, which remains an important goal, workers in the public services are increasingly faced with the tasks of improving their quality. The experience of Bashkiria and of Riazan and a number of other regions, where domestic service shops and receiving centers have adopted work schedules most convenient for the population, and whose doors are open after working hours, without lunch breaks or off-days, deserves widespread emulation. Experience shows that many types of services can be brought directly to the place of work; more receiving centers, cafeterias, and delicatessen stores can be opened at enterprises; and the practice of concluding contracts with stores and domestic service organizations to provide services at the place of work can be expanded. Thus in the Ukraine as of July 1, 1978, operating at enterprises were 863 delicatessen shops, cafés, and stalls offering prepared food and confectionery products, and there were more than 6,000 counters for ordering such products. Some 2,000 stores sell food and consumer goods ordered by workers at the place or work.

One of the ways to make women's work easier, in addition to expanding the scale of public services and improving their quality, is the introduction of household appliances that can halve the time spent on cooking, housecleaning, laundry, and so on. Moreover, the mechanization of household chores cre-

ates conditions for changing the traditional distribution of
household duties between men and women, making it possible
to involve men more actively in time-consuming household
work. To this day Lenin's words are still valid about men who
"calmly look on as women wear themselves down in petty household work. Very few husbands, even among the proletarians,
reflect on how much they could reduce the burdens and concerns
of their wives, and even rid them completely of them, if they
cared to help them in 'women's work.'" [8] We feel that the current process of shaping a new attitude among men toward the
family division of labor should be more actively encouraged by
ideological means and propaganda. Sociological studies show
that in families where both spouses share domestic chores,
more than 60% of the women evaluate their marriage as happy,
while in families where household duties are not distributed fairly,
80% of the women voice dissatisfaction with their marriage.[9]

Obviously the question is not one of painstakingly dividing all
household duties between husband, wife, and other members of
the family down to the last detail. It is, rather, one of a reasonable division of work and creation of the best family atmosphere for all of them. A positive fact worth noting is the apparently greater participation of men in household duties among
younger couples as compared with older families.

All those on whom improving the living conditions of women
at work, in society, and in the family depends should constantly
remember the words of Comrade Brezhnev in his speech at the
Sixteenth Trade Union Congress: we remain indebted to women.
The nation's efforts to carry out the socioeconomic program
envisaged in the decisions of the Twenty-fifth Congress of the
CPSU in the sphere of improving the conditions of work and
everyday life of women will undoubtedly serve as a new source
for the growth of their labor activity for the benefit of our Soviet Motherland.

Notes

1. V. I. Lenin, Poln. sobr. soch., vol. 39, p. 22.
2. Vestnik statistiki, 1978, no. 1, p. 91.

Current Problems of Female Labor

3. Narodonoe khoziaistvo SSSR v 1977 g., Moscow, "Statistika" Publishers, 1978, p. 408.

4. Vestnik statistiki, 1978, no. 1, p. 91.

5. Sovetskaia vlast' i raskreposhchenie zhenshchin. Sbornik dekretov i postanovlenii RSFSR, Moscow, 1921, pp. 20-21.

6. V. I. Lenin, op. cit., p. 24.

7. E. Siullero, Istoriia i sotsiologiia zhenskogo truda, Moscow, "Progress" Publishers, 1973, p. 235.

8. K. Zetkin, Iz zapisnoi knizhki, in "Vospominaniia o V. I. Lenine," vol. 2, Moscow, Gospolitizdat, 1957, p. 490.

9. E. V. Novikova, V. S. Iazykova, and Z. A. Iankova, Zhenshchina. Trud. Semia, Moscow, Profizdat, 1978, p. 60.

2

Socioeconomic Problems
of Female Employment

M. Ia. Sonin

In recent years scholarly attention has increasingly been drawn to the social dimension of the economic development of society. There are objective reasons for this.

In the epoch of building communism in the USSR there is an ever greater need for a social approach to the solution of economic problems. The importance of such an approach is especially enhanced by the expanding scientific-technological revolution, which is fundamentally changing the character of work. From a means of existence work is gradually becoming a prime necessity of life. The balance between these aspects of work is increasingly shifting toward work as a social requirement and as a form of developing human talents, self-affirmation, and the highest manifestation of vitality. All this results in changes in the employment structure.

Since the first years of Soviet power, one of the basic principles of social and economic construction in our country has been de jure and de facto equality of women in all spheres of political, social, and economic life. On this foundation concrete ways of enhancing the social and economic effectiveness of female labor were elaborated. It is work in the socialist sector

Russian text © 1977 by "Nauka" Publishers. "Sotsial'no-ekonomicheskie problemy zaniatosti zhenshchin," in *Izmenenie polozheniia zhenshchiny i sem'ia*, A. G. Kharchev, ed. (Moscow: "Nauka" Publishers, 1977), pp. 22-31.

that, under socialism, gives women both economic independence and the opportunity for self-determination, harmonious development of their personalities, and overcoming de facto inequality in their daily life. Soviet society has recorded a series of historic achievements in solving problems of female labor, achievements that are universally recognized. They include:

— full employment of Soviet women in socially useful activity and the world's highest rate of female employment;

— equal pay for equal work by men and women;

— high level of female educational and occupational training;

— one of the most progressive structures of female employment in all branches of the economy, coupled with the world's highest proportion of women in industrial management, science, culture, and art.

All these achievements are based on a state system of protection of motherhood and children and systematic resolution of the contradictions of female labor. However, some shortcomings in the utilization of female labor resources have not yet been overcome. Principal among them are: (1) the lag of women behind men in the level of occupational skills and, correspondingly, wages; (2) a longer aggregate workday (including household work) for women than for men.

These shortcomings, which are a consequence of a number of contradictory trends in the growth of female employment, breed new contradictions and trends that have to be studied in order to correctly define the ways to further female participation in the socialist sector.

After World War II, in which the Soviet Union suffered huge losses — more than 20 million human lives — an unfavorable, extremely lopsided socioeconomic and sexual population structure developed in our country (notably, 19 million more women than men). At the beginning of 1976 women accounted for 53.6% of the country's population. [1]

By now the surplus of women of able-bodied age has moved into the over-forty age brackets. Here the ratio of men to women (as of January 1, 1974) was: 856 men to 1,000 women in the 40-49 age bracket; 584 in the 50-59 bracket; 511 in the 60-69; and

411 in the 70-79 bracket. In all age brackets under 28, the number of women is slightly smaller than men, and by 28 years the
proportion evens out. [2]

The preponderance of women long affected the dynamics and
character of utilization of female labor resources. During the
war it contributed to the promotion of women to executive positions and into many other fields of highly skilled labor. At the
same time, many women were engaged in heavy, unskilled labor. In 1945 the percentage of women among all workers and
employees reached 56; by 1950 it dropped to 47, and then rose
again to 55 in 1975. [3]

By 1959 the degree of occupational activity among the female
population of able-bodied age, the main indicator of which is the
employment rate, had considerably increased. The proportion
of women employed in the socialist sector among the total number
of women increased from 38.4% in 1939 to 41.5% in 1959 to
44.5% in 1975. [4]

In the past five-year plan period, women accounted for 6.81
million out of a total increase in the work force of 11.97 million
persons. The proportion of women in the total increase in the
numbers of workers and employees was 56.9%, as opposed to
almost 60% in the preceding five-year period. By 1975 the total
female work force numbered 52.6 million, of which 16.7 million
were employed in industry, 4.5 million in agriculture (state
farms), 6.8 million in trade and procurements, 4.9 million in
public health, 6.6 million in education and culture, and 2.0 million in science. [5]

Women now constitute one half of the country's workers and
employees. As compared with 1950, by 1975 the proportion of
women had increased from 47 to 51.5%, although in the production sphere it either remained at almost the same level (46 to
49% in industry and 42 to 44% in agriculture) or declined, as in
construction (from 33 to 29%) and in transport (from 28 to 24%). [6]

The proportion of women in the work force is now highest in
such sectors as health (84%), trade and procurements (76%),
education (73%), communications services (68%), state and economic administration and management (64%), and science (50%),

that is, mainly in the nonproductive sectors, which corresponds to many distinctive features of female labor.

The rise in female employment in 1965-75 was greatest in the spheres servicing the cultural and everyday needs of the population. While the rise in female employment in the sphere of material production as a whole was relatively low (1.3%), in trade and nonproductive branches it was substantially higher (47.9% in trade, 32.8% in education, 35.4% in health, 52.8% in science, and 59.9% in housing and public services). [7]

It should be noted in this connection that over the last few years, wages increased substantially in the branches where the proportion of female labor is highest. Thus with an average national increase in average monthly cash wages of 127.4% between 1950 and 1975, the rise was 233.8% in agriculture (state farms), 131.3% in trade, 111.3% in health, and 90.8% in state and economic administration and management. [8]

Nevertheless the average wage level in branches where female labor predominates still remains somewhat below the overall average.

The educational and occupational skill levels of women employed in the economy are rising. Whereas the proportion of women employed in predominantly manual labor increased (between 1939 and 1959) by 1.2%, the proportion employed in predominantly nonmanual labor increased by 20.4%. [9]

Some 70% of the women working in industry are employed in three branches: machine building and metalworking (30%), light industry (25%), and food (11%), whereas in prerevolutionary Russia women workers were employed mainly in the textile and light industries, where mechanization and wages were lowest.

According to the Central Statistical Administration, in 1973 women in the USSR accounted for 33% of all the engineers, 38% of the technicians, and 16% of the shift, shop, or section superintendents and their deputies. [10]

The proportion of women employed in power and material-handling plant operations increased from 1% in 1926 to 23% in 1939 and to 32% in 1959 (according to the 1959 census). [11]

All this is a clear indication not only of the rise in the quan-

titative indicators of the employment of women but also of the increase in their employment in more skilled and technologically
more modern and sophisticated jobs.

What are the causes and effects of the overall rise in female
employment?

An analysis of the social and economic factors of the growth
of female employment suggests the following six main causes
for this increase in female labor activity:

1. An increased demand for manpower in all branches of the
economy, especially the nonproductive, where the use of female
labor is greatest.

2. Changes in the character of work as a result of the scientific-technological revolution, in particular making it easier.

3. Feminization of education.

4. Demographic peculiarities of the present period (declining
birthrate and family size).

5. The growth of the social and economic need for work,
associated with the growing requirements of the population
for material and cultural wealth.

6. The rise in women's personal requirements associated
with employment.

As noted before, the increase in female employment can no
longer be ascribed to the fact that there are more women than
men among the able-bodied population, since in the most active
age brackets (up to 40 years) the proportion of the female and
male population is equal. The greater numbers of women in
the older age groups contributes to the high proportion of working
women in those groups, but they are not a factor that increases the
employment rate as compared with the previous ten-year period.

The rise in female labor activity should be viewed in close connection with the rise in demand for manpower in the economy,
which affects the involvement of women in the sphere of social
labor and their distribution within that sphere. In 1959-65 the
natural increment in the able-bodied population, which is now
the main source of new manpower for the national economy,
was quite small (these were the years when young people born
during the war came of age). During that period the main

source of manpower for the nonagricultural branches of the economy was the agricultural sector, including private subsidiary farms and households, in which women were mainly employed.

In 1958-61 the absolute size and the share of the natural increase of the able-bodied population dropped sharply, while the share of redistribution of the able-bodied population from household and private subsidiary holdings into the socialist sector increased. During that period, and even more so subsequently, the labor force participation of women (not only widows and unmarried women as a result of the war but also in age groups not affected by the war) increased appreciably.

In discussing the ways in which changes in the character of work (as a result of the scientific-technological revolution, particularly mechanization and automation, scientific organization of work, etc.) affected female employment, we believe that these changes are evident in the following basic indicators: first, reduction of labor costs, especially in the sphere of material production; second, rising occupational skills. These changes are seen, notably, in the accelerated rates of development of those industries that employ highly skilled labor and in which labor costs are lower. It goes without saying that all this contributes to the greater use of female labor. That is why in 1959-70, when the work force in the Soviet Union's machine-building and metalworking industries increased by 1.1 million women and 6.2 million men, the rate of employment of women continued to be high in such branches as electrical technology, instrument building, and ball bearings, i.e., where conditions for employing female labor are most favorable. [12]

This increase is connected with the fact that women perform better than men in many work operations requiring concentrated attention, precision, and deftness (assembly, etc.), resulting in higher quality, less spoilage, saving of materials, higher output, and so on.

However, in the sphere of material production and, even more so, in the service sphere, along with the introduction of the newest types of technology requiring highly skilled workers, there still remain a whole series of nonmechanized types of work requiring few or no skills. The result is a polarization of manpower demand between high and low skills (in labor-intensive jobs). While freeing women from hard work and thereby narrowing the sphere of their employment, we often fail to make up for this by expanding employment in highly skilled jobs, most of which require fewer labor costs. Such jobs are frequently "appropriated" by men, even in those cases when the use of female labor would not only be more suitable for women but also economically more effective.

The structure of female labor is also affected by the higher rate of growth of employment in the service sphere in the last few years.

Work in many service branches usually requires a personal approach, neatness and precision, and relatively little physical labor. This creates indubitable advantages for female labor. Furthermore there are many jobs in services that permit shorter daily or weekly working hours (notably in retail trade, services, etc.), which is very convenient for women. With workers who can be employed during peak periods, when the relative manpower demand is higher, service establishments can keep hours convenient for the populace, since their work loads vary substantially over certain times of the day, week, and year. Unfortunately, part-time work is still rarely used, although the objective prerequisites for it have been created.

The new generations of women desire and can obtain higher occupational skills than the older generation. They no longer regard access to higher forms of education solely, or even predominantly, from the economic point of view. For them higher education is not so much a source of livelihood as an integral part of their general cultural development. More and more girls in our country seek to acquire a higher rather than just a general secondary education.

The accelerated growth in the educational levels of women, as well as the rise in their employment in the sphere of socialized labor, which gives them economic independence, inevitably introduces new elements in their family relationship.

Under the conditions of the scientific-technological revolution, when the importance of intelligence grows and the use of manual labor declines, the question of discovering and utilizing individual capabilities for work acquires prime economic and social significance. This is recognized all over the world. One could say that there is a worldwide search for talented and capable people. The ways and means employed in this search differ fundamentally in different social and economic systems. We have in mind the well-known process whereby the United States plunders other countries, including developing nations, by "buying" ready-made skilled specialists. This business, highly profitable for some countries, becomes a calamity for others.

Our country, like the other socialist nations, follows a different path — that of mass training of its own cadres and revealing its own talents. The task, therefore, is to create equal opportunities for educating such people. In this respect the task of equalizing the skill levels of men and women is of tremendous economic and social importance. The countries of the socialist camp possess great advantages in their capacity to solve this problem. However, these opportunities still remain inadequately utilized. This is evident, in particular, in the absence of a female ergonomics and in the insufficient correspondence between new technology employed in the national economy and social and cultural construction and the specific features of the female organism.

For women to receive sufficiently high occupational skills it is necessary to constantly improve the conditions for them to do so. An important part in achieving this can be played by reducing the aggregate workday, which is still considerably longer for working women than for men. One of the main needs for working mothers is to preserve professional knowledge at a sufficiently high level before, during, and after maternity leave. A related task is supplementary occupational training for mothers after their leave of absence when, having raised children, they want to get jobs at current levels.

Our striving for the full employment of female labor resources in no way implies that such employment must necessarily be continuous or full-time. Exceptions must be made for working mothers, and they are fully justified both economically and socially.

We have briefly reviewed existing trends in the utilization of female labor resources. Let us now try to "forecast" those trends.

The utilization of female labor resources in the near and more distant future will be influenced by two interrelated trends: reduction in the tempo of the natural growth of labor resources, and increased labor activity. The recent reduction in the birthrate will result in a future reduction in the annual increase in male and female labor resources. [13] At the same time, it can be assumed that increased labor activity of the female population will find expression less in an increase in the percentage of women employed in the sphere of social labor than in changes in the sectoral, occupational, and skill structure of their employment, as well as in greater employment of women of retirement age. The skill levels of the female work force will rise at a higher rate than those of males.

The main direction for changes in the sectoral, occupational, and skill structure of female labor should be toward freeing women from heavy work and expanding employment in mechanized jobs.

It is still insufficiently clear which areas of work and which jobs are most in keeping with the general development and rational employment of women. To this day it is not clear, from a theoretical point of view, to what extent the feminization of some trades is inevitable or what the "limits" of feminization are in trades conventionally regarded as purely "feminine." Solution of these problems is an urgent task of scholarship and practice.

Women's work stations at existing enterprises are as a rule less comfortable than men's since they were initially designed for the male organism. The lack of a "female ergonomics" is painfully acute in designing new industrial plants. Even at new plants where it is known in advance that women will be predominantly employed, the machines and equipment often do not correspond to their physical makeup. There are also many shortcomings in the principles of organization of female labor.

A very serious shortcoming in planning the requirements for female personnel by occupation is the divorce of such planning from the demographic structure of the labor resources.

The designing of new enterprises still includes only equipment and manufacturing processes with no reference to the occupational and skill composition of the work force. Yet only an integrated blending of the design of new technology and the makeup of the work force manpower requirements can correctly determine the requirements for the timely training of qualified workers.

The task of completely eliminating the remnants of women's inequality in daily life and creating the social and living conditions making it possible to combine happy motherhood with increasingly active and creative participation in the labor force and in civic activity, science, and art, as set forth in the CPSU Program, is being successfully implemented. In the Report of the Central Committee of the CPSU to the Twenty-fifth Party Congress, L. I. Brezhnev stressed: "The party considers it its duty to display constant concern for woman and to improve her position as a participant in the labor process, a mother, a counselor of her children, and a housewife." [14]

Ever new and more complex tasks arise in solving the problems of female labor, without the solution of which, at the present stage of development, it is impossible to advance rapidly along the road to communism. The main way to assure the ever more active and creative participation of women in social labor today is to raise the skill level of female labor. The educational and occupational training of women must be geared to this, together with the creation of the best sanitary, hygienic, and other working conditions.

When we speak of work, and within it the raising of skills, as an overriding task, we have in mind work that must become a prime necessity of life: communist work. Consequently, the task of equalizing occupational skills is posed not as a tactical objective but as a strategic, long-term task.

The specific problems of female labor are not secondary.

31

M. Ia. Sonin

They can be resolved only within a complex of political, economic, and organizational measures, the preparation of which requires specialized knowledge and a special approach.

Notes

1. SSSR v tsifrakh v 1975 godu, Moscow, 1976, p. 9.
2. Estimated from Narodnoe khoziaistvo SSSR v 1973 godu, Moscow, 1974, p. 34.
3. Vestnik statistiki, 1976, no. 1, p. 85.
4. Zhenshchiny v SSSR, Moscow, 1975, p. 26.
5. Estimated from SSSR v tsifrakh v 1975 godu, p. 175; Vestnik statistiki, 1976, no. 1, p. 85.
6. Ibid.
7. Estimated from SSSR v tsifrakh v 1975 godu, pp. 174-77.
8. Estimated from Trud v SSSR, Moscow, 1976, p. 138; SSSR v tsifrakh v 1975 godu, p. 180.
9. Zhenshchiny i deti v SSSR, Moscow, 1969, p. 66.
10. Zhenshchiny v SSSR, p. 78.
11. Zhenshchiny i deti v SSSR, p. 68.
12. Itogi Vsesoiuznoi perepisi naseleniia 1970 goda, vol. 6, Moscow, 1973, p. 14.
13. In the future industries will apparently introduce integrated mechanization and automation, and the factor of increasing the work force employed in the spheres of material production will no longer be of the decisive importance it is now and will continue to be in the next few years.
14. XXV s''ezd KPSS. Stenograficheskii otchet, vol. 1, Moscow, 1976, p. 111.

3

Features of the Development
of Female Employment

V. G. Kostakov

The basic trends in studies of the problem of female employment are determined by their role in the development and utilization of labor resources. One of the directions of research
seeks to reveal the relationships between general trends in the
utilization of labor resources and the specific features of a
given population group. This has in large measure shaped the
questions taken up in this paper: analyses of changes in the
levels of female employment, factors affecting women's employment in the economy, the distribution of women by industries, occupations, and skills, geographic differences in the
utilization of female labor resources — that is, the most important aspects of the use of labor resources that help most
fully to reveal specific processes connected with female employment.

Another direction of analysis is linked directly with the specific features of female labor resources, which allows for a
comprehensive approach to the evaluation of the employment
situation of women, with due account of sociopolitical, economic,
and demographic factors. This approach considers not only
the need of a woman to combine work and the functions of motherhood, but also the resolution of economic problems which

Russian text © 1976 by "Ekonomika" Publishers. *Trudovye resursy: Sotsial'no-ekonomicheskii
analiz* (Moscow, "Ekonomika" Publishers, 1976), part V, pp. 101-35.

grants ever greater de facto equality of men and women.
Correct understanding of the de facto equality of men and
women, especially in the area of employment, is of great
methodological and practical importance. It is a special
kind of equality, evaluated not according to the degree to which
women's work is identical to men's, but according to the social
consequences of the use of female labor.

Analyses of female employment reveal a number of important
features of the current utilization of female labor resources
and make it possible to draw conclusions regarding ways to
further improve it. The Report of the CPSU Central Committee
to the Twenty-fifth Party Congress noted the great contributions of Soviet women in developing the economy and enhancing the
power of our country. Recognizing that the solution of many
important tasks in all spheres of public life will in the future
continue to depend in many ways on the work of women, "the
party believes its duty is to display constant concern for women
and improve the position of woman as a participant in the
labor process, mother, rearer of children, and housewife."[1]

The greatest changes since the war in the utilization of female labor resources took place between 1959 and 1970. This
discussion concentrates mainly on that period, all the more so
as the 1959 and 1970 census returns are frequently the only
source of information for studying many social and economic
aspects of female labor nationwide and by republic.

1. The Employment Situation of Women
at the Present Stage

Changes in female employment in the USSR have gone through
several stages, corresponding to the specific features of economic development at different periods. These periods are:
the years of the prewar five-year plans (1928-40), the period
of World War II (1941-45), the postwar economic reconstruction
period (1946-50), and the periods 1951-58, 1959-70, and 1971-75.
Each period is characterized by certain peculiarities in the utilization of female labor resources stemming from a number of so-

ciopolitical, economic, and demographic causes. The determining factor in expanding female employment has always been the
need to provide manpower for the economy. At the same time, the
economic need to draw women into the work force corresponded
to one of our state's social tasks: to secure equal social status of
women through their participation in socially productive labor.

The 1959-70 period was characterized by a high rate of change
in the employment situation of women which affected its very
character. A qualitative leap took place in the utilization of
female labor resources, and the degree of socialization of female labor increased substantially.

Between 1959 and 1970 the involvement of female labor resources in the socialized economy and study increased from
72.6 to 89.7%, or 17 percentage points[2] (see Table 1). Such
a substantial peacetime rise in the level of female employment
can only be compared with the period of industrialization and
collectivization, when profound social changes linked with the
development of socialist production occurred.

In absolute figures the number of women of working age
engaged outside the socialized economy, mainly in the home
or in private subsidiary agriculture, declined by 11 million,
and their proportion in total labor resources declined by a
factor of 2.7.

Table 1

Distribution of Women of Working Age
According to Type of Occupation
(in %, according to 1959 and 1970 censuses)

	1959	1970
Women of working age occupied in:	100.0	100.0
The public sector or full-time education	72.6	89.7
in the public sector	68.4	82.1
in full-time education	4.2	7.6
Outside the public sector or education	27.4	10.3

35

High labor participation rates are at present characteristic of almost all age groups of the able-bodied female population: about 90% for women up to 49 years of age. The level decreases only in the preretirement age group, largely because some women between 50 and 54 years old are entitled to earlier retirement or disability pensions. The level of female employment today does not differ much from that of male employment. Whereas in 1959 the gap between employment levels of men and women was 20 percentage points, in 1970 it was only 5 points.

The liberation of female labor resources from the household and private subsidiary agriculture at a time of slow growth in the size of the able-bodied population has enhanced the role of women in replenishing the work force. Except for the war years the 1959-70 period saw the highest proportion of women in the overall growth of the work force: 58% (46% in 1928-40, 28% in 1945-50, 43% in 1951-58). Between 1959 and 1970 the number of women workers and employees increased by 80% (men by 50%), and their proportion in the total labor force reached 51%. The growth in the number of women workers and employees was made possible by the decline in the number of women working at home and on private subsidiary plots, as well as in the socialized sector of agriculture.

It should be noted that the redistribution of female labor resources between the socialized and private sectors may be either absolute or relative, which must be taken into account in evaluating the qualitative composition of additional labor resources. In the first case, when women leave domestic production and begin to work in the socialized sector, there occurs a change in the sphere of activity within the same population groups. In the latter case, when the natural decrease in the female population in the private sector (due to old age, disability, etc.) is not made up in whole or in part by new individuals, the reduction in the number occupied in the household does not involve any shift in the sphere of activity of the given population groups. In 1959-70 most of the decline in the number of women of working age not engaged in the socialized sector or education was due to women who had been occupied in the household or private subsidiary holdings in 1959 and since then found work in the socialized sector, and only a small part was due to natural causes (old age, etc.) largely not made up by an influx of young women. For that reason the major contribution to the work force from this source was of women in the median and older age groups.

The reduction of employment of women in the socialized sector of agriculture was of a somewhat different nature. Young rural women reaching working age only partially made up for the natural reduction in the number of women in agriculture. A fairly intensive outflow of young women from villages to cities took place, which served to increase the number of workers and employees. However, the share of this source in increasing the number of employed women was about one half of that from the transfer from household duties and private subsidiary agriculture.

Consequently the 1959-70 period was characterized not only by an exceptionally high proportion of women in the increment to the work force but also by a change in the qualitative composition of the additional female contingent. In 1951-58 the able-bodied population, including women, increased considerably while the number of women engaged outside the socialized sector remained almost unchanged; this provided for an influx of mainly young people into the economy.

The change in sources of female labor contributed to a substantial change in the age structure of working women: the share of women of median and older ages increased considerably, raising the proportion of less-skilled female labor, since these women were less educated and less trained for jobs. Between 1959 and 1970 the female population in the 30-54 age bracket increased by only 4.7 million, but the number of women from this group employed in the socialized sector increased much more. The difference between the increase in the numbers of women in general and the number of working women was especially marked in the 40-54 age group. The number of women aged 16 to 29 employed in the economy decreased somewhat owing to higher enrollment of young women in full-time education (the number of women students increased 90% between 1959 and 1970) and the sharp drop in the female population in this age group. Even so, the considerable outflow of young women from villages to cities produced an increase in the number of working women in the nonagricultural sector.

Characteristically, in those age groups in which employment increased (30 years and older), women either predominated in the increment (30 to 39 years), or the increment was wholly due to women (40 to 49 and preretirement age). The result was an "aging" of the female work force. The male work force increased mainly due to the influx of young people.

The significant influx of women into socialized production from the private sector in 1959-70 had a major impact on a number of processes in the development of employment as a whole. First, the general level of employment of the able-bodied population increased. The degree of socialization of labor attained virtually its natural limits, which is very important in evaluating the development of socialist production relations and the prospects for utilizing labor resources. The higher the proportion of the population employed in the socialized sector, the stronger the socialist relations of production. On the other hand, a high employment level increases the need for effective utilization of manpower and alters attitudes toward the procurement of manpower for rapidly developing industries.

High female employment means that most able-bodied women work in collectives, participate in social and political life, and are economically independent. Extensive participation of women in social production is of great importance for achieving de facto equality with men as well as for personal development. But in evaluating female employment it is necessary to take the aggregate of social, economic, and demographic processes into account.

It should once again be stressed that a substantial expansion of the rate of female employment took place in the remarkably short period of ten years. But within such a short period society is not always able to develop all branches of the economy to the extent needed to fully meet the demand for services, children's institutions, etc. In 1959-70, when large numbers of women of working age were drawn into the socialized sector, the inadequate level of social services that would enable women to harmoniously combine work and child-rearing led to a decline in the birthrate. It dropped so sharply during these years that in some regions of the country, expanded reproduction of the population began to give way to simple reproduction.

Furthermore the considerable expansion of female labor and high proportion of women joining the work force, coupled with continued differences in the technological equipment of factories and industries, made due consideration of the specific features of female labor difficult.

Thus, attaining high levels of female employment means society must face certain tasks in the future utilization of their labor: it is necessary to enhance its effectiveness, improve the employment structure, improve working and living conditions more than has been done until now, and take due account of the specific features of female labor.

Five years have passed since the last census. The sources of female labor have changed considerably during these years. Household work and private subsidiary holdings have almost completely lost their significance as additional sources of labor. During the Ninth Five-Year Plan period, the labor resources engaged outside the socialized sector and education declined slightly for the USSR as a whole while increasing in the republics of Central Asia and Transcaucasia, sometimes substantially. The role of agriculture as a source of replenishment of the labor force has declined considerably.

The main source of replenishment of the female work force was the increase in numbers of women of working age. Employment of women pensioners increased somewhat. While formerly unskilled and uninteresting jobs, especially in the services, were filled mainly by former housewives or women who worked on private subsidiary holdings, today these jobs are often held by women of pension age.

Owing to specific features in the industrial and occupational distribution of working women and the slow rate of technical reequipment of various branches of the economy, the demand for additional female labor remains high. However, in the Ninth Five-Year Plan the growth of the female labor force began to slow down, with an average annual growth rate of 2.8% in 1971-75, as compared with 3.9% in 1966-70. This is a positive trend in the utilization of labor resources in general and female labor in particular.

It was noted at the Twenty-fifth CPSU Congress that only higher labor productivity can assure performance of society's major socioeconomic tasks. The ever growing role of labor productivity in economic development will in the future lead to a further reduction in the economic demand for female labor. It is important to bear in mind that aggravation of the labor resources problem in the '80s is in many ways due to a sharp drop in the increase in the numbers of women of working age. This gives special urgency to the question of raising the effectiveness of utilization of female labor.

2. Factors Affecting Female Employment

The employment of women is influenced by two groups of factors: those that determine the economic demand for female labor, and those that shape women's demand for work, their attitudes toward work in social production, and choice of occupation. When these factors blend harmoniously, the economy gets the labor it needs, and the women who want it find work. In other words, parity is achieved between the supply and demand of female labor for a given level of employment of women of working age. This is one aspect of female employment that derives from the general requirement for rational utilization of labor resources. The other is associated with the specific features of female labor resources. The achievement of optimum female employment requires not only balanced supply and demand of female labor, with due account of the specific features of its utilization, but also a level of women's employment that assures the socially necessary rate of reproduction of the population and the best upbringing of future generations. Knowing the mechanisms through which these factors affect female employment, it is possible to regulate the employment rate of female labor resources with due account taken of their most rational utilization.

An analysis of the development of female employment, especially over the last fifteen years, shows that production factors are decisive among all the diverse elements affecting changes in the employment situation of women. Under conditions of the steadily rising material and spiritual needs of the population, the demand for female labor is a powerful incentive for drawing women into the socialized sector. The accelerated growth of needs makes the possibility of a supplementary income attractive to many groups in the population.

The demand of various branches of the economy for female labor is in the first place shaped under the influence of the rate of development of the economy and its structure (nationally and regionally), as well as by the occupational composition of the work force as determined by technological progress and the organizational standards of production.

A high rate of economic development has been and remains a constant factor in the growth of female employment. The expansion of production in our country is accompanied by profound qualitative changes in the branch structure of the economy that facilitate the employment of women in the socialized sector. In 1959-70, however, the high level of female employment was to some degree influenced by peculiarities of economic development during that period, which was characterized by exceptionally extensive new construction. This somewhat restricted the material and financial opportunities for improving existing production and raising labor productivity. The result was heavy demand for more labor (both skilled and unskilled). A shortage of male labor resources, as well as the contribution of young people to the rise in male employment, facilitated continued redistribution of male labor into skilled jobs. The result was an increase in vacancies in low-skilled jobs. They were largely filled by women previously occupied in the home

41

or private subsidiary agriculture.

An analysis of changes in the composition of the female work force by trades and skills showed that in 1959-70, half the increase in the number of women employed in nonagricultural branches was in mainly low-skilled, blue-collar jobs. Thus the greatest increase in female employment was registered in such trades as salesperson and cook — 1.5 million persons; 1.1 million in machine-building and metalworking trades; 950,000 office cleaners, janitors, porters, gatekeepers, and cloakroom attendants; 930,000 warehouse attendants, weighers, receivers, distributors, quality inspectors, sorters, and controllers; 700,000 orderlies, attendants, and nurse' aides; 505,000 sewing-machine operators; 437,000 house painters and plasterers.

Obviously the high rates of growth of female employment cannot be associated solely with greater employment in the jobs listed above.

It should be noted that over the examined period, the number of women employed in white-collar jobs also increased at a high rate. Of the eight million women who found employment in mainly white-collar jobs, one quarter were engineering and technical personnel, and almost as many worked in planning and accounting (mainly bookkeepers, economists, planners, tellers). This is, on the one hand, a positive change bespeaking the growing proportion of skilled labor among women. On the other hand, however, a different assessment can be made of the increase in the number of women in these jobs, insofar as it involves the irrational use of labor resources. More extensive introduction of progressive forms of organization of work, computerization, and other gains of scientific-technological progress would reduce the demand for engineers, economists, and especially, accountants.

The influence of production factors on the level of employment of women is especially apparent in the geographic aspect. Disregarding those areas where ethnic family, household, and child-bearing traditions are strong, we note that the higher the regional economy's demand for labor deriving from comprehensive economic development, the higher the employment rate among women. The highest level of female employment is found in the largest cities with diversified economic structures (Moscow, Leningrad). Female employment is lowest in those communities and areas where low production or lopsided industrial development fail to provide adequate opportunities for female labor. In the RSFSR, for example, this is true of a number of oblasts of the Central Black-Earth, North Caucasus, and Eastern regions, the southern and southwestern regions of the Ukraine, and so on. Comprehensive economic development of a town or district, moreover, not only provides jobs for women but also creates favorable opportunities for women to combine work in the socialized sector with household duties.

The high level of female employment in the nation is to some degree due to the imbalance in the sex composition of the population caused by World War II. Under normal conditions, for the same number of women 16 to 54 years of age there would be eight or nine million more men of working age and fewer working women (given the current manpower requirements of the economy). Consequently, the employment level of women would have been some 15 percentage points below the present level, since there would have been no need to employ so many women from households or private subsidiary agriculture. But is it possible to explain the considerable rise in female employment in 1959-70 better by demographic than by socioeconomic factors? If, in the face of demographic disruptions, labor was more efficiently employed in all spheres of the economy, including services, and the rates of growth of productivity were higher, the same levels of output could have been attained without drawing on additional labor sources to the extent this was done in 1959-70.

In planning it is necessary to take more fully into account that various sex and age groups of the population display specific employment characteristics, which makes it inadvisable to replace one group of workers with another, like hiring women instead of men or making up for shortages of young people of both sexes by recruiting older men and women, including

43

pensioners. When the composition of the work force by sex (as well as by age, education, etc.) does not meet the requirements of modern production, poor utilization of labor and lower productivity result. Attempts to use female labor resources not occupied in socialized production must be based on real reserves of labor freed from domestic chores as a result of the expansion of socialist forms of services and child-rearing. Special attention must be given to this in view of the fact that the 1971-80 period, with its high rate of increase in the able-bodied population (both men and women), will be followed by a decade (1981-90) in which the growth in the number of people of working age, especially women, will diminish sharply.

In the future, the growing role of intensive factors will sustain high rates of economic development, permitting a considerable reduction in the demands of the economy for female labor, especially in work that still does not correspond to the current achievements of scientific-technological progress. The growing requirements of some spheres of employment for women workers can be met by the redistribution of female labor among branches and occupations.

While attaching the greatest significance to production factors in the changing patterns of women's employment, it is also necessary to reckon with those factors that satisfy the need to work. It would be unfair to regard the high rate of growth of female employment in 1959-70 as a result solely of production factors. It was also influenced by factors that determine the material and moral incentives for women to participate in social production and services.

At present a woman's wages are of great importance for a family's material well-being. The income of a family of three or four increases by 60 to 70% when the wife also works. In addition, women workers enjoy a number of benefits: paid pregnancy and maternity leave, state-financed maintenance of children in various children's institutions, social insurance vouchers to rest homes and sanatoriums, material assistance, if necessary, from a trade union organization, and opportunities for improving housing and living conditions. All of these strengthen women's interest in working in the socialized economy.

A highly complex question is the effect of the income of workers employed in the national economy on the formation of woman's need to do socially useful labor. Experience shows that higher living standards and higher female employment are parallel phenomena. Naturally, all other conditions being equal, the higher one's average wage, the more material and spiritual values can be acquired; hence higher wages enhance the economic need to work. An important part in this is played by the structure of a family's expenses and the degree to which they satisfy contemporary notions of life style.

Between 1961 and 1970 average wages of workers and employees in the USSR rose 50%. As wages rise, so does the inducement for women to participate in social production. This is confirmed by the fact that highly paid women try to cut down any nonpaid interruptions in their work. It can therefore be claimed that high rates of increase in wages contribute to higher female employment. Furthermore, higher family income makes it possible to rely more on everyday services and catering, reduce the time devoted to household work, and more meaningfully spend the greater free time.

At the same time, sample sociological surveys show that some working women would leave production jobs if their husbands earned more. Many of these women work in unskilled jobs or under poor working conditions. Two factors simultaneously influence the attitudes of this category of working women toward work: the unattractiveness of the type and conditions of work and low wages. One should also take into account the low educational level of these women.

It can therefore be assumed that any substantial rise in a family's income, given the current occupational and skills composition of the female work force, would result in some more poorly educated women leaving their jobs.

As some sociological studies show, the proportion of working women who would like to leave work is not high, although in absolute figures it may run into several millions and appreciably lower the general level of female employment. But wage changes and the growth of family incomes are not arbitrary processes. They depend on our society's economic development; it will probably be more than one five-year period before wages, say, double. At the same time, industry and its technological equipment and organizational forms will continue to improve, the number of jobs with unfavorable working conditions will decline, and the occupational and skills structure of the work force will improve, all of which will undoubtedly enhance the appeal of work. Also, greater development of the service sphere and socialized forms of child care will help to substantially ease and reduce domestic work, thus reducing the working woman's work load. All this will help maintain high employment levels among women of working age.

In our view higher family income, especially at the stage when the structure of consumption is determined less by daily needs and more by durables and expenses on recreation, can have only a short-term effect on a reduction in women's employment. Given sufficiently high earnings of one working member, a family may accept the temporary loss of some income if it is warranted by its interests in raising children or caring for an ailing member of the family (for example, taking a longer leave of absence than provided by labor law to look after small children, leaving work for health reasons, or wider use of part-time work).

It should be noted that for some women work in the socialized economy is the only or main source of subsistence. They are unmarried women, widows, and divorcees, with or without children.

It is not surprising that under socialist conditions, when the distribution of wealth in the society is based mainly on the quantity and quality of labor, the labor activity of the female population is determined primarily by social and economic factors.

Principal among them is the desire to secure higher family income to meet higher demands. But there is also an attendant incentive. This is the woman's desire for economic independence. Although a family's income can be increased by means other than increasing the number of workers, the woman can achieve economic independence only by working. Women's economic independence and, hence, socially productive labor are the material basis for attaining de facto equality of men and women in many spheres of life. It appears to us that today many women fail to realize the importance of this factor, which is obfuscated by family ties. Nonetheless, it is an inevitable concomitant of female employment. Women's attitudes toward work and their assessments of motivations to work change with the increasing well-being of the nation, rising educational standards, higher occupational and skill levels for working women, and better working conditions. It appears that the desire for economic independence will become one of the main incentives for female employment. While based on material considerations, the desire for economic independence is in many ways nurtured by ethical considerations.

The combination of material and moral incentives to work is inherent in socialist relations in general; but as applied to women's work, it is of special significance. A man's obligation to work is a result of the traditional view of his role in the family and society; by the same token, a woman need not work. Yet today almost all able-bodied women do work, and the overwhelming majority of them have no desire to leave work.

The social conditions of our society's development create a favorable atmosphere for fostering new attitudes toward work, which determines a great deal in the occupational activities of women, who usually combine work and motherhood. When we speak of the immediate reasons affecting the growing moral need for women to participate in social production, we note the growth of female employment and the higher educational standards of women.

At first glance there seems to be no connection between the development of moral incentives to work and women's employment. However, the participation of women in social production, even when it is initially prompted solely by material considerations, has a great impact on the development of

47

moral incentives to work. The overwhelming number of employed women develop a life image that includes work in the socialized economy as an essential element. The actual status of women of one generation, even if it was due to economic necessity, is passed on to the next generation as a way of life and is a great incentive in the preservation of high labor activity among women. Women who take part in social labor experience the advantages of work in a collective; they feel public recognition of their occupational activity and their usefulness to society, which also shapes their attitude toward socially productive labor. Finally, it is work that most fully brings out a woman's professional abilities and provides opportunities for realizing her intellectual and spiritual values, which facilitates the development of the personality.

High general education levels supplemented with vocational education make it possible for women to do skilled work. As a result, with the growth of general education, professional work increasingly becomes an ethical necessity for women. In all age groups of women of working age, employment is highest among those having a higher education and lowest among those with primary education or less. The same correlation was found in a survey of nonworking women; the higher the education, the larger the proportion of women who expressed the desire to work. Furthermore, an analysis of the occupational and skill composition of working women revealed substantial differences in the character and conditions of work as a function of the level of education.

It can be concluded from what has been said that the level of women's education offers a general idea of the development of moral incentives to work, despite a certain arbitrariness in this approach. An important factor is the transfer from one level of education to another: from primary to incomplete secondary and then on to complete secondary (general and specialized) and higher education (in 1970 women were approximately equally divided among the three levels of education). In our opinion, among working women with a higher education, moral incentives to work may be of equal or even dominant

significance as compared with economic incentives; for women
with a secondary education they are equivalent. Women with
a low education level have fewer grounds to attach any significant meaning to moral factors in their work, since most of them
do low-skilled jobs. Furthermore low education levels coupled
with age (in 1970 almost half the working women in the 40-49
year age group and two thirds in the 50-54 group had no more
than a primary education) reduce the prospects of raising their
educational standards and occupational training. As a consequence these women have virtually no prospects for job promotion, which also affects their attitudes toward work.

Despite the fact that the proportion of women with a primary
education or less is still fairly high, the rise in the educational
level of the female population in 1959-70 was considerable.
This was reflected in rising female employment. Between 1959
and 1970 the proportion of women with a higher, secondary, or
incomplete secondary education among all women of working
age increased 50%. Among young women (up to 35 years) the
proportion with a higher or full secondary education (general
or specialized) more than doubled. In the older age groups
the proportion of women with primary education or less declined considerably: from 74 to 48% in the 40-44 year group,
from 87 to 49% in the 45-59 group, and from 89 to 69% in the
50-54 group.

The inevitability of a woman combining work in the socialized
economy with motherhood gives great importance to demographic factors (family composition and size) in the changing patterns
of female employment. Socioeconomic conditions also play an
important part in this.

Analysis of the relationship between female employment
and demographic processes shows that family composition and
size are secondary to material and moral incentives in the expansion of female employment. But when all other conditions
are equal, demographic factors determine the working woman's
status, her work load, with all the attendant consequences for
her employment and starting a family. The level of public services play an important part in this. By the early '60s, when

49

many nonworking women began to join the work force, public forms of satisfying various needs were poorly developed.

Later the service sector developed at a fairly rapid rate; but demand also increased rapidly, as more and more women joined the work force. In 1960-70 employment of women in the service sphere increased at the same rate as the total number of women workers and employees: by 60%. That is why, despite some improvements in public services, the present level has not removed the problem of housekeeping.

Naturally, with inadequate public services high employment among women is more often than not explained by the predominance of small families. According to the 1970 census, 83% of all families in the country had one or two children or none at all: more than three quarters were families consisting of one couple with or without children or of mothers (fathers) with children, that is, families with no household help within them. Since childless families are typical mainly of women of younger and older ages, family women in the age cohort of highest labor activity (25-45 years) are even more homogeneous in the number of children (one or two), and hence in the amount of housework.

Large families are still common only in areas of the country inhabited by nationalities with stable family and domestic traditions and high birthrates. Whereas 89% of Russian and Ukrainian (ethnically homogeneous) families and 93% of Estonian and Latvian families are small or childless, the proportion is only 34% among the Tadzhiks, 36% among Uzbeks, and 43% among Kirghiz. Large families predominate among the indigenous populations of Central Asia and Azerbaidzhan, which is the main reason for the low employment rates among women in those republics.

The age of children is also an important factor in female employment. The hardest time for a woman to work is when her children are small. According to the 1970 census there were 30 million children under seven years of age in the country, the overwhelming majority of them children of working women, insofar as 82% of the women of able-bodied age work. Just

over nine million children attended preschool institutions. It
should be borne in mind that the mothers of small children are
usually young women at the peak of their creative powers (the
overwhelming majority of children up to three years old belong
to women 20 to 34 years old). It is not surprising that with a
shortage of preschool children's establishments, these women
desire a minimal number of children in the family.

There is a heated debate over the reasons for the country's
declining birthrate in recent years. In our view the connection
between the level of employment of women in the socialized
economy and the birthrate is obvious. And it is important to
take into account that women today prefer work, insofar as
it permits them to satisfy a wide range of material and moral
interests, while the need for motherhood can be satisfied with
the minimum number of children. That is why the main efforts
in the search for ways to combine female employment and motherhood should be aimed at improving conditions for aiding in
child care and education, as well as household work, to leave
working women sufficient free time for harmonious development. The Tenth Five-Year Plan envisages a number of measures aimed at improving the position of working women: introduction of partially paid leave to care for children up to
one year old, high-priority programs for building children's
preschool institutions in areas with high female employment
and in major industrial centers, and further development of
the service sector, with special attention to improving the
quality of its work.

3. Women's Vocational Specialization

The development of women's occupational specialization
is characterized by the ever greater penetration of female labor into different types of work. Our country's experience
long ago proved the practical expedience and feasibility of overcoming the traditional division of labor between men and wom-
en and the possibility of women performing many jobs of great
complexity or responsibility. Women work on a par with men

V. G. Kostakov

for the benefit of our society's social and economic progress.

Women now account for almost, or more than, half the work force in all leading branches of the economy except construction and transport. Industry, with its diversified structure, is the largest sphere of female employment, in which 28% of all working women are occupied (see Table 2). We find 30% of the women working in industry engaged in machine building, 25% in the textile and garment industry, 11% in the food industry, and 34% in other industries (printing, porcelain and earthenwares, chemicals, etc.).

Table 2

Women's Employment by Sector
According to the 1959 and 1970 Censuses
(% of total female work force)

Branch	1959	1970
Material production	80.5	72.4
industry	21.9	27.9
construction, transport, mail and communications	7.8	9.3
agriculture and forestry	43.9	25.2
trade, public catering, procurement, material supplies	6.7	10.1
other branches	0.2	0.6
Nonproduction branches	19.5	27.6
health, sports, social security, education, science, art	14.5	20.7
public housing, utilities and services, administration, banking and finance, public organizations	4.8	6.5
unclassified	0.2	0.4

Second in number of working women is agriculture, though its importance as a factor in female employment is steadily declining. In only eleven years between 1959 and 1970, the

52

number of women working in agriculture declined by more
than one third, while employment in nonagricultural spheres
increased 60%. Still, it must be noted that agriculture continues to divert a substantial portion of female labor resources,
with 25% of all working women engaged in it.

Women predominate in the highly important spheres of sociocultural and everyday services. Twenty-one percent of all
working women work in education, culture, sports, art, and
public health. Another significant sphere of the economy with
respect to the scope of female labor is trade and public catering, which accounts for 10% of the working women.

According to the 1970 census, women were extensively represented in many leading industrial and humanitarian occupations. They account for 44% of engineering and technical personnel, 35% of agronomists, 45% of livestock specialists, 38%
of lawyers, 43% of college and university teachers, 74% of
secondary general school teachers, 74% of doctors, and 82%
of economists. There are quite a few trades in which women
are employed almost exclusively: in the textile and garment
industries, some agricultural occupations (milker, poultry
tender, vegetable farm worker), saleswomen, waitresses,
drafters, nurses, pharmacists, counselors at preschool establishments, librarians, telephone operators, accountants, tellers,
typists, stenographers, and other occupations.

Despite the extensive penetration of female labor into various spheres of employment, the proportions of men and women
vary greatly from industry to industry and occupation to occupation. However, the important social principle — assuring the
equality of women and men — is more than an arithmetic equality,
an equal representation of women in all occupations. The important thing is for women to receive the necessary vocational
training, to work in healthy conditions, and to perform the same
skilled work as men. If the occupational specialization of wom-
en meets these requirements, it can be considered optimal, regardless of the proportions of women in various jobs and occupations.

At the same time, proportions of men and women in various
types of work should develop with due consideration of the re-

quirement of the industry or service for the personal qualities of the worker of a given sex and age. One should also not overlook so important an aspect of work as the social and psychological climate in the collective (comradely mutual assistance and mutual understanding, attentive attitudes on the part of the management, etc.). Harmonious blending of the efforts of workers of different sex and age groups in the production collective makes it possible more fully to take the specific traits and features of each into account and contributes to the creation of a favorable work environment.

The proportion of men and women in various jobs is in many respects determined by the level of female employment, the nature of work and conditions in various branches and occupations, and differences in wage payments in different branches. Women constitute one half the national work force; and if they were evenly distributed by branches and occupations, the percentage would be fairly high everywhere. However, there are jobs that are more suitable and jobs that are less suitable for women. As a consequence the percentage of women is higher in some trades and professions and lower in others; and with a high percentage of women in the work force, many occupations and even branches become predominantly female.

Is this in keeping with the social and economic purpose of different types of labor? Undoubtedly there are trades that most fully suit the psychophysiological characteristics of the female organism, for example, jobs requiring great accuracy and attention, which should result in high female employment in such jobs. But this does not mean that only women can perform them; rather the character of work is more suitable to a woman's temperament and more satisfying for her than for a man.

However, when a certain sex or age group predominates in a production collective, difficulties arise, for example, in the organization of work (women with children may refuse to go on business trips or to accept changes in work schedules, a preponderance of young people may mean numerous requests for leaves of absence, for study, etc.). And when a preponderance of women (or men) becomes typical of an enterprise, or, even more so, a community, serious social and demographic problems may arise.

Furthermore there are types of work whose socioeconomic significance requires that they be equally shared by men and women (for example, education and public health). Education is more than just learning; it is also the rearing of new generations, in which women and men should participate equally. Public health is one of the main social branches of the economy the effective functioning of which determines the health and physical fitness of people, the principal productive force of society. The nature of work in public health also presumes a more harmonious blending of male and female labor, insofar as today there are more women doctors than men.

The high level of female employment in the economy, where there are jobs with different working conditions, many of them ill-adapted to the psychophysiological characteristics of the female organism, results in a concentration of female labor in unsuitable jobs. Considerable differences in wage payments in different branches economically consolidate the occupational specialization of men and women. With time the practice of job recruitment by sex begins to determine the occupational orientation of women and men.

Under the conditions of the scientific-technological revolution and a planned economy, it is possible to regulate the composition of the work force by sex and by types of work by varying the socioeconomic parameters of occupational orientation, choice of occupation, and place of work, reducing differences in wage payment by branches, and changing the character and conditions of work. Technological innovation makes it possible, on the one hand, to expand female employment in branches and jobs where women are rarely or never employed and, on the other, to enhance the attractiveness to men of jobs in which the proportion of women is now high. Still, varying proportions of men and women in different branches, trades, and occupations are inevitable. It is, however, hardly correct to preserve considerable differences from one branch to another. Differences in the proportions of women within certain occupations may vary more than from one branch to another, but they can level off within an enterprise or branch despite the existence of jobs filled mainly by men. Moreover, the distribution of women by branch and occupation should be such as to take into account the specific features of the female organism and not to place women in less skilled jobs.

In evaluating the skill structure of the female labor force, it is worth considering separately jobs involving mainly mental functions and jobs with predominantly manual functions, performance of which requires different levels of general and specialized education. Of the total female work force, 32% do white-collar jobs and 68%, manual jobs. Women are more extensively employed than men in jobs in which mental work predominates. Almost three fifths of the total white-collar work force are women, while among manual workers they make up less than half (according to the 1970 census).

The high rate of employment of women in jobs requiring a higher or specialized secondary education is a major social achievement. Fifty-nine percent of all specialists employed in the economy are women.

However, the higher proportion of specialists among working women as compared with men is due to the large number of women with a secondary specialized education. Whereas in 1972 for every 100 women specialists with a higher education there were 173 with a specialized secondary education, among men the proportion was 100 to 117. In some branches, especially public health, the difference in this ratio is even higher. Major occupational groups with a high proportion of women are engineers and technologists, teachers, counselors, doctors, bookkeepers, and economists (see Table 3).

Characteristically, today the number of women specialists having a higher education is growing at a faster rate in industrially developed branches: construction, communications, industry (3.2, 3.1, and 2.8 times, respectively, as compared with a 2.3-fold growth for the economy as a whole in 1959-70). This is an indication of the growing role of women in the development of industrial branches of the economy under the conditions of the scientific-technological revolution. High

Table 3

Occupational Breakdown of Women in Mainly White-collar Jobs, According to the 1959 and 1970 Censuses
(% of total)

	1959	1970
1. Managers of governmental offices and their subdivisions	0.7	0.4
2. Functionaries, managers, and administrators of party, Komsomol, trade union, cooperative, and other public organizations	0.3	0.3
3. Managers of enterprises and their subdivisions	1.4	1.4
4. Engineering and technical personnel	16.2	20.4
5. Agronomists, zootechnicians, veterinarians, foresters	1.6	1.2
6. Medical workers	15.1	13.2
7. Scientific workers, teachers, counselors	19.0	18.4
8. Workers in literature, printing, and the press	0.5	0.4
9. Cultural and enlightenment workers	3.3	2.8
10. Workers in art	0.6	0.5
11. Workers in wholesale and retail trade, public catering, procurement, and supply	4.3	4.4
12. Law and justice personnel	0.2	0.2
13. Planning and accounting personnel	24.9	22.9
14. Public utilities and services personnel	0.5	0.6
15. Typists, stenographers, secretaries, clerks, agents, expediters	5.3	5.0
16. Others	6.1	7.9

rates of growth in the numbers of women specialists (with higher or secondary education) were also noted in housing, urban and domestic services, trade, and public catering.

At the same time, it should be noted that women specialists and other women white-collar workers often perform lower level jobs than men. Thus women are still underrepresented in leadership positions (even in fields where they predominate among the rank and file). Among managers of enterprises and their subdivisions, only 16% are women, and only 25-29% of the principals of eight-year and secondary schools are women. The proportion of women among state and collective farm managers remains very low: 4%. Sample surveys show that within the same occupation, women tend to work at lower levels than men. The skill levels of women white-collar workers are heavily influenced by the fact that in all branches of the economy except construction, the proportion of people with a higher education is lower among women than men. The differences are greatest in branches of the nonproductive sphere.

In nonmanual jobs the proportion of women is very high among secretaries, clerks, typists, stenographers, cashiers, tellers, and bookkeepers. These jobs are often held by women with fairly high educations but lacking work experience. Some 2.5 million women hold such jobs.

At the present stage in the development of the productive forces, the economy is still in need of blue-collar workers who create material wealth. For that reason it is impossible to solve the problems of female employment without employing women in industrial occupations. As noted before, most women doing predominantly blue-collar jobs work in machine building and metalworking, the garment industry, construction and textiles, many of them in such leading trades as metal-cutting and woodworking machine operator, machinist, apparatus tender, weaver, spinner. In other branches of the economy many women employed in blue-collar jobs are also highly skilled workers in leading production sectors. At the same time, many women blue-collar workers have low skills. The closest attention must be given to the skill distribution of women workers, insofar as more women work in blue-collar jobs, and differences in their job skills indicate incomparably greater differentiation in the character and conditions of work than differences in the job qualifications of specialists.

A general idea of the extent of low-skilled labor among working women can be gained from data on the number of working women having no more than a primary education. The 1970 census revealed that 35% of all working women fell into this group. They usually hold jobs requiring no special training. The largest group of women with low education was farm workers in nonmechanized jobs. Among other occupational groups we should note office cleaners, janitors, hospital attendants, general laborers, warehouse workers, gatekeepers, watchwomen, weighers, examiners, laundresses, ironers, sweepers, dishwashers, and so on. The percentage of men with primary education or less in the male work force is approximately the same, but occupationally they are distributed differently, with many holding mechanized jobs requiring vocational training (tractor operators, drivers, turners, fitters, electricians, bricklayers, etc.). That is why, in our view, the proportion of low- and unskilled workers among men is considerably lower than among women.

Educational level is of great importance in occupational specialization in general, but among men a relatively low education is frequently no obstacle to the acquisition of a more or less skilled occupation. For women a low level of education usually results in the simplest jobs. An important factor here is that men with a low education began to work young and could take vocational training both full-time, in vocational schools, and on the factory floor. Many women with low education began to work later in life, which made it harder for them to acquire vocational training, while some forms of vocational education providing opportunities for high-skilled jobs were virtually closed to them.

Some part in this was played by the traditional notion that women are less-skilled workers, based on the fact that for many years women's education lagged behind that of men. Not infrequently married women demand less of their jobs than do men.

59

The growth of educational levels creates a real prerequisite for raising the skill levels of working women. It is important to make use of the potentialities for work provided by general education, which inevitably involves the expansion of vocational training for women. At present fewer girls than boys take vocational training after finishing school. To an important extent this is linked to the prevalent view that some types of work in which many women with secondary education are employed do not require vocational training (secretary, typist, clerk, some jobs in the service sector). But the absence of suitable training reduces efficiency and the quality of service, which increasingly conflicts with the rising requirements of the economy and the population.

An important prerequisite for the occupational specialization of women is due consideration of the specific features of the female organism. Labor legislation prohibits female labor in physically arduous and hazardous jobs and underground (except for light service jobs), and it restricts female labor on night shifts, except for plants where this is a technological necessity. As a result most women work in areas and jobs where working conditions are favorable for the female organism.

However, uneven technological development in industry and the services still makes it necessary to use heavy physical labor, work in unfavorable production conditions (high or low temperature, vibration, noise, poor ventilation, etc.), and finally, work in aesthetically unattractive jobs. Given the high rate of female employment, some women are still employed in jobs where working conditions do not meet the specific requirements of the female organism. Most frequently they are poorly mechanized auxiliary jobs, as well as some jobs in certain machine-building plants, the chemical industry, and a number of construction jobs. Some of the traditional forms of female employment (weaving, some jobs in the meat and dairy industry, retail trade, especially fruit and vegetables, and preparation of food) also do not fully meet conditions for employing female labor.

Female employment in jobs with unfavorable working condi-

tions is due to a number of reasons, primarily the shortage of
men during and after the war, the impossibility of equally
mechanizing all types of work, and also failure to take due consideration of the sexual composition of the population in planning new production facilities. Quite often women themselves
accept such jobs when they are close to home and more highly
paid or offer shorter working hours or better retirement benefits. Sample surveys indicate that a large proportion of women
holding jobs with unfavorable working conditions are single or
divorced with two or more children and are in the median
or older age groups with low education, that is, groups within
the female population who, for family reasons, attach greater
significance to material considerations and the availability of
free time.

The implementation of a number of technical and organizational measures at the present stage will help create more
favorable working conditions for women. Primary among them
is extensive mechanization of manufacturing processes requiring considerable physical effort, to which special attention was
given at the Twenty-fifth CPSU Congress. An important requirement that could be considered in drawing up technological
policies is the adaptation of technology to the characteristics of
the female organism, as is already obligatory in designing
farm machinery.

Enterprises can play an important part in creating the necessary
working conditions for women by utilizing a larger part of the
Production Development Fund to improve working conditions
for positions in which many women work. Unconditional
observance of labor legislation aimed at protecting women's
health is also a necessary and quite realistic measure.

Scientifically based recommendations regarding the occupational specialization of women could be of great importance.
Requirements involving the personal qualities of workers
should be included in the occupational profiles on the basis of
which worker training is done. Recommendations for the occupational specialization of women should be reviewed regularly,
since scientific-technological pregress continuously intro-

duces changes in the character and conditions of work.

4. Regional Differences in the Utilization of Female Labor Resources

The utilization of female labor resources at the present stage is characterized by substantial differences in the level of their employment from one republic to another and, in the final analysis, by differences in their role in the economic development of different regions.

The high level of female employment nationwide in the Soviet Union is due to the higher than average rates of female employment in a number of republics where a considerable portion of the able-bodied female population lives. The 1970 census showed that the difference between the highest and lowest levels of female employment in the republics was 19 percentage points. In comparison with 1959, female employment had risen in all republics; but the differences between republics changed only slightly, which is indicative of the operation of fairly stable factors.

According to the 1970 census the highest levels of female employment were in Moldavia, Estonia, Belorussia, the RSFSR, Latvia, and the Ukraine (1.5 to 2 points above the national index, except for the Ukraine). These republics account for four fifths of the female population of working age. Economic and demographic conditions in all of them have a great deal in common. The only significant difference is Moldavia, where the high level of female employment is due to the fact that a large portion of the able-bodied women live in rural communities and work in agriculture, where working conditions make it possible for them to combine work with household duties.

The lowest levels of femal employment (8 to 15 points below the national average) are found in Azerbaidzhan, Tadzhikistan, Georgia, Turkmenia, and Armenia. Somewhat apart from this group is Georgia, where the birthrate is substantially lower than in the other republics, and the demographic factor has a much smaller effect on female employment; on

62

the other hand, private subsidiary agriculture plays an important role.

Intermediate in levels of female employment are Uzbekistan, Kazakhstan, Kirghizia, and Lithuania, where it is 1.5 to 5 points below the national average. The first three republics, moreover, tend toward the group of republics with high levels of employment, and Lithuania toward those with low levels. Female employment in Kazakhstan and Kirghizia is higher than, say, in Tadzhikistan or Turkmenia because they have a higher percentage of Russian women, whose employment is higher than that of indigenous women. The lower employment of women in Lithuania as compared with the other Baltic republics is due to the effect of private subsidiary agriculture and a higher birthrate.

The varying levels of employment of women of working age in different republics are not only due to differences in their distribution between the socialized sector and the household and private subsidiary agriculture sector. The level of female employment in the socialized economy is also a function of the branch and occupational structure of employed women. The lower the level of employment, the comparatively fewer the number of women who work in industrial branches and the greater the proportion in agriculture. The relationship is most obvious in republics with stable family and household traditions (the republics of Central Asia and Azerbaidzhan). Thus the proportion of women working in industry in Tadzhikistan, Uzbekistan, and Turkmenia is less than half that in the RSFSR, Estonia, or Latvia, and the proportion of women in agriculture, on the contrary, is 2.5 to 3 times higher. Since work in agriculture, especially on collective farms, is generally seasonal, often part-time, and with a high proportion of manual jobs, high employment in agriculture tends to reduce the relative social and economic significance of socially productive female labor. Furthermore work in agriculture still means living mainly in rural communities, where life is less dynamic and more persistent in the preservation of old family traditions and mores, which to a certain degree prevents the redistribution of labor resources between town and country and retards the further growth of the participation of the female labor force.

In the republics where female employment is relatively low, this is true not only of industry but also of such major branches in the service sphere as retail trade, public catering, housing, and public utilities and services. This is probably due to both the lower levels of development of these branches and to the greater interest of men of indigenous nationalities in work in the service sector. Whereas nationally the percentage of women in retail trade and public catering in 1970 was 77%, it was 41% in Tadzhikistan, 46% in Azerbaidzhan and Uzbekistan, and 56% in Turkmenia. The relationship between the level of female employment and women's participation in the republics' sociocultural development is not so apparent as in the aforementioned branches because employment in public health, education, and culture is to a large extent influenced by population size and structure.

Both high and relatively low levels of women's employment in different republics are due to objective causes, i.e., they correspond to specific features in the development of each region. That is why any geographic comparison of female employment can be only relative (not simply a low level of female employment in say, the republics of Central Asia but a relatively low level as compared, for example, with Estonia or the RSFSR).

Nationwide trends in changes in female employment are apparent in all the republics; more in some and less in others. In 1959-70 the demand for labor rose rapidly in all republics. Moreover, the work force in the republics of Central Asia, Transcaucasia, and Kazakhstan increased at a faster rate than in the central regions due to continuing industrialization and the need for an adequate supply of jobs to meet the high rate of increase in the able-bodied population. Whereas in 1959-70 the number of women in blue- and white-collar jobs increased 1.5 times in the RSFSR, Estonia, and Latvia, the increase was 2.5 times in Armenia and more than double in Kazakhstan, Kirghizia, Azerbaidzhan, and Tadzhikistan.

The Development of Female Employment

This provided a real basis for a substantial increase in female employment. In most republics, including the republics of Central Asia (except Tadzhikistan), Armenia, and Georgia, the level of female employment grew 11 to 15 points, and in Kazakhstan more than 20 points. In all republics the absolute number of women occupied outside the socialized sector and education declined, and relatively fewer young women remained locked in household duties or private subsidiary agriculture.

Consequently the relatively low levels of female employment in some republics cannot be explained by lower rates of economic development and the absence of sufficient scope for the use of female labor or of demand for female labor. However, the need for additional manpower, including female labor, was met not only from local labor resources. Many jobs were taken by newcomers from the central regions of the country, which affected female employment in those as well as other republics.

If the needs of the economy were met in the republics of Central Asia solely from local labor resources, the level of female employment in these republics would have been somewhat higher.

Differences in female employment from one republic to another are due to factors that affect the development of people's need to work and are largely sociodemographic in character. The 1970 census showed that despite the relatively favorable conditions for drawing unemployed women into social production (mostly women under 40 years of age), family considerations remain the main restricting factor. That many young and middle-aged women fall into this category is due to demographic causes: the higher the number of women with children under 16 among nonworking women, the higher the proportion of women up to 40 years old within the nonworking population. According to the 1970 census, nationwide the greater part of nonworking women had children under 16 years of age. The proportion of nonworking women with children is approximately the same in the republics with high levels of female employment, where families with small children usually predominate. In the republics of Central Asia and Transcaucasia (with the exception of Georgia), the proportion of women under 40 among nonworking women is higher than the national average, as is the proportion of women with children under 16 (the overwhelming number of women in these republics have three children or more.)

A large proportion of the nonworking women in the republics of Central Asia and Transcaucasia live in rural localities. They have low social mobility, no industrial work habits, and are reluctant to change their way of life. But the demand for female labor is growing in all branches except agriculture. Besides, for many nonworking women in republics with favorable climatic conditions, income from private subsidiary agriculture reduces the material incentives to work in the socialized sector. Although nationwide the proportion of rural inhabitants not working in the socialized economy, whose main source of income is private subsidiary agriculture, is comparatively small, in a number of republics in Central Asia and Transcaucasia it is significantly higher.

In the republics of Central Asia and Transcaucasia, old family and domestic traditions that influence the formation of young women's life style still persist. Many young women of indigenous nationalities marry early and settle into the domestic economy immediately after school, without taking any vocational training or working in social production. In the central and western regions of the country, girls start working after completing school; and if they leave work, it is usually to have a child. Naturally, these two groups of women later display different attitudes toward employment in social production.

Some analysts, referring to the relatively high proportion of nonworking women in some republics, claim that they have untapped labor reserves. Indeed, if in some regions (for example, Moscow) almost all women of able-bodied age work in the socialized sector, why can't this be attained in other regions?

A certain proportion of able-bodied women remains, and will for sometime continue to remain, outside the socialized economy, fulfilling the functions of motherhood. Therefore, as

long as differences in the birthrate exist in different parts
of the country, there will be regional differences in employment
levels among the female population. Today birthrates vary
widely from one area to another. These differences are expected to remain for the coming fifteen to twenty years. The
social and demographic factors that determine regional peculiarities in the use of female labor resources are very stable,
as indicated by the almost sixty years of development of our
society. It is therefore wrong even to pose the question of
attaining identical levels of female employment in different
republics now or in the near future. Moreover, to take as a
guideline the female employment levels found, for example, in
many regions of the RSFSR, Estonia, or Latvia means to ignore
sociodemographic processes in the development of society. At
the same time, some economic and social measures can be applied to gradually even out the levels of female labor participation in different republics. In areas where high female employment is accompanied by low birthrates, it would be useful to
reduce the demand for female labor by technologically reequip-
ping industry. This would make it possible to create better
conditions for women to harmoniously combine motherhood
with employment in the socialized sector. Providing working
women with a preferential work regime could play an important role. Such a measure could reduce somewhat the levels
of female employment in regions where it is now very high.
At the same time, the structure of the nonworking population
would change as the significance of all factors other than demographic ones in not seeking employment would disappear.

As the demand for female labor declines, it will be possible
to extend part-time work for more women. Moreover, more
part-time employment may well help improve service work
by reducing peak loads.

The growth of intensive factors in the development of the
economy will raise its efficiency and hence create greater economic opportunities for increasing the free time of working
women. Higher incomes, greater satisfaction of daily needs
in the service sector, and an adequate system of children's

preschool institutions, that is, the creation of better conditions for bringing up children, can (and will) decisively influence women's attitudes toward the number of children in a family.

As for regions with relatively low levels of female employment and high birthrates, social and economic development will undoubtedly result in a reduction of the birthrate within the next fifteen or twenty years. Further industrialization in the republics of Central Asia and Transcaucasia, urbanization, better geographic distribution of industry taking into account local demographic and ethnic characteristics of local labor resources and the rising cultural, educational, and occupational level of the population will effect both a reduction in the birthrate and higher women's employment.

The formation of a rational optimum pattern of women's employment by region could be greatly facilitated by drawing up long-term balance sheets of labor resources by sex. They would help relate possible women's employment to both socio-demographic and economic factors (the existence of spheres of employment in the first place) and outline measures to ensure optimum employment. For this it is necessary to regularly draw up ex post balance sheets of labor resources by sex (at least once every five years) for the end of the five-year period.

Some elements of the long-term balance sheets of female labor resources are already being elaborated by scholarly and planning organizations, e.g., household employment of able-bodied women taking demographic factors into account (small children, family size, etc.). An attempt is being made to forecast the proportion of women going into education and the distribution of women's employment by branch. However, there is still a great deal of methodological work to be done in this field, and methods of labor accounting must be improved.

Notes

1. Materialy XXV s"ezda KPSS, p. 85.
2. In the 1970 census employment was counted in terms of physical persons regardless of whether the person worked the full year or only part. Therefore in terms of the average annual number of employees, the employment of women is somewhat lower.

4

The Educational and Occupational
Skill Level of Industrial Workers

A. E. Kotliar
and S. Ia. Turchaninova

1. The General Educational and Occupational Skill
Level of Female Industrial Workers

The rising level of technical equipment, mechanization, and automation of production processes, which provides the material basis for the growth in number of skilled workers, imposes higher demands on workers' cultural and technical levels.

"Modern industry," it was stressed in the report of the Central Committee of the CPSU to the Twenty-fifth Party Congress, "imposes ever greater demands not only on machines and technology but most of all on the workers, on those who create the machines and operate that technology. Specialized knowledge and high levels of occupational training and general culture are becoming essential to the successful work of ever greater segments of the work force."[1]

In other words, higher skill levels are not only essential for the national economy and industrial production in particular, but they are also of prime importance for the development of man and for his personal improvement. It is from this perspective that one should examine the task of raising the skill levels of women workers as one of tremendous economic and sociopolitical importance.

The generally lower level of skills among female workers

Russian text © 1975 by "Statistika" Publishers. *Zaniatost' zhenshchin v proizvodstve* (Moscow: "Statistika" Publishers, 1975), pp. 57-104.

A. E. Kotliar and S. Ia. Turchaninova

is a historical legacy from capitalist production which, typically, utilizes female labor almost exclusively in unskilled jobs.

During the years of the five-year plans, enormous changes have taken place in the cultural and technical levels of women workers. This is a result of a deliberate policy in the fields of both general and specialized education and female employment.

The qualitative improvement of the female work force can be seen in the growth of the share of women among mental workers, in the changing ratio between women occupied in manual and nonmanual work, and finally, in the growing number of women in highly skilled occupations and among specialists with a higher or specialized secondary education.

Thus census data show the rising proportion of women among nonmanual workers, from 33.5% in 1939, to 54% in 1959 and 59% in 1970.[2]

The growth in women's general education and occupational-technical levels promotes the role of female labor in the area of predominantly mental work. In 1970 there were almost 10 million women specialists with a higher or specialized secondary education employed in the nation's economy, and they accounted for 59% of the work force in that category.[3] This means that virtually every fifth working woman is a specialist with a higher or specialized secondary education. The number of women specialists with diplomas increased 11.5 times between 1940 and 1970; whereas in 1939 only 104 out of every 1,000 gainfully employed women had a higher or secondary (complete or incomplete) education, by 1970 they already numbered 651.[4]

In industry more than 40% of the engineers and technicians are women.[5] More and more women perform creative and administrative work. Today women account for 32% of the executive personnel in socialist industry.

In the course of the five-year plan years, the level of skills of women workers in industry has also substantially increased, and there is every reason to affirm that this growth will continue at an ever higher rate. This is because in modern industry general and vocational-technical education is the foun-

dation of worker skills, and educational levels are steadily
rising. For example, in 1970 almost two thirds of all textile
and garment workers, trades in which female labor predominates, had a higher or secondary (complete or incomplete) education, whereas in 1959 this was true of only half the work
force.[6] The level of skills is rising accordingly. Thus, according to data from the Central Statistical Administration of
the USSR, in the ten years between 1962 and 1972 the mean
skill rating of workers in the textile industry rose from 3.5
to 3.7. [7]

Today the proportion of persons with a higher or secondary
education among working men and women is approximately
equal: 718 and 717, respectively, per 1,000 persons of each
sex. In industry the average educational level of women workers is somewhat higher than among men. Thus in industry as
a whole, 73.2% of the female workers have more than an elementary education, as compared with only 69.8% among male
workers. In machine building 77.7% of women workers and
only 74.5% of men workers had a higher or secondary (including incomplete secondary) education. In light industry the gap
between the educational levels of workers by sex is even higher,
with 74.5% of the women and 65.3% of the men workers having
an education above primary school level. [8] The gap between
the educational levels of women and men is narrowing because
women with a low level of education (primary or less) are
gradually leaving the work force due to age, [9] while the number of women attending educational institutions is increasing
faster than the number of men. For example, between 1960
and 1970 the number of women studying in vocational-technical
schools increased almost fivefold, while the number of men
only doubled; enrollment in specialized secondary schools increased 2.5 and 1.8 times, and in institutions of higher learning
2.2 and 2.1 times, respectively.[10]   As a result the proportion
of women among students in the 1972/73 academic year was
50% in institutes of higher learning and 53% in technical
schools. [11]

The proportion of girls is increasing among students of

Table 1

General Education Levels of Industrial Workers
(% of total)

Branch of industry	Grades 1-4		Grades 5-8		Grades 9-10 (11)	
	men	women	men	women	men	women
Machine building	9.6	6.0	55.2	46.5	35.2	47.5
Garment	—	5.0	—	55.0	—	40.2
Textile	17.7	16.6	64.0	55.2	18.3	28.2
Meat and dairy	21.6	23.8	48.4	54.1	30.0	22.1
Baking	35.3	21.2	54.7	56.5	10.0	22.3

vocational-technical schools — an indication of a substantial improvement in the occupational training of women workers. In 1970 girls accounted for 30% of the enrollment at schools in the vocational-technical training system. [12] At the same time, more than half the pupils in the senior grades of general education schools were girls. This means that at present most girls acquire a secondary education. This is confirmed by sociological studies done by us in 1970-72.

In particular, it was found that almost 70% of the young women workers (up to age 25) at the surveyed factories had completed nine or ten years of schooling. Among male workers in the same age bracket, only 55% had a nine- or ten-year education. This is because some young men leave school and start working at an earlier age, thereby postponing completion of their education until they are 25 or 30.

In the coming years the number of skilled workers with complete secondary education will increase. This will be facilitated by the growing number of schools in the vocational-technical training system that offer a secondary education along with vocational training.

However, the educational level of women workers in the older age brackets is much lower, and the drop from the younger to the older groups is quite sharp.

According to the 1959 census, almost half the women aged 40-45 lacked even an elementary education, whereas among men in the same age bracket the percentage was only 18.[13]

The sharp difference in the educational levels of women of different generations is an indication of the results of the tremendous effort made by the party and government to achieve genuine equality among men and women, notably in the sphere of education.

At the surveyed industrial enterprises, in the 25-44 age bracket the proportion of men and women with nine or ten years of schooling was almost the same: 26.8 and 27.8%, respectively. But in the over-45 bracket 10% of male workers and only 6.8% of female workers had completed nine or ten years at school.

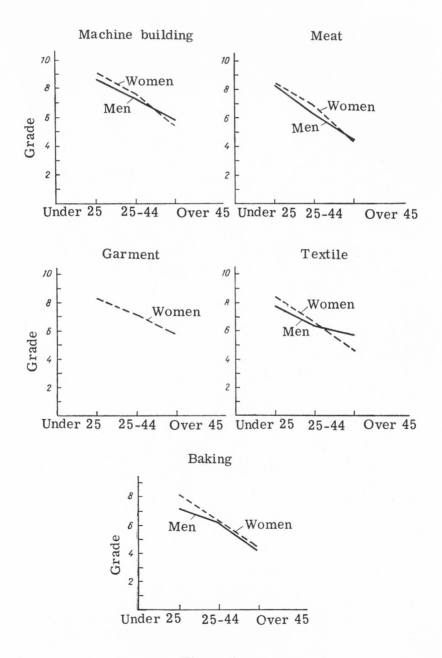

Figure 1.

Differences in the level of general education among workers of different sex, by age groups in each of the surveyed industries, are shown in Figure 1.

In industry there are substantial differences in the levels of general education of women workers from one branch of industry to another.

The highest levels of general education were found among women workers at machine-building and garment enterprises, where most had at least seven or eight years of schooling and more than 40% had finished the ninth or tenth grade.

The growing integrated mechanization and automation of manufacturing processes at machine-building enterprises require not only greater occupational training of workers but higher general education levels as well. New workers in the machine-building industry come largely from graduates of vocational-technical and general education schools because many of the popular trades at machine-building plants are regarded as highly prestigious by young women.

The garment industry also attracts primarily young women for a number of specific reasons (workers must have good eyesight, be especially neat and conscientious). It is the predominance of young people among women workers at machine-building plants and garment factories (the average age of women workers is 28 to 30) that contributes to the high level of general education of women in these industries.

The general educational level of women workers at textile mills was found to be lower than in the machine-building industry. Most women workers had six or seven years schooling. This is in part due to the fact that the workers are generally older (average age of women workers is 33), and a substantial portion of the younger workers come from rural localities and have lower educational levels than city youth. For example, almost 70% of the young workers (under 20) at textile mills in Ivanovo are new residents, many of them from rural areas in the Volga-Viatka region, Northern Urals, and other economic regions.

The lowest general education level among women workers

at the surveyed establishments was found in the food industry: at meat-packing and baking plants. This is due to the older age of workers. Young people are reluctant to seek jobs in the food industry, especially at meat-packing plants, where mechanization is low, and the very nature of the work is often unattractive to women (for example, cutting carcasses). The majority of women in the food industry are in the median age bracket (38-40) with fifth- or sixth-grade education. Here the proportion of women with only a primary education is largest (about 24%), and those with nine or ten years' schooling is lowest (22%).

The following specific features were found with regard to regional differences in the general education of women workers at surveyed enterprises in large and small cities.

In the study it was found that in all the surveyed towns and cities regardless of size, the level of general education of women workers tended to be higher in enterprises of the predominant industries.

In the large cities (Vladimir, Rostov-on-Don, and Vladivostok), machine building is the predominant industry, and the female work force in it is younger and has a higher level of general education than at enterprises in the secondary industries of such cities, such as the garment, food, and other industries (see Table 2).

In small towns where female employment predominates (Viazniki, Kansk) and in which light industry is the leading branch, the level of general education of women workers in it is higher than in other industries. Characteristically, at such enterprises in small towns, the education of women workers is higher than at similar enterprises in the larger cities of the same region. Thus at a textile mill and garment factory in Viazniki (a small town), the general educational level of women workers is higher than at similar enterprises in Vladimir and Ivanovo (see Table 3). This is because enterprises of the leading industry (and in Viazniki light industries predominate) attract the younger and, as a rule, better educated women.

Table 2

Educational Level of Workers at Enterprises of Primary and Secondary Industries in Cities of Various Size

Type of city	City	Enterprises of primary industry	Level of education, by grade	Enterprises of secondary industry	Level of education, by grade
Large	Vladimir	"Auto Instruments" Plant	7.3	Garment factory	6.9
Large	Rostov-on-Don	State Bearing Plant (GPZ-10)	8.4	Dairy	7.3
Large	Vladivostok	"Radio Set" Factory	8.3	Garment factory	8.2
				Meat-packing plant	5.8
Large	Sverdlovsk	—		Bakery	6.4
Medium	Artem	—		Bakery	5.6
				Garment factory	7.6
	Artem			Bakery	5.3
Medium	Kansk	Garment factory	7.4	Meat-packing plant	6.1
Medium	Kansk	Knitwear mill	6.8	Bakery	5.4
Medium	Asbest	—		Bakery	6.1
Small	Viazniki	Flax-spinning mill	6.6	Meat-packing plant	5.9
	Viazniki	Garment factory	7.7	Bakery	5.6

77

Table 3

Comparison of Educational Level of Young Workers in
Cities of Different Size

Industry	Percentage of workers up to 25 educated through grades 9 and 10			
	large cities		medium (small) cities	
	men	women	men	women
Garment	—	55.6	—	46.5
Textile	42.0	61.0	31.5	52.5
Meat and dairy	82.0	100.0	20.0	40.0
Baking	—	57.5	—	33.8

The proportion of women workers under 25 at the Viazniki flax-spinning mill is 41.5% while at a cotton-weaving mill in Ivanovo it is only 29%. The general educational level of women textile workers in the smaller town is accordingly higher than in the larger city. At a garment factory in Viazniki the general educational level of women workers is also higher than in a similar plant in Vladimir: 7.7 and 6.9 grades, respectively.

However, the education of young people up to 25 is generally higher in large cities than in towns.

The reason is that in small towns, where the network of secondary and higher educational institutions is much less developed, young people often fail to see any prospects for continuing their education and tend to leave school and start work at an earlier age. This ultimately is also indicated by the fact that in small towns the proportion of young people up to 25 among workers with a nine- or ten (eleven)-year education is higher than in large cities. The reason is that in large cities, a large proportion of the contemporaries in this age bracket go on to study at specialized secondary or higher educational institutions or already work as specialists, whereas in smaller and medium-sized towns they are employed more often as factory workers.

In comparing the general educational standards of male and female workers at the surveyed enterprises, it was found that in the branches and subbranches where women workers predominate, their educational level is considerably higher than that of men.

Thus at machine-building enterprises (the "Auto Instruments," "Radio Set," and GPZ-10 Bearing plants), the average level of general education is 7.3 grades for men and 7.8 for women; at textile mills it is 6.4 and 6.8 grades, and at bakeries, 5.2 and 6.4 grades, respectively. Only in the meat-packing industry was the general educational level of women 0.4 grades lower than that of men (and the women workers were generally older).

The differences in the level of general education of men and women are one of the manifestations of the feminization of secondary education.

However, the levels of production skills among women work-

A. E. Kotliar and S. Ia. Turchaninova

ers at the surveyed enterprises were everywhere lower than those of men.

Since statistical reports provide no data about the skill levels of industrial workers by sex, we shall examine this question on the basis of our own studies done in 1970, 1971, and 1972.

We found that the skill levels of women workers were below those of men at almost all enterprises. Only at one, the flax mill in Viazniki, was the mean skill [and wage] rating of women slightly higher than that of men (3.6 and 3.4, respectively). The difference in mean skill ratings of men and women at the surveyed enterprises in the machine-building and food industries ranged from 0.6 to 1.4 grades. Even in the traditionally "female" textile industry, the skill ratings of women were lower, albeit insignificantly (0.1 grade), than those of men.

The greatest difference between the occupational levels of men and women workers (see Table 4) is found in machine building, where it is almost 1.5 skill grades.

Among the surveyed women workers in machine-building, more than 67% had the lowest skill ratings (I and II), and only 5.5% had ratings IV to VI; among male workers only 23% had ratings I and II, and more than half had ratings IV to VI.

The low occupational standards of the female work force at the machine-building plants studied is indicated by the fact that out of 1,500 women workers at the "Auto Instruments" Works in Vladimir, only eight were rated in the fifth skill rating, and among 140 grinding machine operators at the Rostov GPZ-10 Bearing Plant, only one had reached the fifth rating. Not a single woman worker at the plants surveyed had the highest, sixth skill rating.

The low occupational levels of women workers at machine-building plants is in large measure due to the fact that women are predominately employed in the mass trades, such as assembler, sorter, and other jobs in the first through third skill rating. Women accounted for as many as 96% of the assemblers, and the mean skill rating for that occupation was only 1.9.

At the same time, there are still very few women occupied in such highly skilled jobs as adjusters who handle maintenance

80

Table 4

Mean Skill Ratings of Men and Women Workers in Industry
(surveyed enterprises)

| Industry | Mean skill rating | | | Difference in mean skill ratings of men and women workers |
	all workers	men	women	
Baking	4.0	4.5	3.9	0.6
Meat and dairy	3.5	4.0	3.1	0.9
Textile	3.7	3.8	3.7	0.1
Garment	3.4	—	3.4	—
Machine building	2.6	3.5	2.1	1.4

81

Table 5

Skill Ratings of Male and Female Workers in
Machine-Building Factories (%)

	Total	Skill ratings					
		I	II	III	IV	V	VI
Men	100	5.8	17.2	24.6	26.6	21.1	4.7
Women	100	29.1	38.6	26.8	4.4	1.0	0.1
Percentage of women in respective wage grade		89.9	79.9	66.0	22.6	7.8	3.8

and setting up of equipment. For example, at the surveyed factories, of the 135 adjusters employed, only six were women (4.5%), and they were in lower skill categories than the men (the mean skill ratings were 3.7 and 4.2, respectively). In other mass machine-building trades, such as grinding or drilling machine operator or electroplater, women had the lowest ratings and were inferior to men in skills and the complexity of job assignments. For example, the mean rating for male electroplaters was 2.3 and only 1.6 for women; for grinding machine operators it was 2.9 and 2.0, respectively.

The difference in the occupational skills of men and women, it should be noted, is due not only to the fact that men perform more complex jobs; they are also employed much more extensively in arduous and hazardous jobs. The current system of skill rating takes into account both the complexity of a job and its difficulty and hazardousness.

Thus a comparison of the occupational skills of men and women workers at the machine-building plants surveyed revealed a considerable lag in female worker skills. The predominance of female labor in this leading industry in manual, low-skilled jobs is indicative of inefficient use of female labor, low mechanization in largely female jobs, and furthermore, a lack of concern for such problems as raising the skill levels of women workers on the part of factory managers and public organizations.

The lag in the occupational levels of women workers in the food industry (bakeries and meat-packing plants) is smaller than in machine building. The difference between the mean skill ratings of all men and women workers surveyed in the meat and dairy industry was found to be not more than one rating (see Table 6). In the bakery industry the majority of women workers (78.2%) had skill ratings III, IV, and V, while about the same proportion of men (77.0%) were in the two higher ratings, IV and V. Also, 13.6% of the women workers were doing low-skilled jobs (first and second skill grades), as against only 2.4% of the men.

The picture of job rating of men and women is similar in the meat-packing industry.

Table 6

Skill Ratings of Male and Female Workers
in the Food Industry (%)

		Skill ratings					
		I	II	III	IV	V	VI
Baking industry	Men	0.5	1.9	7.5	37.1	39.9	13.1
	Women	3.9	9.7	21.1	27.8	29.3	8.2
Percentage of women in respective skill rating		96.0	93.7	89.1	68.6	68.1	64.5
Meat and dairy industry	Men	—	4.2	27.1	31.2	34.4	3.1
	Women	0.5	8.9	63.5	23.4	3.2	0.5
Percentage of women in respective skill rating		100	80.9	82.4	60.0	15.3	25.0

An analysis of skill levels in selected mass, basic production jobs in the food industry also reveals differences between
males and females. For example, in meat processing the mean
skill rating of male workers is 4.6, as against only 3.6 for
women.

In the textile industry women workers enjoy relatively high
occupational levels (mean skill ratings of 3.7), and there is
virtually no difference in the occupational levels of men and
women in this traditionally "female" industry. Women workers
in the leading jobs, such as weavers and spinners, have high
ratings (averaging 4.8-4.9). The majority of women workers
at textile mills were in the third and fourth skill rating (86.7%),
while only 8.3% were in the lowest ratings.

When comparing the distribution of men and women workers
by skill ratings, attention should be drawn to the proportion of
men and women in the highest ratings (V and VI). Whereas
among women textile workers only 5% were in that category,
the percentage among men was 44.5%. The explanation for this
can be found in the occupational composition of male and female
workers. As mentioned before, in the textile industry male
workers are employed in equipment maintenance and set-up
(auxiliary operations), while on the main production line they
are assistant foremen with a mean skill rating of 5.6 (of 58
assistant foremen only seven were women).

It is interesting to compare the occupational levels of women
workers in similar enterprises located in cities of different
size. Such a comparison was possible with garment factories
and bakeries, which were surveyed in both large cities and
small (medium) towns.

A clear-cut pattern is quite apparent here: the occupational
levels of women workers in larger cities are invariably higher
than in small (medium) urban communities.

What are the explanations of the observed differences in occupational levels in different cities and, more important, between men and women at the same enterprise?

We know that a number of factors contribute to the development of occupational skills — notably, general and specialized

Table 7

Skill Ratings of Male and Female Workers
in the Textile Industry Enterprises Surveyed (%)

| | Total | Skill ratings | | | | | |
		I	II	III	IV	V	VI
Men	100	14.8	11.1	12.0	17.6	18.5	26.0
Women	100	–	8.3	50.0	36.7	3.3	1.7
Percentage of women in respective skill rating		30.0	66.2	80.5	57.8	77.4	32.2

education, general and work experience, age, family status, and so on. The influence of these factors on occupational skills spans all industries. They are also interrelated, and it is not always possible to demonstrate the effect of each factor in "pure form" on a worker's occupational skills. Moreover, there are other factors, such as type of production, complexity of manufactured product, form of work remuneration, system of worker training, and others.

The current lag in the occupational levels of women workers is due to the sociodemographic features of the female and male work force and the consequent different effect of these factors on the occupational level of men and women workers.

An analysis of the effect of age on the occupational levels of men and women workers showed that rises in skill levels of women workers occur more slowly and within narrower limits than for men.

It can be seen from Table 8 that up to age 19, the bulk of both men and women workers (up to 75%) do jobs in the first and second skill ratings. Occupational rating increases with age. However, whereas by age 30 (the 25-29 age bracket) 52% of the male workers have reached skill ratings IV and V, among women the percentage is only 4.4%. At the same time, in the low ratings (I and II) in the 25-29-year age bracket, one finds 17.5% of the male workers and 70.8% of the female workers. We thus see a clear slowing down in the rise of occupational levels of women between the ages of 20 and 29, which is due to the effect of such factors as family situation. Marriage and the appearance of children impose an additional strain on working women that impedes their occupational advancement. Conditions have yet to be created in which a majority of women can combine work, family duties, and advanced training at courses or schools. The change in the family status of working men, on the contrary, is an incentive to earn higher wages, thereby stimulating occupational advance.

Another characteristic feature to be noted is that whereas men continue their occupational advancement after 30 and tend to slow down only after 40, the job rating of most women over

87

Table 8

Breakdown of Occupational Levels by Sex and Age among Workers of Machine-Building Enterprises Surveyed (% of total in given age bracket)

Age	All men	Skill rating						All women	Skill rating					
		I	II	III	IV	V	VI		I	II	III	IV	V	VI
19 and under	100	20.9	56.4	13.6	7.3	1.8	—	100	54.8	22.0	15.6	0.6	—	—
20–24	100	5.2	30.0	37.9	23.1	3.8	—	100	38.8	38.6	20.6	1.9	0.1	—
25–29	100	3.3	14.2	29.5	32.2	19.7	1.1	100	27.6	43.2	24.5	4.1	0.3	0.3
30–39	100	4.6	11.3	22.0	28.2	29.0	4.9	100	19.7	38.1	35.1	5.2	1.8	0.1
40 and over	100	5.0	7.8	19.7	29.3	28.3	9.9	100	15.4	41.7	31.6	9.1	2.0	0.2

30 who have attained skill rating III tends to remain almost un-changed. In what is called the age of "occupational maturity" (30-39 years), 62.1% of the male workers are in the highest skill ratings (IV, V, VI), as against only 7.1% of the female workers.

The same dependence between skill level and age of women workers as in machine building (slower and shorter period of advancement as compared with male workers) can be found in other industries. However, in industries with a high proportion of female employment (garment, textile, baking) the dependence is less pronounced. In these industries women's skill levels advance at almost the same rate as men's, and this continues after ages 30-40. Accordingly, in the older age brackets from 22.5 to 36.2% of the women workers in the garment, textile, and bakery industries had high skill ratings (V and VI).

Table 9

Percentage of Highly Skilled Workers among
Men and Women Aged 40 Years and Older

Industry	Percentage of workers in skill ratings V and VI	
	men	women
Garment	—	22.5
Textile	43.5	33.4
Baking	55.7	36.2
Meat and dairy	48.9	5.2
Machine building	38.9	2.2

An analysis of the effect of length of service on the skill levels of workers showed that they invariably rise with general experience and occupational length of service in all age brackets. As we know, a person's general work experience counts less in occupational advancement than length of service in a specific occupation.[14] We attempted to determine the ex-

A. E. Kotliar and S. Ia. Turchaninova

tent to which occupational length of service influences the occupational advancement of working men and women. We found,
in particular, that the effect of this factor was less pronounced
for women than for men. The accumulation of experience,
knowledge, and work habits in a given trade appears to be slower
among women. Thus at machine-building plants, the occupational level of women workers after ten years in the same trade
had hardly changed. This is seen in the following figures: in
a group of women workers whose time in a particular occupation was up to three years, 76% were in skill rating I and II;
among those with three to five years of service, the percentage
was 70.7%; and in the five to ten years' group, 68.8%. Only after ten or more years work in the same trade did some 50% of
the women workers attain the third skill rating. Among male
workers at the machine-building plants surveyed, 71.4% were
in skill ratings III and IV after three to five years' service,
and only 18% were in ratings I and II. Among men with a service record exceeding ten years in their specific trades, 78.2%
were rated in skill ratings IV-VI, and about 10% were in ratings
I-II.

A comparison of the length of service of men and women in
the same skill ratings for several occupations shows that men
tended to attain higher ratings 1.5 to 2 times faster than women,
as is shown for assemblers in Table 10 (compiled from a survey of the "Auto Instruments" Plant in Vladimir).

Table 10

Work Experience for Male and Female Assemblers
in the Same Skill Rating (years)

Trade	Sex	Skill rating		
		I	II	III
Assembler	male	1.5	4.6	8.9
Assembler	female	4.6	8.9	14.5

90

It can be seen from Table 10 that a woman working as an assembler for 4.6 years is still in the first skill rating, whereas a man has already reached skill rating II; a woman attains rating II after 8.9 years, by which time a man has reached rating III, and so on. In other words, a woman has to work half again as long as a man to attain a higher skill rating.

A survey of young workers (up to age 30) made by the Central Scientific Research Laboratory of Labor Reserves in 1971-72 at 105 industrial enterprises in the Russian Federation revealed that with almost the same average service record at a given enterprise (men 2.8, women 2.6 years), the advancement of women up the wage scale was much slower. Thus whereas in the course of his work at the given enterprise one out of every four male workers under age 30 raised his skill rating twice or more, only one out of nine women workers achieved as much.

A worker's skill level is influenced to a varying degree by his or her general and specialized education. Specialized (vocational) training has a very direct and more immediate effect on occupational skills. General education does not directly raise skill levels, insofar as they are an expression of mastery of specific forms of concrete work that depends primarily on vocational training and length of service in the given trade. However, general education facilitates more rapid mastery of specialized knowledge and work habits and attitudes, and in this sense it is the foundation on which work skills form and develop.[15] It should also be noted that the role of both general and specialized education as a factor in occupational advance is in large measure dependent on the quality and degree of mechanization of work. Where manual labor predominates, the role of education in occupational advancement is restricted, and skills depend almost solely on the worker's experience, which corresponds to his length of service.

This is clearly seen in comparing the effect of general education and length of service on the qualification of workers (men and women) performing assembly, mainly manual, operations (the comparison is based on a survey of the Vladimir

91

A. E. Kotliar and S. Ia. Turchaninova

Table 11

Comparison of Education, Length of Service, and
Skill Rating of Assembly Workers (by sex)

	Skill rating					
	I	II	III	IV	V	VI
Men:						
education, grades	8.1	9.1	8.0			
length of service, years	1.5	4.6	8.9			
Women:						
education, grades	8.3	8.1	7.4			
length of service, years	4.6	8.9	14.5			

"Auto Instruments" Plant).

It can be seen from Table 11 that the skill rating of assemblers is affected not so much by level of education (which is approximately the same for everyone) as by length of service.

In highly skilled trades, however, high general educational levels together with occupational training acquire primary importance in raising job ratings. Thus highly skilled women workers (fifth and sixth skill ratings) in the textile and bakery industries also had a better general education than workers in the first and second skill ratings.

Vocational training is acquired either in apprenticeship, subsequently supplemented by on-the-job advanced training, or in the system of vocational-technical education (vocational-technical schools and technicums). An analysis showed that the most effective training is provided by vocational-technical schools.[16] Surveys conducted at several plants showed that there was a high proportion of vocational-technical school graduates among women workers in the higher skill ratings (see Table 12).

A stable and fairly close relationship (coefficient of paired

92

Table 12

Proportion of Vocational-Technical School Graduates among
Female Workers of Various Trades and Skill Ratings (%)

Trade	Enterprise	Skill rating					
		I	II	III	IV	V	VI
Sewing machine operator	garment factory, Vladivostok	—	5.1	7.7	41.0	40.1	—
	garment factory, Artem	—	—	11.7	23.2	11.2	—
Weaver	weaving mill, Ivanovo	—	—	—	41.7	28.2	—
Baker	bakery, Sverdlovsk	—	—	—	16.7	33.3	—
	bakery, Asbest	—	—	—	9.1	25.0	50.0
	bakery, Viazniki	—	—	—	—	—	20.0

correlation + 0.61) was found between vocational school training and the skill rating of sewing machine operators.

It follows that worker training in the system of vocational-technical education is preferable over other types of training, since it gives the worker a high level of theoretical and practical training. It is especially favorable in training women workers, as it usually falls in the period of their lives (16-20 years) when most are not yet additionally burdened by family and children. The team apprenticeship method on the factory floor is less suitable for women workers and restricts subsequent occupational advance because most women usually limit themselves to the primary stage of apprenticeship. Opportunities for advanced on-the-job training at schools or courses are usually restricted because most working women between the ages of 25 and 35 are too busy with family chores and bringing up children to both study and work. The existing system of on-the-job advanced training is ill adapted for working wives and mothers, and the question of creating a suitable system in our country still remains unresolved. In some socialist countries, for example, the German Democratic Republic, factories run special groups or classes during working hours for working women with families; average monthly wages are maintained. Depending on the features of production organization, factories in the GDR adopt different variants of instruction for family women. For example, at the electro-chemical works in Bitterfeld there are special women's groups at the advanced training courses that have one whole day of classes per week during working hours, and students receive their average pay. At office equipment factories in Sommerd [?], family women attend advanced training courses operating during nonworking hours, but they are given equivalent time off from work. Another important aspect for women is that the training of skilled workers in the GDR is broken down into several stages, the number of which depends on the trades and skills they teach and the type of enterprise. In this system the teaching process is so organized that after each stage, a worker can perform specified jobs and is issued a certificate

94

to that effect. Advanced training is gradual, moving from
stage to stage. If there is a break in studies due to the birth
of a child or other family circumstances, they can subsequently
be resumed at the next stage. For example, at a factory in
Zwickau the study program for training skilled women workers
is broken down into four stages of ten weeks each.

At the factories we surveyed in the Russian Republic, apprenticeship was the dominant form of vocational training.
Moreover, the proportion of women trained by the team apprenticeship method on the factory floor was substantially
higher than on-the-job training of men. Thus whereas the
proportion of men who received their occupational training
through apprenticeship ranged from 60% (in maching building)
to 88% (in meat packing), among women it ranged from 78%
(in the textile industry) to 97% (in meat packing) — see Table 13.

It should be noted that men are much more persistent in continuing their occupational training at advanced training courses
and schools (five times more in machine building, roughly two
times more in the bakery, meat, and dairy industry, one and a
half times more in the textile industry). These figures indicate that the system of advanced training at factories does not
take the features of female labor into account and is thereby
less accessible to the majority of women who had received
their initial occupational training on the factory floor. This
was also confirmed in a poll of workers (see Table 14).

As Table 14 shows, at almost all enterprises, with the exception of bakeries, fewer women than men saw any opportunity
for advancing their occupational skills. This subjective evaluation of the opportunities for advanced training by men and
women is additional indication of the lack of equal opportunity
for the occupational advance of women workers. This is also
confirmed by current data on worker education at the surveyed
factories, which reveal that women study less than men (with
the exception of the textile industry).

Most of the currently studying workers are in the low-skilled
category. Thus at machine-building plants 95% of the women
workers now studying belong to the first skill rating. This in-

Table 13

Distribution of Workers by Sex and Form of Occupational Training
(% of total surveyed in given industry)

| | | Form of occupational training | | |
	apprenticeship	advanced training courses or schools	vocational-technical school	technicum
Machine building:				
men	59.5	26.7	11.0	2.8
women	87.5	4.8	5.6	2.1
Garment:				
men	—	—	—	—
women	87.4	2.3	9.8	0.5
Textile:				
men	75.7	8.5	12.0	3.8
women	77.9	5.5	16.2	0.4
Baking:				
men	68.4	15.8	10.0	5.8
women	81.7	7.0	9.2	2.1
Meat and dairy:				
men	87.9	6.6	4.4	1.1
women	96.9	3.1	—	—

Table 14

Assessment of Possibilities for On-the-job Advanced
Training by Male and Female Workers

	Percentage of workers who see opportunities for advanced training	
	men	women
Machine building	51.8	32.4
Garment	—	26.2
Textile	26.0	17.3
Baking	7.2	16.3
Meat and dairy	18.8	8.5

Table 15

Percentage of Male and Female Surveyed Workers
Currently Studying

	men	women
Machine building	13.9	8.8
Garment	—	11.5
Textile	6.9	13.0
Baking	8.4	5.9
Meat and dairy	10.6	2.7

dicates that the majority of those studying are young women
not yet burdened by families. But older women workers in the
median skill ratings (third or fourth grade) are no longer able
to combine work with studies.

However, it is not only family duties and the difficulty of
combining them with work and studies that prevent women
workers from raising their skills. Much in this field depends
on how female personnel are employed at factories and on concern for the features of female labor. Polls conducted at factories indicate that men and women generally assess differently their opportunities for professional advance.

97

Table 16

Responses of Workers Currently Studying to a Question Concerning the Prospects for Professional and Occupational Advancement

(%)

"Do you see an opportunity for professional advancement at your factory?"	Workers currently studying							
	at advanced training courses		at young worker schools		in technicums and institutes		total	
	men	women	men	women	men	women	men	women
Yes	70.6	40.9	67.6	48.6	67.4	57.3	68.6	50.7
No	10.3	18.2	9.8	27.8	13.0	15.7	10.8	20.5
Don't know	19.1	40.9	22.5	23.6	19.6	27.0	20.5	28.8
Total	100	100	100	100	100	100	100	100

We see that some 70% of the male workers currently studying see opportunities for professional and occupational advancement at their factory, whereas only half the women workers
share such expectations. Moreover, only 40 out of every 100
women attending advanced training courses think it will help
them win promotion. This shows that for many women workers
at the surveyed factories there is no promise in advanced training at work, which undoubtedly discourages women from combining work with study. Another factor retarding the growth in
women's occupational levels is the tendency of plant management to underestimate the importance of improving female
workers' skill,[17] and sometimes simply to understate their
skill ratings. Thus at some of the surveyed machine-building
plants, we found women workers with a secondary technical
education employed in jobs rated in the first to third skill
ratings. Only 3% of women worker graduates of technicums had the highest, fifth, skill rating, and 25.3% had rating IV.

It should be noted that problems of raising the general educational and occupational levels of women workers do not go
unheeded at the leading industrial enterprises in the country.
The collective agreements and social development plans of
many of them provide for worker training and retraining. The
scale on which workers are involved in various forms of training at industrial enterprises is tremendous. At the Belorussian Red Labor Banner Automobile Works, for example, almost 40% of the workers are studying to complete their education or raise their skills. In five years (1971-75) more than
7,500 workers will have completed production courses and communist work schools, and 480 will have acquired secondary
trades. The factory also operates a young workers' school,
vocational-technical schools, and a branch of the Belorussian
Polytechnical Institute and the Minsk Automotive Technicum,
providing opportunities for all workers, including women, to pursue their general and occupational education. The results of this
important work in personnel training are apparent — by 1975, 62%
of the women workers will hold skilled jobs, as against 53% in 1971.

99

A. E. Kotliar and S. Ia. Turchaninova

At the Volga synthetic fibers plant more than 12,700 workers, some 10,000 of them women, will have taken retraining courses and acquired higher job ratings.

The Urals railway car factory in Nizhnii Tagil attributes great importance to the education of female workers. Some 4,000 women are covered by various forms of education: night institutes, technicums, and young workers' schools; and 2,500 women attend advanced training courses. Many industrial enterprises consider it necessary to create favorable conditions for combining work and study, for which they set up study centers, such as the part-time basic school for young workers at the Solikamsk pulp and paper mill or the part-time technicum and school at the Ivanovo worsted mill, where school and work schedules are dovetailed to assure convenient hours. At the mills of the Voronezh "Trikotazh" Association, virtually every third young worker, most of whom are women, has acquired one or two secondary trades.

Questions of raising the occupational and skill levels of women workers are acquiring mounting significance because the Ninth Five-Year Plan provides for an extensive program of retooling and reequipment, especially in the light and food industries, where female labor predominates. Higher technological standards of production will require higher occupational standards of the work force, which undoubtedly will promote a substantial rise in productivity. Women themselves will benefit from higher skills because they will be able to leave the physically arduous jobs to which many workers with low general educational and occupational standards are relegated; this will open up opportunities to them for more meaningful work. It should be noted that the collective agreements and worker training and retraining programs in most of the social development plans of the industrial enterprises we surveyed did not pay special attention to organizing women's studies. It is not surprising that shortcomings in this field often remain unexposed.

The sociobiological features of the female work force and the importance of enhancing the efficiency of female labor suggest the need for comprehensive production and social development plans of enterprises, especially those employing large numbers of women, to place emphasis on measures aimed at raising the skill level of women and improving their working conditions.

Work Schedules in Industry and Female Labor

One of the ways of assuring the best utilization of female labor is the adoption of work schedules that enable women to combine work with fulfillment of their family, especially maternal, responsibilities and ensure high and stable working ability for as long as possible.

At present, with an average workweek of 40.7 hours in industry,[18] the most common work schedules provide for a five- or six-day workweek in one, two, or three shifts.

Most industrial enterprises have a two- or three-shift schedule, the most convenient for the workers being the former, with no night shift.

Industrial enterprises with three shifts operate according to a number of different schedules. The most widely used, especially at textile mills, are the so-called Ivanovo, Leningrad, and Krivtsov schedules, in which the choice of shifts is determined by local and production characteristics and the personal interests of the workers. These schedules, in various degrees, reduce the number of night shifts and provide for different variants of two off-days per week. For example, the Ivanovo schedule, first introduced at the P. Kamenskii Weaving Mill in Gorno-Pavlovsk, substantially reduces the number of night shifts (to two a month) and provides for two successive sliding off-days, however, at the expense of regular weekend holidays. This schedule has been adopted by most textile mills operating on a five-day week schedule.

The Leningrad schedule, used extensively at textile mills in large cities, has more night shifts than the Ivanovo schedule, but it retains the regular off-days for all.

101

Another schedule that is being used provides for a five-day workweek with four shifts a day. It is used mostly at continuous operation factories with hazardous conditions and a shorter workday.

The negative aspect of three- and four-shift schedules is the existence of night shifts, which are most unsatisfactory for women, since they aggravate labor conditions by breaking the normal diurnal life pattern.

Without setting ourselves the task of an exhaustive analysis of the problem of work schedules, let us examine some problems of the organization of working time for women workers in RSFSR industry: nighttime employment of women, work schedules used at some factories with high concentrations of female labor, evaluation of those schedules by the women themselves, and some questions of female labor involving reduced working hours or work at home.

Night shifts exist for either technological (continuous manufacturing processes in metallurgy, chemical manufacture, oil extraction, cement production, etc.) or economic reasons (the need to achieve production quotas without increasing manufacturing capacities, machine-tool plant, etc.). Approximately 40% of all industrial enterprises operate continuously throughout the week.[19] They are mainly in the iron and steel, nonferrous metals, oil, chemical, pulp and paper, power, cement, and glass industries, in which from 30 to 50% of the work force performs continuous manufacturing processes. In other industries where three-shift schedules are used, as in the textile and food industries, no more than 10% of the workers perform continuous technological processes; and the need for three shifts, and consequently night shifts, is dictated by economic considerations.

At the time of the survey, almost 25% of the women industrial workers were employed at factories with three-shift schedules, that is with night shifts, although at only one third of these factories was the schedule due to technological reasons.

To determine the attitude of working women to different work schedules, we analyzed five types of schedules used at twenty-one

102

surveyed plants with noncontinuous production processes:

Schedule type 1: One shift, five-day week. All surveyed meat-packing plants worked according to this schedule.

Type 2: Two shifts, five-day week. This schedule was in force at machine-building plants and all the garment factories, except one in Viazniki.

Type 3: Two shifts, six-day week, at the Viazniki garment factory.

Type 4: Three shifts, five-day week, with sliding off-days. This schedule operated at bakeries, dairies (in Rostov-on-Don), and the S. M. Kirov Weaving Mill in Ivanovo.

Type 5: Three shifts, six-day week, at the flax-spinning mill in Viazniki.

The factories were classified according to the work schedule involving the majority of workers.

Workers at plants with a noncontinuous manufacturing process operating a five-day working week have two days off, and those with a six-day week have one day off.

With one- and two-shift work schedules, fewer than 6% of all women workers are on average regularly engaged in three shifts. The proportion of women among the workers on night shifts is only 1%. With a three-shift working week (with both five and six working days) the majority of workers (from 53% at the Rostov dairy to 92% at the Viazniki flax-spinning mill) work regularly in three shifts, i.e., they have night shifts. True, the percentage of women on the night shifts is 60%, although the factories are typically "female" enterprises.

What do the workers think of different shift schedules, and to what extent are they satisfied with their work schedules? A poll revealed that the extent to which working men and women are satisfied depends in the first place on the extent to which the shift schedules fit in with their changing daily living pattern. Women, however, are more sensitive to the work scheule, and being "doubly employed," they resent to a greater degree night shifts and off-days that do not coincide with the off-days of other members of the family.

Table 17

Classification of Surveyed Enterprises
According to Schedule Type (%)

Schedule type	Enterprises working on the schedule	Share regularly working					
		one shift		two shifts		three shifts	
		total	women	total	women	total	women
1 – 1 shift, 5-day week	Meat-packing plant (Kansk)	75.3	73.0	23.3	24.3	1.4	2.7
	Meat-packing plant (Viazniki)	75.4	82.1	20.0	15.3	4.6	2.6
	Meat-packing plant (Vladivostok)	83.0	70.0	14.5	23.5	2.5	6.5
2 – 2 shifts, 5-day week	Garment factory (Vladimir)	3.1	1.9	96.4	97.6	0.5	0.5
	Garment factory (Vladivostok)	20.2	17.0	79.8	83.0	—	—
	Garment factory (Artem)	3.5	2.0	96.5	98.0	—	—
	Garment factory (Kansk)	4.1	3.2	95.9	96.8	—	—

Garment and knitwear factory (Kansk)	20.0	16.0	70.0	76.0	10.0	8.0
"Auto Instruments" Plant (Vladimir)	49.0	43.0	44.0	55.0	7.0	2.0
"Radio Set" Plant (Vladivostok)	56.7	47.2	30.4	51.9	12.9	0.9
Bearing Plant GPZ-10 (Rostov-on-Don)	49.1	36.4	35.4	61.1	15.5	2.5
3 — 2 shifts, 6-day week						
Garment factory (Viazniki)	—	—	100.0	100.0	—	—
4 — 3 shifts, 5-day week, sliding off-days						
Kirov Weaving Mill (Ivanovo)	16.0	6.5	2.0	2.2	82.0	91.3
Dairy (Rostov-on-Don)	29.0	22.0	27.0	28.0	44.0	50.0
Bakery (Sverdlovsk)	25.4	12.0	1.0	3.0	73.6	85.0
Bakery (Asbest)	25.0	16.4	17.6	22.4	57.4	61.2
Bakery (Viazniki)	31.6	9.4	7.1	11.5	61.5	79.1
Bakery (Artem)	32.6	25.7	4.7	5.7	62.7	68.6
Bakery No. 2 (Vladivostok)	39.1	31.0	8.8	4.2	52.1	64.8
Bakery (Kansk)	—	—	44.0	37.0	56.0	63.0
5 — 3 shifts, 6-day week						
Flax-spinning mill (Viazniki)	17.0	5.0	5.0	3.0	78.0	92.0

A. E. Kotliar and S. Ia. Turchaninova

Table 18

Degree of Acceptance of Work Schedule by Workers
(by sex) (%)

Type of schedule	% of total factory work force on given schedule	% of workers satisfied with work schedule	
		men	women
1 — 1 shift, 5-day week	80.0	90.0	83.0
2 — 2 shifts, 5-day week	75.0	87.0	71.0
3 — 2 shifts, 6-day week	100.0	92.0	77.0
4 — 3 shifts, 5-day week	65.0	71.0	51.0
5 — 3 shifts, 6-day week	78.0	70.0	13.0

As the table shows, men are much less sensitive to differences in work schedules, and they voice no special preference
for any of the work schedules adopted at the surveyed plants.
(It should be borne in mind that the survey covered only predominantly "female" enterprises.) Their evaluations range
from 92% satisfied with the two-shift six-day week schedule
to 70% accepting the three-shift six-day week. This comparative "tolerance" of men for work schedules suggests that the
task of raising the shift coefficient in industry is best solved
by utilizing male manpower.

The polled working women at enterprises using the first,
second, and third types of work schedules (one- or two-shift
work with a five- or six-day working week) expressed the highest degree of satisfaction. These schedules suit women best,
and most of them (70 to 90%) are satisfied with them. In the
case of three shifts, for both a five- and six-day working week
(types 4 and 5), acceptance of the schedule by women workers

is much lower (an average of less than 35%). This is because of night shifts and sliding off-days, which are most inconvenient for family women.

Among women working at factories with a three-shift schedule there is a substantial difference between the assessments of those with a five-day working week (type 4) and those with a six-day week (type 5). Whereas 51% are content with a five-day week, the six-day week is acceptable to only 13% of the women workers. The reason for this difference is that the type 5 schedule does not provide for a second off-day, and 61% of the women have to work nights more than ten times a month. With a three-shift, five-day working week (type 4) the workers have two successive off-days and a smaller number of night shifts (see Table 19).

Night shifts are the main reason for dissatisfaction among women workers with three-shift schedules. Hence the direct and very close connection between the degree of dissatisfaction with the work schedule and the number of night shifts per month. This can be seen in comparing the proportion of working women satisfied with the work schedule of three-shift enterprises and the number of night shifts per month.

Table 19 shows that three shifts with a five-day week (type 4) is more acceptable (64% to 31%) than with a six-day week (type 5), which only 13% of the polled women found acceptable. The workers at the flax-spinning mill in Viazniki, where this schedule is used, have only one day off a week, and each woman has to work ten to twelve night shifts a month. Hence the dissatisfaction of most of them.

Prominent among the enterprises operating according to the type 4 schedule is the Kirov Weaving Mill in Ivanovo, where the women showed a relatively high degree of acceptance of the schedule (64%), which closely approaches the percentages for establishments working one or two shifts. The reason is that the mill has a three-team shift schedule with sliding off-days that reduces the number of night shifts to two per month (the so-called Ivanovo schedule). With this schedule the workers work two eight-hour shifts four days a week and three

Table 19

Attitude of Women Workers to Three-shift Schedule,
Depending on the Number of Night Shifts (%)

| | Women satisfied with schedule | Women working night shifts | | | |
| | | | shifts per month | | |
		total	fewer than 5	5–10	more than 10
Type 4 schedule					
Kirov Weaving Mill (Ivanovo)	64.0	100	100.0	—	—
Bakery (Asbest)	60.0	100	30.0	70.0	—
Bakery (Artem)	47.0	100	17.0	83.0	—
Bakery (Kansk)	36.0	100	—	100.0	—
Bakery (Vladivostok)	44.0	100	—	100.0	—
Bakery (Viazniki)	34.0	100	3.0	97.0	—
Bakery (Sverdlovsk)	31.0	100	2.0	98.0	—
Type 5 schedule					
Flax-spinning mill (Viazniki)	13.0	100	11.0	28.0	61.0

shifts the fifth day, with a seven-hour night shift. One week the workers have two successive days off after five working days, and the next week they also have two successive days off, but after six working days. However, the main drawback to this schedule is sliding off-days, as indicated by 75% of the women workers who expressed dissatisfaction with the schedule. The main reason for dissatisfaction at the other enterprises was night shifts (from 70% of the workers at the bakery in Asbest to 97% at the bakery in Vladivostok).

The second reason for dissatisfaction was sliding off-days, and other reasons accounted for no more than 25 or 30% of the total.

The survey also revealed that working women of all ages were equally dissatisfied with night shifts.

An attempt was made in the course of the survey to correlate the work schedule with the physical state of women workers at the end of a shift. We know that a worker's physical state may depend on a variety of factors: socioeconomic, demographic, age, sex, marital status, type and conditions of work, and so on. The work schedule is a component of working conditions that affect the workers' physical state, and there is a definite and discernible link between them. At enterprises with three-shift work schedules, most women complained of considerable fatigue by the end of the working day. Thus whereas not more than 40% of the women workers at meat-packing plants, garment factories, and machine-building plants (with work schedule types 1, 2, and 3) complained of considerable fatigue by the end of a shift, in factories with three-shift schedules almost 60% of the women workers felt very tired, with the exception of the Ivanovo weaving mill, where only 30% of the women felt very tired by the end of the working day (see Table 20).

Table 20 reveals a marked difference in the physical state of workers by the end of the shift at two different textile mills: whereas at the Ivanovo weaving mill only 30% complained of considerable fatigue, at the flax-spinning mill in Viazniki more than half (59%) complained of great fatigue by the end of the shift, and the proportion among women dissatisfied with the

Table 20

Physical State by End of the Workday of
Women at Enterprises Surveyed

| | % of workers reporting considerable fatigue | |
| | among all women workers of factories with the given schedule | among women dissatisfied with the work schedule |
Type of schedule		
1 — 1 shift, 5-day week	42.0	66.0
2 — 2 shifts, 5-day week	37.0	49.0
3 — 2 shifts, 6-day week	40.0	57.0
4 — 3 shifts, 5-day week	46.0	62.0
including: bakeries	58.0	72.0
Kirov Weaving Mill in Ivanovo	30.0	50.0
5 — 3 shifts, 6-day week	59.0	77.0

work schedule reached 77%. This suggests that the large percentage of workers dissatisfied with the three-shift, six-day
week schedule (87% of all women workers) is due, in part,
to the considerable physical strain it imposes. A comparison between these two textile mills with respect to the
physical state of their workers by the end of a shift and the
degree of satisfaction with their work schedules leads to the
conclusion that urgent steps should be taken at the Viazniki
flax-weaving mill to establish a more favorable work schedule

that would reduce the number of night shifts and thus the physical strain on workers.

Interestingly, in 1969 the Viazniki flax mill did introduce the Ivanovo work schedule, thereby reducing night shifts. However, after several months the workers requested a return to the former three-shift, six-day schedule. A study revealed that the decision to return to the old schedule, with which most of the women workers are now dissatisfied, was prompted by the fact that the social and cultural establishments and everyday services in Viazniki were not prepared for the introduction of a five-day workweek, the workers were not prepared psychologically for the changeover (the flax mill was the only enterprise in the town to go over to the five-day week), and the local characteristics of a medium-sized town (one third of the women working at the mill are from surrounding villages) had not been taken into consideration. All this contributed to disaffection with the new schedule, although it was an improvement over the previous one. Consequently, it is essential to prepare the ground before introducing changes in work and recreation schedules.

Summing up the materials of our survey, we can conclude that one-and two-shift schedules with a so-called "pure five-day week," providing regular off-days (Saturday and Sunday), are best for women workers. The schedule with two successive off-days is, in the view of experts, most suitable from both the economic and physiological point of view. This schedule does not disrupt the established pattern of work and helps maintain high labor productivity throughout the week because the two days' rest helps restore working ability. This schedule is especially favorable for women because it allows more time for domestic duties, bringing up children, and recreation.

In view of the unfavorable economic and social consequences of employing women, especially those with children, on night shifts, the Soviet government has decreed in the Principles of Labor Legislation that women may not be employed at night jobs, except in branches of the economy where this is required by extreme necessity, where it is permitted only as a temporary measure.

In other words, the overriding principle in improving work schedules for women workers is the continuing reduction of night work. This principle is pursued on a planned basis in all industries. It is geared to the expansion of the economic potential and the rising levels of mechanization and automation of production. A variety of measures is being taken to reduce night work for women, depending on the industry, type of manufacture, proportion of women in the industry, local conditions, etc. In some industries, such as metallurgy, chemicals, oil, etc., where night shifts are necessary because of the continuity of the production process and the proportion of female labor is not high, women are gradually being transferred from continuous process sections and replaced by men. In other industries where night shifts are operated for economic reasons (for example, shortage of machine tools) and the proportion of women in the work force is high, production expansion and raising of labor productivity is accompanied by the introduction of schedules reducing the number of night shifts. Thus in the textile industry 80% of the enterprises that have adopted the five-day week operate according to the Ivanovo schedule.

Measures are now being elaborated at all leading industrial enterprises to reduce night work for women, along with the development and introduction of work schedules more convenient for women workers. Social development plans of many industrial plants provide for specific measures to reduce female employment on night shifts. Thus at enterprises in the pulp and paper industry, reduction of third shifts has been achieved by introducing new, highly efficient equipment, semiautomatic lines, and better equipment) for handling materials. For example, at the Malin paper mill in the Ukraine, replacement of old reel-slitting machines with improved models made it possible to eliminate the third shift and transfer the 300 women who operated the machines to a two-shift schedule.

The social development plan at the Kondopoga pulp and paper mill provides for the transfer, during 1971-75, of women workers in some trades in the sheet paper shop (cutters, packers, sleeve gluers) to two shifts. The introduction of the two-

shift schedule without night shifts, and with general off-days
for all, is being effected under the social development plans of
the twisting-weaving, finishing-rewinding, and other shops of
the Volzhsk synthetic fibers mill. A similar process is due to
be completed by 1975 at the spinning and weaving mills of the
"Rigas Textils" Works in Riga, etc.

Many textile mills, besides introducing work schedules reducing the number of night shifts, operate various types of
shift work and rest schedules for women in the main trades
which provide for varying working weeks, shift hours, rest
periods, and lunch intervals.

Introduction of additional work breaks, for exercise, ten-
minute rest intervals in the middle of the first or second half of the
working day, extension of the lunch break to 40-60 minutes,
etc., has made it possible for weavers and spinners to increase
productivity by an average 2-3% and considerably reduce fatigue.
Such work and rest schedules have been used successfully at
the Kherson and Krasnodar cotton mills and other textile
enterprises.

In those industries and types of production where it is not
yet impossible to eliminate or reduce night shifts, their unfavorable effects for women are reduced by giving them additional vacation days and pay for night work, as provided by the
decisions of the Twenty-fourth CPSU Congress and the Session
of the USSR Supreme Soviet in November 1971.

In the future, with the creation of the economic prerequisites
for building a communist society, real opportunities will appear
in our country for reducing the working hours of all working
people, as provided for in the CPSU Program. The resolution
of this important social problem has already begun, and it has
primarily affected women with children.

Because the health of mothers and children is a prime concern, women workers are not only transferred to easier jobs
when necessary, but job intensity is reduced without affecting
their pay. Nursing mothers have their working day reduced
by one hour (the time of additional breaks for feeding the child),
and they cannot be given night jobs. Furthermore women have

113

an option of additional unpaid leave until the child is one year
old, that period being included in the length of service. Many
young mothers now avail themselves of this option.

The first to benefit from further reductions of working hours
and from longer vacations should be working mothers.

A question of interest in the search for rational work schedules is the introduction of part-time and at-home work. Soviet
labor legislation provides for the possibility of contracts between workers and management that stipulate part-time workdays or weeks. Remuneration in such cases is on a per-hour
or piece-rate basis. The Code of Labor Laws of the RSFSR
states that "part-time work does not entail for workers and
employees any restrictions in length of annual vacation, length-
of-service record, or other work benefits." [20] Part-time
workers enjoy all the benefits established for a given category
of workers. They receive temporary disability benefits, full
vacation, and their general and specific length of service ac-
cumulates, with all the consequent benefits with respect to pay
raises and pension plans.

Among those who opt for part-time work are students, pensioners, housewives, and mothers of small children. Some cannot work a full day for health or family reasons, others because
they are studying.

A sample survey carried out by the Sector of Labor Resources in the Service Sector of the Central Scientific Research Laboratory of Labor Resources showed that most of
those working, or expressing the desire to work, shorter hours
were women (90% of those who would like to work part-time in
both the service sphere and industrial establishments). Almost
half the women workers who would prefer part-time work had
children of preschool or elementary school age.

For most women part-time work enables them to devote
more attention to bringing up children at home, caring for ailing or senior members of the family, and having more free
time for rest and developing their talents. This conclusion is
confirmed by an analysis of the main reasons motivating the
desire of women workers to work shorter hours: more than

46% of those polled spoke of the need to look after children or ailing members of their families, as well as the need for time for housework or tending subsidiary farm plots; 6.5% cited the difficulty of combining work with studies; and 4.5% said that they could afford to earn less. [21]

Soviet and foreign authors sometimes claim that shorter working hours are equivalent to discrimination against women, since they consolidate the remnants of their family inequality and reduce the economic role of female labor. It is hard to accept this view. Shorter working hours rid the woman of work in "two shifts," on the job and at home.

Polls of women workers at the Moscow Watch Factory No. 2[22] and enterprises in Moldavia with a high proportion of women employees[23] revealed that some 6-12% would prefer to work part-time. Most of them were mothers of one or two children of preschool or elementary school age and would expect to work shorter hours temporarily, for not more than three to five years, while their children grew up a little.

In the sociological study by the Sector for Labor Resources in the Service Sphere of the Labor Resources Laboratory, some 20% of the workers would like to work part-time, but only half could afford the loss in pay this would entail.

Bearing in mind that each year some 10% of women workers leave their jobs for family reasons,[24] we can assume that many of them would have stayed on if they had the option of part-time work. In the future, when more shops, sections, or even entire factories will have schedules providing for part-time work, many women may well choose to continue on their jobs after they have children. This will make it possible for working women to reduce the breaks in their service records for maternity reasons and help reduce turnover in the female work force. Part-time working women will not lose their trades or skills and will remain within the worker collective. Furthermore, work at the factory or at home will make it possible for women to contribute to their family budget. This is confirmed by a poll of part-time workers: 53% continued or had come back to work because they needed the additional

115

money for their family budget, 32% felt the need for daily work or contact with their work collective or love for their trade, and 12% had to work part-time to reach the required service record entitling them to pension benefits. [25]

On the other hand, the economy can benefit substantially from the introduction of shorter work schedules and the utilization of female labor because this draws a portion of the housewives into social production and can provide additional working hands for both industrial enterprises and those in the nonproductive sphere experiencing acute shortages of manpower and where part-time work is most widely employed. However, the overwhelming majority of housewives who would like to work in the economy can do so only if special conditions are created, since about half of them have no specialized training, more than 30% never worked or stopped working more than four years ago, and almost 25% have three or more children. [26]

Earlier sociological surveys of nonworking women in small and medium-sized towns in the Russian Federation, Baltic republics, Georgia, and Moldavia showed that 25% would like to work in various branches of the economy provided they could do so on a part-time basis or at home. [27]

A survey carried out in nine oblasts of the RSFSR revealed that half of the housewives who would like to work on a part-time basis wanted to work in industry, the others in the service sphere.

But in order to draw them into the economy it is necessary to organize workplaces with preparatory training programs, shorter working hours, and enrollment of children in preschool institutions, etc. Furthermore, when considering the problem of the efficiency of part-time work, one should not overlook the law of the correlation between the intensive and extensive aspects of labor. Karl Marx formulated it as follows: "The first result of a reduction in the working day is based on the self-evident law that the ability of manpower to function is in inverse proportion to the time it functions. Hence, within certain limits, what is lost in the time it is active is made up in its intensity." [28]

Studies show that the productivity of a worker working shorter hours is higher than that of one working a full shift. This is indicated by the experience of garment workers in Estonia: given the same organizational and technological conditions, two workers at the same workplace turn out in half a shift 20% more than one worker during a full shift. This is added confirmation of the economic expediency of expanding the scale of part-time work.

In our country some positive experience with part-time work has already been accumulated at public catering establishments, public services and utilities, mail and telephone services, and public transportation in Moscow and other major cities. Part-time work schedules are in effect at a few garment, knitwear, and textile factories in Moscow, Kishinev, Georgia, and Estonia. However, this form of work organization is still not widespread enough. In the RSFSR, for example, no more than 10,000 people, 70% of them women, have part-time or at-home jobs.[29]

Estimates made by the Sector of Labor Resources in the Service Sphere of the Labor Resources Laboratory show that by the end of the Ninth Five-Year Plan, the scale of this form of employment should increase. In 1970 only some 0.1% of the work force in the RSFSR was employed in part-time jobs; by 1974 the percentage rose to 2.0-2.5%. This means that from 1972 to 1975 some 60,000 to 65,000 people formerly doing domestic work or cultivating private plots began working part-time in industry in cities of the RSFSR.[30]

What is holding back the expansion of part-time employment? First, the industrial enterprises and organizations themselves have no idea of their needs for part-time workers. The All-Union Council of Trade Unions has recommended that the managers of enterprises and organizations in need of manpower determine the production sectors and specific workplaces at which part-time workers can be employed, and that state labor resources committees and their local bodies provide extensive and timely information about part-time work opportunities and conditions.

Only lack of adequate information about part-time work opportunities and the rights and benefits provided for this cate-

gory of workers can explain why, in a poll of people seeking
employment taken during the 1970 census, only 4.7% out of almost a half-million nonworking able-bodied urban residents of
the RSFSR cited a part-time workday (or week) as a condition
for taking a job.

Employment of workers in part-time jobs in the service
sphere often runs into difficulties owing to the unwillingness
of people to work half a shift because of low pay.

Another important question is the form of record-keeping
for part-time workers. For if employment records do not account separately for part-time workers, this reduces the productivity estimates for the given enterprise, since the part-
time worker produces less than the full-time worker. In January 1972 the Central Statistical Administration of the USSR
introduced separate records for part-time and full-time workers in trade, public catering, public service, mail and telephone
service, and local industry. The system was introduced for
other industries in 1973. The Central Statistical Administration has now drawn up a new system for evaluating work productivity that takes into account part-time workers at all enterprises.

This, however, has not eliminated all the difficulties. In industry there are still few specialized factories or shops that
have work schedules with combined shifts or half-shifts. Also,
it is difficult for the average industrial enterprise to employ
people working five or six hours a day because of the difficulty
of organizing work during the remaining hours without letting
equipment stand idle.

The organization of part-time work depends in many respects
on the organization of the manufacturing process. Experience
shows that industries with unit or small-series production can
utilize part-time workers on a much larger scale than in those
with large-series and mass-production output. That is why
some enterprise managers fearing complications in work organization are in no hurry to introduce part-time schedules,
and industrial ministries and departments are unenthusiastic
about introducing this form of work at their subordinate en-

terprises. Often the management of a factory, reluctant to
burden itself with the organizational concerns entailed in creating conditions for part-time workers, refuses to employ
them, thereby failing to realize the economic effect this form
of employment can yield. Thus in one survey it was found that
more than 12% of the workers who would like to work part-time
could not do so because of objections by management. Yet manpower shortages at enterprises in many industries, public services, and public catering could be substantially alleviated by
employing part-time workers. It would seem appropriate for
local soviets to work out special measures to expand this
form of employment and draw up lists of occupations and workplaces at enterprises where it would be expedient to employ
part-time workers.

Of great importance for attracting housewives to jobs in industry, communications, transportation, and public services
on both a full- and part-time basis, or to doing work at home,
is the organization of a special system of job-training courses.

Overcoming these shortcomings in the organization of part-
time work will promote the extensive development of this form
of manpower utilization. And Soviet women workers will receive "new opportunities for bringing up children, for greater
participation in public life, rest, recreation, and studies, for
greater access to the benefits of culture."[31]

Notes

1. Materialy XXIV s"ezda KPSS, p. 41.
2. See Zhenshchiny i deti v SSSR, Moscow, 1969, p. 66; V. A. Boldyrev, Itogi perepisi naseleniia SSSR, Moscow, 1974, p. 76.
3. Computed from census data and data in Vestnik statistiki, 1974, no. 1, p. 86.
4. See Vestnik statistiki, 1974, no. 1, p. 82
5. See Zhenshchiny i deti v SSSR, p. 102.
6. See Vestnik statistiki, 1973, no. 11, p. 86-87.
7. See Vestnik statistiki, 1974, no. 7, pp. 93-95.
8. Ibid.
9. In 1975 the difference in educational levels of men and women will remain only in the over-50 age brackets.

10. See Zhenshchiny i deti v SSSR, p. 56.

11. See Vestnik statistiki, 1974, no. 1, p. 88.

12. See Narodnoe khoziaistvo SSSR v 1970 g., Moscow, 1971, p. 528.

13. See Itogi Vsesoiuznoi perepisi naseleniia 1959 goda. SSSR (Svodnyi tom), Moscow, 1962, pp. 74-75.

14. See V. A. Zhamin and G. A. Egizarian, Effektivnost' kvalifitsirovannogo truda, Moscow, 1968, p. 160.

15. Some authors believe that today every year of general educational school is equivalent to an increment in occupational skills 5.8 times greater than one year of work, and the effect of education in the eighth through eleventh grades is even higher (see V. A. Zhamin and G. A. Egizarian, op. cit., p. 180).

16. Extensive studies carried out in the USSR indicate that instruction in a factory training school gives a worker an advantage in occupational advancement over workers with apprenticeship training (see V. V. Krevnevich, Vliianie nauchno-tekhnicheskogo progressa na izmenenie struktury rabochego klassa SSSR, Moscow, pp. 350-51; Iu. F. Novgorodskii, N. N. Ottenberg, and N. M. Khaikin, Tekhnicheskii progress i sovershenstvovanie podgotovki rabochikh kadrov, Moscow, 1973, p. 86).

17. Similar examples have appeared in the periodic press. See A. Levina, "Pokushenie na razriad," Rabotnitsa, 1971, no. 7.

18. See Narodnoe khoziaistvo SSSR. 1922-1972, p. 352.

19. See N. Tarasenko, "Za naibolee ratsional'nyi rezhim raboty predpriiatii," Ekonomicheskaia gazeta, 1969, no. 21, p. 4.

20. Kodeks zakonov o trude RSFSR, Moscow, 1972, art. 49, p. 24.

21. See A. Novitskii and M. Babkina, "Nepolnoe rabochee vremia i zaniatost' naseleniia," Voprosy ekonomiki, 1973, no. 7, p. 137.

22. See M. Sonin, Aktual'nye problemy ispol'zovaniia rabochei sily v SSSR, Moscow, 1965, pp. 152-53.

23. See N. Shishkan, Sotsial'no-ekonomicheskie problemy zhenskogo truda v gorodakh Moldavii, Kishinev, 1969, pp. 75-76.

24. See N. Shishkan, "Nepolnyi rabochii den' dlia zhenshchiny v usloviiakh sotsializma," Ekonomicheskie nauki, 1971, no. 8.

25. See Voprosy ekonomiki, 1973, no. 7, p. 137.

26. See Narodonaselenie, Moscow, 1973, p. 29.

27. See N. Shishkan, "Nepolnyi rabochii den'."

28. K. Marx and F. Engels, Sochineniia, vol. 23, p. 421.

29. See B. Sukharevskii, "Nepolnyi rabochii den'; ego granitsy i effektivnost'," Literaturnaia gazeta, 1972, no. 11, p. 10.

30. See Voprosy ekonomiki, 1973, no. 7, p. 138.

31. Materialy XXIV s''ezda KPSS, p. 75.

5

Raising the Skill Level of Women Workers

N. M. Shishkan

Many studies carried out in the socialist countries indicate that the occupational qualifications of women in them are higher than in capitalist countries. The proportion of women among engineering and technical personnel is increasing. Whereas in the United States the proportion of women among engineers is 1%, in the USSR women account for about 35% of the design and project engineers and more than 45% of the process engineers. Women account for some 40% of all the technicians. Important changes have taken place in the distribution of the female labor force among different trades and occupations. More and more of them are working as setters-up of equipment, chemical installation supervisors, machinist instructors, machine-toll operators, electricians, and in other trades directly associated with scientific-technological progress. Their proportion has increased among machine operators and workers with high skill grades. [1]

The number of women among scientific workers is growing rapidly, having increased eightfold between 1950 and 1974. [2]

Nevertheless women's skill levels remain considerably lower than those of men. This is seen, in the first place, in the lower

Russian text ©1976 by "Shtiintsa" Publishers. *Trud zhenshchin v usloviiakh razvitogo sotsializma* (Kishinev: "Shtiintsa" Publishers, 1976), pp. 137-45.

121

skill grades of the jobs they hold. Thus women account for 70-80% of the workers with first and second category skill grades, and from 5 to 35% of the workers with fifth to sixth and higher skill grades. In agriculture the proportion of women with some occupational skill or specialization is even lower; lower still is the proportion (under 20%) in occupations directly associated with scientific-technological progress. This proportion is especially low in rural areas. In the villages we surveyed — Sukleia, Ialoveny, Karpineny, Kriuliany, and others — the share of women among machine operators does not exceed 2-3%.

Although the proportion of women among scientific workers is growing, there are still substantially fewer women than men among candidates and, especially, doctors of science and academicians.

The proportion of women among graduate students has remained virtually unchanged in recent years. It was 27.3% in 1965 and 27.9% in 1974. [3]

There are fewer women than men among teachers in higher schools and among managerial personnel. Thus among directors of enterprises 9% are women, 10% among deputy directors and chief engineers, and 16% among shop superintendents, shift and section supervisors, and their deputies.[4]

The level of qualifications, as we know, has decisive importance in the task of raising productivity and wages. The reasons for the lag of women behind men in this field vary, but the most significant appear to be the following:

First, in the branches of material production, higher skill grades are established for more substantial types of work requiring technical knowledge. In spite of the growing percentage of women among workers in mechanized jobs, most of them continue to be employed in the less mechanized areas of production. Moreover, of the total increase in the numbers of manual laborers between 1962 and 1969, 96% were women. [5] One of the main reasons for this is that despite the high rates of mechanization of production processes and work, the proportion of mechanized labor is still growing comparatively slowly. Between 1959 and 1972 the average annual increase was 0.7%.[6] During this same period a significant number of former housewives and women who had worked private subsidiary plots, with no specialized education or training, joined the work force. Historically men more than women have been associated with the manufacture and use of implements of labor, first primitive, then more and more sophisticated machines and automatic devices. Even today boys are more technically inclined than girls.

The historical conditions of life activity have also engendered the equation of female labor with manual labor and male labor with mechanized. It is therefore no accident that mechanization is often accompanied by the transfer of women to auxiliary, manual jobs that do not require great skills. Unfortunately such attitudes are not infrequently shared even by some economists. Thus B. D. Breev, analyzing qualitative changes in labor resources as a result of the growing proportion of men, writes: "The growing proportion of men among those joining the work force means that many jobs that are today held by women will tomorrow be taken over by younger men.... It is necessary to plan in advance measures for the unrestricted replacement by men of jobs held by women. Such measures, in our view, could in the first place include the introduction of new tools, integrated mechanization and automation of production processes" (my emphasis. — N. Sh.).[7]

A similar attitude to the question is taken by K. Taichinova. "It should be borne in mind," she writes, "that with the industrialization of agricultural production, the employment opportunities for female labor directly in agriculture will decline first."[8] Of course, at the present stage in the development of technology, one can to some extent agree with such assertions.

The machinery introduced into production does not always make it possible to take account of specific features of female labor. If we analyze the manufacture of products in the major branches of machine building and metalworking, it becomes apparent that their manufacture and utilization require mainly male labor. This includes power, metallurgical, coal and ore-mining machinery, equipment for oil and gas extraction and oil refining, for land improvement, lumbering, construction and road building, the tractor and farm machinery industries, etc., operation of which presumes primarily the employment of male labor.

At the same time, it should not be forgotten that instrument building is developing at a faster rate than machine building and metalworking, and the manufacture of equipment for the chemical, light, and food industries is expanding at a rapid rate. [9] Here the opportunities for utilizing female labor are greater both in the manufacture of such equipment and in its industrial applications.

In integrated mechanization, and even more so automation, of production, the spheres of employment of female labor should be expanded, not reduced.

Identification of manual labor with female and mechanized with male work leads in practice to a state of affairs in which women sometimes perform jobs involving considerable physical exertion and the lifting of loads; but as soon as these jobs are mechanized, women are shifted to other jobs. Thus, for example, as long as cows are milked, fed, and watered manually, tending them is seen as a woman's job; as these processes are mechanized, it becomes a man's. Of course, it is wrong to identify manual with unskilled labor, as we often find in the literature. As K. Varshavskii correctly notes,[10] manual labor can be unskilled or very highly skilled indeed. Therefore, in our view the content of work is best characterized by grouping workers according to the degree of mechanization and occupational training and skills.

With all this in mind, we applied a methodology developed by Leningrad scholars to group the workers of a number of enterprises according to the content of their labor. [11]

I. Manual labor without the use of machines or mechanisms, or with them but not requiring special occupational training (unconstrained rhythm of work).

II. Work on a conveyor requiring a constrained rhythm of work, skilled or low-skilled.

III. Work on machines and installations requiring specialized vocational training.

IV. Work on semiautomatic machine tools, usually requiring extensive occupational training (semiconstrained rhythm of work).

V. Manual work not involving machines or mechanisms but using tools and requiring extensive occupational training (unconstrained rhythm of work).

Both women and men were employed in all the groups, but women considerably predominated in groups I and II, and men in groups III, IV, and V. Thus since women are employed mainly in lower skilled jobs, their wage ratings are on the whole lower than those of men.

Second, lower skilled jobs, especially auxiliary ones, by virtue of their routineness, do not stimulate a creative attitude toward them and provide no incentive for continuing education and raising skills. This is confirmed not only by our studies but by studies by other economists and sociologists as well.

Third, technological progress implies interest not so much in attained levels of skills as in higher levels, in raising educational standards and continued advanced occupational training, focusing on the mastery of a broad spectrum of technical knowledge.

Our studies, carried out in Moldavia, show that women raise their educational level less than men, even though as a rule more of them want to continue their education (see Table 1).

This is due to the fact that in view of the specific features of the female organism connected with the function of childbearing, women's work in social production is periodically interrupted. Frequently these interruptions are much longer than provided by maternity leave. Up to 15% of new mothers leave work to look after an infant.

A women who is on maternity leave and subsequently looking after children usually drops out of studies, which was confirmed by data obtained by us at surveyed enterprises in the republic (see Table 2).

Women with small children spend more time on housework

Table 1

Comparative Data on Education and Advanced Training of Men and Women
(% of total surveyed)*

	Enterprise									
	"Vibropribor" (Kishinev)**		"Elektrotoch-pribor" (Kishinev)**		"Elektromash" (Tiraspol')**		Kirov (Tiraspol)**		40 years of VLKSM***	"Stiaua Roshie"***
	men	women	men	women	men	women	men	women		
Have 10 years or more education	70.0	80.0	40.0	67.0	80.4	76.8	60.0	60.6	45.6	61.3
Studying part-time	29.0	23.0	30.1	33.0	32.3	14.5	34.0	20.0	53.0	36.0
Would like to study	61.0	63.0	44.2	46.3	54.2	58.4	65.0	61.6	35.2	56.1
Difference (between 3 and 2)	–32	–40	–14.1	–13.3	–21.9	–43.9	–31.0	–41.6	+17.8	–20.1

*The table is based on data obtained by the departments of labor safety and political economy of the Kishinev S. Lazo Polytech-nical Institute (with the participation of the author).
**1970.
***1974.

Table 2

Effect of Number of Children on Continuation of Education
by Women (in %)

	Total	Of whom, studying
No children	100	28.0
1 child	100	13.0
2 children	100	9.0
3 children	100	7.0
4 or more children	100	0.6

than those without children. Therefore they have much less
free time than men. Shortage of time is especially significant
in the case of scientific workers. It is the main obstacle to
women's advancement to managerial positions.

Fourth, there are shortcomings in worker training in general,
and in training women in particular. Thus the proportion of
women learning occupational skills in the vocational education
system is growing in all countries. However, their proportion
in the numbers needed to meet new demands for skilled workers is still small. The proportion of women who learned a
trade in the system of vocational-technical schools does not
exceed one third of the total number of students, and in some
schools it is even lower.

Differences in the proportions of girls and boys among students are, on the one hand, natural, insofar as some schools
train workers for strenuous jobs (bulldozer operators, structural steel assemblers, plumbers, press operators, etc.) in
which employment of women would not be appropriate. On the
other hand, the proportion of women among students for some
trades is considerably below their proportion among the workers employed in those trades.

The overwhelming majority of women receive their occupational training as apprentices. This makes it possible for them

only to acquire certain skills, without adequate theoretical
training, which reduces the effectiveness of applying the
achievements of science and technology. Yet the basic trends
in the country's long-term economic development require highly
skilled workers, primarily in view of the continued development of machine building and metalworking. Enterprises, however, do little to promote social planning in personnel training;
in particular, only the total numbers of workers in various
types of training are planned, without breaking them down according to trade and sex. But the role of social planning is
tremendous.

The attitudes of factory management play a great part in
realizing female workers' desires to continue their education.
As can be seen from the figures in Table 1, fewer workers at
the "40 Years of VLKSM" factory would like to continue their
education than at the "Stiaua Roshie" works (this is because
at the Tiraspol factory the level of education is lower, hence
there is less need to raise it). Yet the number of women workers continuing their education exceeds the number who want
to. This is a result of the great concern of the factory management for organizing advanced training.

It is impossible to overcome the difficulties in organizing
worker training and advanced training without improving vocational selection and orientation services. Taking due account of a person's abilities in choosing an occupation is
of tremendous social and economic importance. As E. I.
Stezhenskaia, head of the Labor Hygiene and Physiology Laboratory of the Gerontology Institute of the USSR Academy of
Medical Sciences, notes, a person's longevity and ability to
work depend in many ways on the degree to which his intellect and
character are attuned to his chosen activity. If it fits, the probability is greater that he will keep on working longer and will derive
pleasure from his work. [12] When a job is interesting, a person will also naturally seek to improve his skills on his own.

Much has been done in the past five years in our country and
the individual republics to improve vocational selection and
orientation. In Moldavia a great deal has been achieved in this

field by the Tiraspol Communist Party Committee and the State Committee of the Moldavian SSR Council of Ministers on the Utilization of Labor Resources.

On the whole, however, the problem is still being overcome slowly. It is the duty of the general education school to take account of the inclinations and abilities of young men and women and their health and psychological qualities, because few young people can master all trades. [13] A special physiological laboratory set up at the Institute of Child and Adolescent Hygiene of the USSR Ministry of Public Health under Doctor of Medicine I. D. Kartsev has been operating for many years. However, its experience is often neglected by schools and medical establishments.

Under the conditions of the expanding process of integration of the socialist countries, with growing specialization and cooperation of production, it would be expedient to expand the division of labor in personnel training as well.

And finally, fifth, women's advancement to more skilled jobs and, especially, managerial positions is still blocked by remnants from the past in approaching women as housewives and viewing their participation in social labor as a temporary and passing phenomenon. [14]

Yet, as many special studies show, [15] women possess many qualities essential for leadership: political activity and communist humanism, sensitivity to interpersonal relations, adherence to principles, sense of duty and responsibility, etc. What women sometimes lack is courage, knowledge, and organizational abilities in posing and resolving complex questions. This can be completely overcome by specialized training and better organization of time for managerial workers. Their working day, as we know, is virtually unscheduled. In addition, it is not always devoted to immediate duties. This negatively affects the amount of spare time, which is less for women than for men.

An analysis of the factors affecting advanced training of women indicates that to improve the situation, it is necessary to draw up not only general measures (scientific-technological

N. M. Shishkan

progress, changes in the character and content of work, better training of personnel) but also specific measures that take account of, and overcome, existing contradictions between a woman's work and her duties as a mother, between the working woman and the housewife.

Notes

1. Voprosy ekonomiki, 1973, no. 11, p. 60.
2. Zhenshchiny v SSSR, Moscow, 1975, p. 81.
3. Ibid., p. 84.
4. Ibid., p. 80.
5. Voprosy ekonomiki, 1974, no. 4, p. 37.
6. Ibid., 1973, no. 11, p. 47.
7. Voprosy teorii i politiki narodonaseleniia, Moscow, 1970, p. 128.
8. Voprosy ekonomiki, 1974, no. 6, p. 59.
9. Narodnoe khoziaistvo SSSR v 1973 godu, Moscow, 1974, p. 277.
10. Ekonomicheskie nauki, 1973, No. 6, p. 84.
11. Chelovek i ego rabota, Moscow, 1967, ppl 367-71.
12. E. I. Stezhenskaia, Literaturnaia gazeta, 1968, no. 32, p. 12.
13. R. K. Ivanova, Nauchno-tekhnicheskaia revoliutsiia i ee vlianie na izmenenie kharaktera obshchestvennogo truda, Moscow, 1974, p. 46.
14. Stroitel'stvo kommunizma i razvitie obshchestvennykh otnoshenii, Moscow, 1966, p. 355; Rabotnitsa, 1968, no. 1, pp. 10-12.
15. Bolgarskaia zhenshchina, 1975, no. 1, p. 4.

6

The Utilization of Female Labor in Agriculture

M. Fedorova

Extensive involvement of women in public life and the socialized sector of the economy has become a constant socioeconomic rule in all socialist countries, in both city and countryside.

As a result of the implementation of a comprehensive program for developing the socialized sector of agriculture, important changes have taken place in the structure of rural labor and opportunities for its employment. The sex structure of the agricultural labor force, which during the war and the first postwar years was characterized by an especially high proportion of women, has evened out considerably. The number of able-bodied women not employed in the socialized sector has declined sharply. At the same time, the average annual employment of women on collective farms has increased, which is favorably reflected in their annual incomes. This is indicated by the data in the table on page 132.

An analysis of general trends in the development of production indicates that the proportion of women working in agriculture is on the average higher than the proportion of women working in the national economy. In number of women work-

Russian text © 1975 by "Nauka" Publishers. "Ispol'zovanie zhenskogo truda v sel'skom khoziaistve," *Voprosy ekonomiki*, 1975, no. 12, pp. 55-64.

	1960	1965	1970	1974
Proportion of women working on collective farms (%)	56	55	53	51
Proportion of man-days worked by women in total expenditure of labor (%)	49	48	47	47
Yearly employment:				
Men:				
man-days	232	222	233	244
%	100	96	100	105
Women:				
man-days	170	170	185	204
%	100	100	109	120
Proportion of man-days worked by women to man-days worked by men (%)	74	77	80	84
Number of able-bodied women who did not work a single man-day (% of 1960)	100	70	40	33
Payment per man-day (rubles)	1.40	2.68	3.90	4.55

ing in the socialized sector, agriculture is second to industry. In 1974 the proportion of women in the total labor force of collective farms was about 51%, increasingly approaching the average in industry, where the proportion of women was 48-49%; on state farms it was 45%. This trend must be taken into account in long-term planning.

The continued intensification of agriculture, based on the extensive introduction of the achievements of scientific and technological progress, will naturally lead to considerable reductions in the numbers of farm workers, both male and female. However, even with the evening out of the sex structure of the population by natural growth, it would not be in the best interests of either agriculture or other branches of the economy if the reduction of the labor force in the socialized sector of state and collective farms was predominantly at the expense of female labor.

The optimum variant of utilization of female labor in agriculture in relation to the total work force cannot be much lower than in the sphere of material production in other branches of the economy. This is required by the demands of production itself — the territorial isolation and distribution of the rural population — as well as by the need of correct demographic policies.

As a result of general demographic changes and the institution of a number of economic measures, the sex structure of the work force in the economy as a whole and in various branches has been evening out in recent years. This process will become more pronounced in the long run. In particular, it is necessary to improve the age and, especially, sex structures of the labor force in the nonproductive sphere. Changes in the overall size of the work force and its sex and age structure will be considerably affected by the erosion of established territorial and ethnic characteristics in the organization of production and the formation of families, which hampers the rational redistribution of manpower. As a result agriculture continues to experience a shortage of manpower in a number of regions of the country.

Studies of the utilization of female labor in our country's agriculture under the conditions of scientific and technological progress show that in many cases, skilled female labor does not yet occupy an appropriate place in the main branches of the socialized sector. As the agricultural labor force decreases both absolutely and relatively, female labor is shifting increasingly into the sphere of "services" in rural communities or to other branches of the economy. The current situation can hardly be considered justifiable either economically or socially.

The practical necessity of employing female labor on machines and mechanized equipment is dictated by the requirements of production itself, particularly the still unresolved

problem of operating machines in two shifts. Due to the shortage of machine operators, tractors, harvester combines, and
other complex machinery are not used efficiently enough, which
leads to delays in field work, failure to meet requirements of
agricultural technology, and ultimately, lower profitability.

The changes taking place in the material and technical bases
of collective farms and state farms, as well as in the character
and special features of production relations in developed socialist society, enhance the role of skilled labor in agriculture.

Generational change in agriculture under the conditions of
the scientific and technological revolution enhances the acuteness of all these problems and makes it imperative to institute
a number of organizational and economic measures. Middle-
aged and elderly women now predominate in the agricultural
labor force. Between 1967 and 1970 the proportion of women
40 to 54 years old increased from 40.5 to 43.9% on collective
farms, and to 42% on state farms. At the same time, the outflow of young women from agriculture to other spheres of the
economy increased. The 1970 census revealed that the proportion of children up to age 15 is higher in rural communities
than in the cities, but since then the proportion has changed
sharply. In the last few years the mobility of young women
has been greater than that of young men.

In the four years between 1967 and 1970 the proportion of
young men of ages 16 to 24 on collective farms increased from
14 to 15%, whereas the proportion of young women in the same
age group declined from 14.8 to 13.8%. On state farms the proportion of people up to age 20 is 8.4% among men and 8.2%
among women; the respective figures up to age 29 are 16.6 and
14.8%. Among state farm workers there are 28% more men
than women up to age 29. The process is now gaining in mo-
mentum, especially in some areas of the Non-Black-Earth Region and Siberia. The age structure of women working in nonagricultural enterprises and offices is more favorable. Here
the proportion of women up to age 25 is 21%, between 25 and 39
it is 42.7%, and over 40 it is 36.4%.

One of the main reasons for the outflow of young people with secondary or incomplete secondary education from rural communities is the conditions and nature of farm work and the restricted opportunities (especially for young women), as compared with those they have in cities, for choosing an occupation and acquiring or continuing vocational and general education.

As an essential branch of the economy, agriculture must have a continuous supply of able-bodied, skilled workers in optimal age and sex ratios. The development of such labor-intensive spheres as horticulture, viticulture, and the cultivation of medicinal herbs also requires qualified personnel. This is especially important in regions with large underutilized manpower reserves (Moldavia, Central Asia).

As regards women, the socioeconomic task is to assure efficient utilization of skilled female labor in agriculture under the conditions of scientific and technological progress. Performing this task effectively depends heavily, in the first place, on changing rural working and living conditions. Of special importance in the set of measures concerned with this is the improvement of work organization, a higher rate of construction of housing and of cultural and domestic amenities and services in rural communities, and planned organization of efforts to build up and maintain a cadre of skilled workers, particularly female machine operators.

Getting young people consistently interested in agricultural careers is a problem with all farm workers, but it is especially acute with regard to women, most of whom are employed in low-skilled, manual jobs. In 1972 only 11.3% of the women working on state farms in crop farming and livestock worked on machines or mechanized equipment (the percentage for agriculture as a whole was 25%); in crop farming, where about two thirds of all the women work, the proportion of mechanized labor was 1.9%, and in livestock it was 28%. Three percent were manually employed servicing machines and mechanisms, and 85.7% were entirely manually employed. In some republics the proportion of women employed on manual jobs is even higher, at times reaching 90-98%.

At the same time, the proportion of women to the total labor

force in some specific fields was: milkers 98%; poultry tenders 94%; vegetable and fruit farming 74%.

The proportion of women among tractor and combine operators on collective and state farms is no higher than 0.5-0.6%.
There are few women among managerial personnel and specialists. Women account for 1.5% of collective farm chairmen
and directors of state farms, 17% of crop-farming and livestock
team leaders, and 36% of agronomists, zootechnicians, and
veterinary workers. Thus in agriculture there has evolved a
de facto, unjustified segregation of male and female labor in
terms of mechanized and manual work.

One of the reasons for this situation is the inadequacy of
the material and technical base of agriculture and the absence
of integrated mechanization despite the high levels of mechanization of some jobs. Animal husbandry is among the least
mechanized branches of the economy. In 1973 the degree of
mechanization of such labor-intensive processes as feeding
cattle, cleaning sheds, and milking was, respectively, 21%, 46%,
and 74%; only 20% of all cattle farms and 46% of all pig-breed-
ing and poultry farms were fully mechanized. In sugar beet
farming 80% of all the work is done by hand, despite the high
level of mechanization of some processes in this branch.

However, unfavorable conditions for mechanized labor and the
imperfections of farm machinery from the standpoint of sanitary and hygienic working conditions and reducing the work-
load have a negative effect both on the utilization of both male
and female labor and on the prevention of turnover of young
machine operators, especially women. Recent studies and re-
views of practical experience [1] indicate that work stations and
working conditions of tractor and combine operators are far
from adequate and are especially unfavorable for women. At
present, by all indications of hazardousness (vibration, gas
emission, dust, grime, etc.) working conditions of farm machinery operators are far inferior to normative requirements.
It is not accidental that many press reports have been appear-
ing citing structural defects in the apparently most up-to-date
tractors, harvester combines, and other machines, especially

from the point of view of maintenance and field repairs. Tests have confirmed that such claims by farm workers are justified. In only ten months during 1974 the Kuban Tractor and Farm Machinery Testing Institute issued recommendations for the suspension of production of many much-needed machines due to their low quality. The need to improve the consumer quality of farm machines is an issue that has been raised repeatedly.[2] It has been noted that up to 200 structural defects that make repairs difficult have been found in several makes of tractors. Fifty such defects were found in combines, and ten to fifteen in such relatively simple machines as sowers and plows. Maintenance work for Soviet-made grain-harvesting combines is 50% higher than for the best foreign makes of the same class. The maintenance of new combines at top performance during peak operation periods requires 184 maintenance operations before work each day, and up to 300 operations every fourth day. It has been found that machine operators spend as much time on repairs and maintenance of tractors, combines, and trailer implements as on work in the field. Higher machine reliability and the separation of maintenance as an independent branch are essential initial prerequisites for the best utilization of labor with machinery.

The growth of mechanization in agriculture sometimes becomes a factor that worsens poor working conditions and is a source of harm to the organism, causing occupational illness. Thus higher engine power and speeds of new tractors and other machines increase vibration and noise.

Such developments must be countered by more stringent controls at all stages in the manufacture and testing of farm machinery as well as by strict observation of the "Uniform Occupational Safety and Hygiene Requirements for Tractors and Farm Machinery" approved by the Ministry of Agriculture of the USSR, the All-Union Agricultural Equipment Administration, and others back in 1966.

At the present levels of mechanization and quality of equipment in animal husbandry, the growing intensity of labor often leads to higher incidence of ailments of the hands and arms and lumbar and sacral vertebrae among milkmaids. Such develop-

ments can be alleviated by establishing an extensive network
of disease-prevention centers equipped with physiotherapeutic
apparatus as the material-technical base is improved. Such
institutes are currently operating successfully in a number of
regions of the country.

Another important cause of inefficient utilization of female
labor is poor organization of training of women for agriculture
at all initial and advanced levels, both vocational and general.

Education Levels of Urban and Rural Dwellers
(number of persons with higher, complete, or
incomplete secondary education
per 1,000 working people)

	Sex	Urban	Rural	Rural as % of urban
1959	both sexes	564	316	56
	men	537	337	63
	women	597	294	49
	women as % of men	112.4	87.2	
1970	both sexes	748	499	67
	men	740	517	69
	women	755	481	64
	women as % of men	102.0	94.9	
1970 as	both sexes	132.6	158.6	
% of 1959	men	137.8	151.9	
	women	126.4	165.3	

It can be seen from the table that between 1959 and 1970
(the period between the last two national censuses), the
educational level of the rural population rose considerably.
The number of working people with higher and secondary education increased by more than 50%; moreover, the increase
in rural communities was greater than in the cities (58.6% as
against 32.9%), and among rural women it was higher than
among men (65.3% and 51.9%). Nevertheless, in 1970 more than
half the working women in rural communities still had only a

primary education or less (32.5% with primary education).

In the prime working age groups (25-29 and 30-34 years), 66-67% of the rural working women had an incomplete secondary or primary education. Even in the 20-24 year age group the proportion of the latter was 50%. This group of women will predominate among women of working age in the near future. But even today, under the conditions of scientific and technological progress, inadequate general education in the countryside is an obstacle to the rapid acquisition of the necessary work habits and occupational skills. Experience suggests that urban dwellers, who have better general education and established careers, master rural trades faster, notably skilled trades as mechanics and operators in agrarian-industrial complexes. As integrated mechanization, the influx of new and more sophisticated machines and equipment, and new, progressive technologies gradually change agricultural labor into a variety of industrial labor, the problem of supplying agriculture with skilled workers becomes more and more acute.

In the long run the changing character of work in agriculture will require that all farm workers have a secondary education and specialized training in a wide range of new trades (machinists, operators, technicians, electricians, etc.).

The list of agricultural occupations for which skilled workers must be trained by vocational-technical schools is extensive. Furthermore, 75% of the trades recommended by the State Committee of the USSR Council of Ministers for Vocational and Technical Education to be offered in rural vocational-technical schools provide for the training of men and women on an equal basis. In reality, however, men continue to this day to predominate in training programs for tractor operators and drivers (82% in 1973). The proportion of machine operators and mechanics in animal husbandry (most of them men) is only 2.6%. The proportion of a number of other categories of unmechanized skilled jobs, for example, fruit and vegetable farmers, viticulturists, and horticulturists, is also small: only 1.6%. No rural women are being trained to become skilled personnel in the nonproductive sector.

M. Fedorova

The proportion of young women enrolled in rural vocational-technical schools since 1953 (when such schools were first opened) has never risen above 9.5%. At the same time, the number of young women in urban vocational-technical schools is nine times higher than in rural ones. The percentage of young women studying urban-type specialties in technical schools is rising at an especially rapid rate, and in 1973 they accounted for more than half the students (55.1%). A high proportion of students of urban vocational-technical schools come from the countryside. Thus in 1973, 160,000 of 320,000 students admitted to secondary vocational-technical schools were from rural areas. Of them, 58,000 enrolled in rural vocational-technical schools, and 102,000 (almost two thirds) entered urban secondary vocational-technical schools to acquire urban specialties. Rural young people prefer to enroll in vocational schools training skilled workers for industry rather than agriculture in large measure because existing working conditions and organization in agriculture, especially in animal husbandry, make skilled farm jobs unattractive.

The share of women among skilled personnel trained in the network of agricultural higher schools (32%) and technicums (36%) is also lower than the nationwide average for all specialties (50 and 53%). The shortage of skilled personnel, especially at intermediate levels, is already resulting in inefficient use of new machinery in animal husbandry, with some newly acquired expensive machines remaining in warehouses. As of January 1, 1974, there were 19,000 idle milking machines and units on farms. In some cases installed mechanisms are operated inefficiently. Thus in Kostroma Oblast at the beginning of 1972, the whole complex of machinery at 100 livestock sections with comprehensive mechanization was operational at less than half the time owing to the absence of skilled personnel.[3]

One of the main reasons for the lag in vocational training of rural residents, especially women, is the fact that in planning and forecasting jobs and job training for the villages, the traditional divisions of areas and jobs into "male" and "female," based on antiquated notions about equipment and jobs, are per-

petuated. It is therefore necessary to fundamentally change the
system of planning and training skilled rural personnel to con-
form to the new conditions and demands of scientific and technological progress. The social development plans of agricultural enterprises and districts must include provisions for
training and steady employment of skilled personnel; they should
provide for occupational training in the nonproduction sphere
and industries servicing basic production at enterprises and
in rural agricultural complexes. To stimulate the growth of
job skills and retain skilled personnel in farming, it would be
useful to consider actual general and occupational education as
one of the criteria in assigning job ratings. The current Instruction of the USSR Ministry of Agriculture on assigning
milker job ratings should be revised, as it provides only for
service record, meeting of planned quotas, and raising the productivity of the herd as criteria.

In the future, rural vocational schools should be located primarily in large rural district centers, because it has become
apparent that young people who learn rural trades under city
conditions get used to urban living standards and are reluctant
to remain in the villages. An equally complex and urgent task
is inducing trained, skilled women workers to stay in the countryside. This problem is closely linked with improving the organization of work and life in the countryside.

Women workers who perform field work spend the fewest
days working per year, and those in animal husbandry spend
the most. In crop farming the employment of female labor declines sharply once the cycle of field work is completed. The
data indicate that in December, in some republics, it is 30-
32 points below the employment of men. In Azerbaidzhan,
Tadzhikistan, Armenia, and Georgia, half the women working
in social production in July do not work at all in December.
Whereas nationwide women worked 204 man-days in 1974, the
figures for the above republics were, respectively, 166, 151,
158, and 128 man-days. This is explained by the different
jobs done by men and women at the present level of technical
development and the availability of jobs for women in rural

141

areas and, in the Central Asian republics and a number of Transcaucasian republics, also by the survival of national traditions, the character of rural families, and the organization of private subsidiary agriculture and of the household.

An analysis of the utilization of annual working time in animal husbandry shows that as a result of unused holidays, it considerably exceeds the optimum employment of workers and employees in industry and agriculture, especially machine operators. This is seen in the table below.

Annual Employment of Able-bodied Female
Collective Farmers in Animal Husbandry
(man-days)

	1965	1970	1974
Milkers	333	318	314
of whom, employed in machine milking	311	305	308
Calf tenders	324	318	315
Poultry tenders	302	300	299

The table shows that the levels of employment of milker attendants and calf and poultry tenders has not diminished much, and that in the absence of change in other conditions of work and organization, the effects of mechanization are still insufficient.

There are now many types of work organization for milkers at dairy farms with mechanized milking facilities. One-shift work is typical. A common drawback of one-shift work is the haphazard use of working time, with an early start and late end to work. The total workday, with necessary breaks, actually lasts thirteen to sixteen hours, although true working time is seven or eight hours. Only the best farms work a two-shift schedule efficiently, and most farms have still not introduced it. Such organization of the working day is an obstacle to acquiring a general or vocational education, which reduces the attraction of work in animal husbandry for skilled young workers.

142

An analysis of the organization of two-shift work at 87 dairy farms in different parts of the Russian Federation showed that the better organization of work led to an increase in young people seeking jobs. The number of workers under the age of 30 doubled. Better organization of annual and daily work schedules is an important task, and this also applies to the development of agroindustrial complexes.

In the organization of work and production it is essential to be guided by scientifically based, rational schedules of work and rest for different categories of workers in both livestock and crop farming, taking into account the effects of the work environment on workers. It is necessary to change technologies, work organization, and schedules in livestock farming and other branches to enable workers freed from heavy labor to have a well-scheduled workday, full rest hours, and genuine free time for pursuing general and vocational education and cultural development. The problem is especially acute with respect to women's work in agriculture.

Observance of these requirements is especially important for women machine operators. There are now some 7,000 women machine operators working in the fields of collective and state farms in the Russian Federation, and more than 3,000 in the Ukraine. More than 56,000 young women are learning to operate farm machines at courses and in vocational schools in the RSFSR. Family teams (links) have proven to be an efficient form of work organization in the Altai area and the Ukraine.

There are many positive examples of the creation of female tractor brigades. In Rostov Oblast more than one quarter of the mechanized brigades and links are female. In the Millerovo District of this oblast there is no farm without a woman's tractor brigade or link, and some even have two. This movement has been steadily expanding from year to year. At present twenty-nine brigades work 30,000 hectares of plowland. Women machine operators work according to a system that provides for remuneration directly in proportion to the harvested crop.

An analysis of many years of work by such teams shows that women tractor operators usually have good harvests on

their fields. About one quarter of them have been cited for their labor achievements and decorated by the government for their
work. These achievements are the result of the purposeful
policies of local party and government organizations aimed at
creating the necessary favorable conditions for women to work
with machines and mechanized equipment. They are largely
based on successful implementation of decrees of the party and
the government on the utilization of female labor in agriculture.

The decree of the CPSU Central Committee and the USSR
Council of Ministers "On More Extensive Involvement of Women
in Skilled Labor in Agriculture" provided for, first, assigning
women machine operators to machines with the most up-to-date
seats and cabs, starting devices, controls, and maintenance
systems; second, setting production norms for women operating tractors and complex farm machines 10% below the prevailing
norms; third, an additional vacation of six working days for
women operating tractors and harvester combines. The decree
of the CPSU Central Committee, USSR Council of Ministers,
and the All-Union Central Council of Trade Unions "On Measures for Improving Working Conditions and Stabilizing Mechanized Personnel in Agriculture" provides, in addition to
necessary measures aimed at raising the level of work organization for machine operators, for improving living, cultural,
personal, and domestic services: faster construction of well-
appointed housing, dormitory facilities, preschools, field stations, cafeterias, medical and disease-prevention establishments, and other cultural and public projects. Beginning in
April 1975 women tractor drivers and machine operators with
fifteen years experience have enjoyed special retirement benefits, drawing pensions from the age of 50 (instead of 55) provided they have worked for twenty years overall.

Thus in Millerovo District, Rostov Oblast, comfortable field
stations and heated garages were built for all brigades, hot
food was provided, and kindergartens and nurseries were
opened. All women machine operators work in two shifts.
Maintenance is provided by specialized teams of mechanics
and repairmen.

Effective participation in socialized labor, increased general education and vocational training, and the harmonious development of rural workers also depend in large measure on freeing time from household duties and work on private subsidiary plots. While female employment in the socialized sector in the RSFSR was on average 30% below that of men, employment in private subsidiary agriculture was three times higher, excluding household work and looking after children. The overall work load for women in social production, given the existing organization of work in agriculture combined with work on private plots and unfavorable housing and living conditions, leads to nervous strain and limits the free time needed for personal development.

Thus the training and employment of skilled workers, especially the vocational training of women in the countryside, do not yet meet the requirements of scientific and technological progress, because these questions have still not been given the necessary attention at all stages.

Improvement in the material and technical base presumes that the training of skilled personnel should proceed rapidly, keeping ahead of this process. Only in this way can the effective use of new machinery and its extensive introduction be assured.

In order to improve the training and utilization of skilled women workers, centralized, planned management in agriculture as it applies to the recruitment and employment of skilled women workers should be enhanced, taking fuller account of the prospects of scientific and technical progress and the tasks of technical and technological development. The number, composition, and profile of women sent to rural vocational-technical schools, specified according to trades and occupations, should be made an integral part of long-range and current plans.

Consequently only the comprehensive solution of social and economic problems, including those of demography, organizational and technical measures, and specific working and living conditions, can assure the necessary effective participation

M. Fedorova

of women in social production on collective and state farms.
At the same time, the participation of skilled women workers
in social production and management helps increase the effectiveness of agricultural production.

Notes

1. See Materialy konferentsii "Gigiena truda v sel'skom khoziaistve," Saratov,
1973; Snizhenie sel'skokhoziaistvennogo travmatizma, Kiev, 1974.
2. See, for example, Izvestia, January 27, 1975.
3. Pravda, February 15, 1972.

7

The Twenty-fifth Congress of the CPSU and Current Problems of Employment of Female Labor in the Republics of Central Asia

R. A. Ubaidullaeva

At the Twenty-fifth CPSU Congress, special attention was given to the need to study fundamental socioeconomic problems of communist construction in the USSR. An important place among them belongs to the question of labor resources. Its significance was reemphasized at the October 1976 Plenum of the CPSU Central Committee. Addressing that meeting, L. I. Brezhnev especially stressed the need for more effective utilization of labor resources.

One of the most pressing aspects of the problem is rational utilization of available female labor resources. It should be noted in this connection that at the present stage of mature socialist society, when cardinal problems of drawing women into social production have been successfully resolved and opportunities have been created for combining work in social production with motherhood and raising children, mounting importance attaches to the most rational employment of female labor in the economy under the regional conditions of individual republics, economic areas, and urban and rural communities.

For a number of reasons stemming from specific features of historical development, demographic processes, economic

Russian text © 1976 by "Uzbekistan" Publishers. "XXV S″ezd KPSS i aktual'nye problemy ispol'zovaniia zhenskogo truda v respublikakh Srednei Azii," *Obshchestvennye nauki v Uzbekistane*, 1976, no. 12, pp. 14-19.

structures, and the like, the problem of assuring fuller employment of the able-bodied population, women included, in social production remains an important one for the republics of Central Asia. At the same time, the high rates of development and structural changes in the economies of the Central Asian republics call for more effective utilization of the female labor resources already involved in production. The reason is that given the relatively high proportion of women employed in household work and on private subsidiary holdings and the oversaturation of agriculture with labor resources, industries experience a shortage of skilled manpower. In Uzbekistan the shortage is 134,800 workers in industry, 153,400 in construction, and 528,600 in the republic's economy as a whole.

The role of female labor in the economy increases rapidly with the growth of the industrial potential of the Central Asian republics, the blossoming of their cultures, and the rising standards of general and specialized education. Between 1940 and 1974 the proportion of women in the work force increased from 39 to 50% nationwide, 21 to 42% in the Uzbek SSR, 29 to 39% in the Tadzhik SSR, 36 to 40% in the Turkmen SSR, and 29 to 48% in the Kirghiz SSR.

We can see that within the Central Asian region, the process of female involvement in social production was most intensive in Kirghizia and lowest in the Turkmen SSR. Evidently this could be explained by the specific features of demographic processes in Turkmenia. However, analyses show that the birthrate and natural population growth are highest in Tadzhikistan. Thus in Uzbekistan there are 34.2 births per thousand inhabitants, 37 in Tadzhikistan, 30.5 in Kirghizia, and 34.3 in Turkmenia. It follows that the reasons for the slow growth in the rate of involvement of women in social production in the Turkmen SSR should be sought in social conditions and the branch structure of the republic's economy.

The figures cited above also show that the proportion of women in the work force of the republics of Central Asia remains lower than for the Soviet Union as a whole. This is due to a number of circumstances, primarily the great household work load borne by local women, large families, and the lower level of development of the service sphere.

Thus in the republics of Central Asia, the problem of optimum employment of women remains a pressing one. At the same time, in the economic literature it is assessed differently in different studies. Some scholars hold that all women of able-bodied age should participate in social production; according to others, a differentiated approach should be taken to the problem; yet others take the view that participation of women in social production should gradually be reduced.[1]

We support the second view and think that it is necessary to take into account a number of regional features in the reproduction of the population and labor resources (high birthrate, stable natural rate of population growth, large families, etc.). In addition, there are a number of socioeconomic, historical, natural-geographic, and ethnic-psychological factors involved. In aggregate they make for the lower mobility of the female population in Central Asia. Thus the nonmobile proportion of female labor resources is 59% in the Uzbek SSR, 78.7% in the Tadzhik SSR, and 8.7% in the Ukrainian SSR.[2]

The prime factor here is the large families typical of the local population. Thus 70-80% of the women engaged in household duties or working on private subsidiary holdings in the republics of Central Asia have three to six children or more.

The rational employment of women of indigenous nationalities calls for the solution of a number of socioeconomic problems, in the first place, acceleration of the development of public services and children's and preschool institutions. At present the availability of children's preschool institutions in the republics of Central Asia does not exceed 20%, as compared with 40% for the Soviet Union as a whole. If we take into account that there are no immediate prospects for any tangible reduction of the birthrate in these republics, the rate of growth of children's preschool institutions in the Central Asian republics provided by the Tenth Five-Year Plan is clearly insufficient. In Uzbekistan, for example, to reach the present national average, the enrollment of children in kindergartens and day nurseries should be 1,113,200 in 1980. Consequently, the accelerated rate of growth of children's preschool institutions remains a prime task in the solution of the social problems of female employment in the Central Asian region.

All conditions and opportunities should be provided to keep young women of able-bodied age from sinking into housework or work on private subsidiary holdings.

This problem, which is directly linked to the development of the sphere of application of labor, the service sphere, and occupational guidance work with young women, is especially acute in rural communities, where the bulk of the indigenous population resides.

Under the conditions of Central Asia, the problem of the development of the sphere of communal and social services is an important socioeconomic problem; the rational employment of female labor in social production depends on its solution. Lenin's words that "for us the question of improving basic living conditions for the great majority of the population is fundamental" remain relevant to this day.

In his speech at the October 1976 Plenum of the CPSU Central Committee, L. I. Brezhnev stressed that "to attract and hold personnel, especially in remote areas, it is important to show greater concern for people's housing, working, and living conditions."[4] This is primarily true of women workers.

One of the regional peculiarities of the republics of Central Asia is the high proportion of women employed in agriculture. On collective farms women account for 49% of the total number of workers in the Uzbek SSR, 44% in Tadzhikistan, 49% in Turkmenia, and 42% in the Kirghiz SSR.

Female employment in agriculture has increased substantially over the last few years. Thus in Uzbekistan the number of working days per woman increased from 187.5 in 1965 to 193.0 at present. However, this rise accompanied a slow rate of growth in labor productivity. Thus between 1970 and 1974 the average increase in productivity on collective farms for the country as a whole was 14%, but only 4% for Uzbekistan. We see that the problem of releasing labor, especially female,

from agriculture is being solved very slowly in the republics
of Central Asia.

There are many densely populated regions and districts in
Central Asia with considerable labor reserves on collective
and state farms and in small and medium-sized towns, while
at the same time, as noted before, many industries and services
are short of manpower. But even in those regions where agriculture has labor reserves, they are inadequately employed
in other branches of the economy. Thus out of 5,867 workers
employed by new industrial projects in the Ferghana Valley,
only 5-7% were former collective farmers.[5]

Our studies show that the movement of women collective
farmers into nonagricultural branches of the economy in the
republics of Central Asia is hindered by an absence of specialized knowledge and industrial work habits. That is why
the majority of women collective farmers who have taken up
nonagricultural jobs are employed in subsidiary jobs or as
apprentices. In our survey we found that 60% of the women
collective farmers who had gone to work in industry were
listed as apprentices. As a consequence the former collective
farm woman gets much less for her work than she did at the
collective farm. Thus an important factor in drawing female
labor resources from agriculture in densely populated areas
is the creation of a better complex of living conditions in the
cities. Another aspect of the problem is the need to provide
vocational training opportunities for young women in rural
communities, which requires expansion of the system in rural
localities, collective farms, state farms, and district centers.
Finally, the third essential condition for drawing female labor
from agriculture in the densely populated regions of the Central Asian republics is the geographic proximity of new industrial projects and service establishments. When there are industrial establishments in the vicinity, collective farm women
readily go to work at them.

For example, 20% of the able-bodied members of the Leningrad Collective Farm in Izbaskan District, Andizhan Oblast,
which is located within one to five kilometers of a number of

industrial installations and facilities, left the farm to find jobs
at them; on the Gulistan Collective Farm, located in the same
district but away from major centers, only 0.8% of the members
went to work at nonagricultural establishments.6

All other conditions aside, locating industries in areas with
relative manpower surpluses is a realistic means of raising
the employment in the industrial branches of the economy and
the services sphere of the rapidly growing able-bodied population, women included, of the Central Asian republics. The
most suitable industries in this respect are the local, light,
food, electrotechnical, and some other branches. Those industries which can employ at-home or part-time workers should
undergo particularly broad development.

The Basic National Economic Development Guidelines for
1976-80 note the need "to create more opportunities for women
with children to work a shorter workday or workweek, and also
to work at home."7 Such extremely important measures are
also provided for in the Tenth Five-Year Plan, approved recently by the Fifth Session of the Ninth Convocation of the USSR
Supreme Soviet.

So far, at-home work has not been sufficiently used as a
form of organization of female labor in the republics of Central
Asia, even though in these republics, with their high birthrates
and large families, at-home work is a very convenient and realistic form of rational employment of female labor.

Modern technological progress is an important factor that
can help make women's work easier. Between 1959 and 1970
the proportion of women employed at mainly nonmanual jobs
in the republics of Central Asia increased from 17.25 to 24.1%.
The rate of growth of female employment in the sphere of mental work is almost double that in the sphere of physical work.

Nevertheless there still remain many unresolved problems.
The situation is especially unfavorable with respect to the proportions of women in manual and mechanized jobs. Thus in
Uzbekistan about half the women working in industry perform
manual labor, and 12% of them are employed in arduous manual jobs. In agriculture most women still do manual work.

One of the main reasons is the inadequate level of vocational training of women. As a consequence many working women have low work ratings. Thus in Uzbekistan's machine-building industry the average wage grade of women is 2.5, as opposed to 2.9 for men; the respective figures are 3.0 and 3.5 in the building materials industry, 3.1 and 3.3 in the food industry, 2.5 and 2.9 in the woodworking industry, and so on.

Raising the occupational qualifications of working women in the republics of Central Asia is of tremendous importance because it entails profound social consequences. For that reason one of the fundamental tasks in the rational employment of female labor in the Central Asian region is the elaboration of measures that would help raise the levels of general and vocational education of working women. It is also necessary to draw up and implement a system of measures aimed at rapidly taking women off hard manual jobs. This system should include three elements: (1) mechanization and automation of production; (2) expansion of the list of jobs where the employment of female labor is forbidden; (3) expansion of the training of skilled women workers in the system of vocational-technical schools that also provide a secondary education.

As noted before, the rational employment of female labor in social production requires the creation of the necessary socio-economic conditions enabling women to combine work with motherhood and raising children; it also requires the creation of conditions facilitating her personal development. Lenin repeatedly emphasized the need to rid women of petty, stultifying, unproductive work.

An important condition for changing this is rational utilization of a woman's nonworking time. This problem, which is of exceptional importance under the conditions of the republics of Central Asia, has regional aspects that flow from the historically formed traditions of the peoples of Central Asia, ethnic-psychological factors, demographic processes, and so on. Women here spend much more time on household chores and bringing up children and correspondingly less time satisfying their spiritual needs. Thus, according to our studies,[8] working women in industry in Uzbekistan had 19.5 free hours a week, as opposed to 34 hours for men, and in Tadzhikistan, respectively, 18.3 and 24 hours.

A reduction in working time that allows for an increase in free time is an important factor for radically improving working conditions for women; they are one of the prime prerequisites for the development of the socialist way of life and the personality of women. It should be noted that this important and topical problem has not yet been duly reflected in scholars' studies on Central Asia.

Solution of the problem of rational employment of female labor under the regional conditions of Central Asia calls for the elaboration and implementation of a number of socioeconomic measures aimed at creating the most favorable conditions for the working woman and "improving her position as a participant in the labor process, as a mother, a counselor of her children, and a housewife."[9]

Also of importance in this connection is enhancing the role of planning organizations in the distribution and employment of female labor resources, especially in rural localities and small and medium-sized towns. There is an urgent need to draw up balance sheets of labor resources for individual establishments, districts, and cities, with a breakdown according to sex. Such balance sheets should be drawn up at least once every three to five years.

To draw up an integrated program for rational employment of female labor and improvement of working conditions, it is necessary for the central statistical administrations of the Central Asian republics and scholars to undertake a joint sociological survey of organizations and working conditions for women in the economies of these republics.

These are but some aspects of studies of the problem. A profound and comprehensive elaboration requires an integrated approach and the joint efforts of experts in different fields: economists, sociologists, physicians, psychologists, etc. Only in this way can we provide a firm scientific base for solving the whole set of socioeconomic questions of rational utilization of female labor, taking into account the specific regional conditions of the republics of Central Asia.

Female Labor in Central Asia

Notes

1. See Voprosy ekonomiki, 1967, no. 2; Proizvodstvennaia deiatel'nost' zhenshchin i semia, Minsk, 1972; E. Z. Danilova, Sotsial'nye problemy truda zhenshchiny-rabotnitsy, Moscow, 1968.

2. N. A. Sakharova, Optimal'nye vozmozhnosti ispol'zovaniia zhenskogo truda v sfere obshchestvennogo proizvodstva, Kiev, 1973.

3. V. I. Lenin, Poln. sobr. soch., vol. 45, p. 248.

4. Pravda, October 26, 1976.

5. The survey covered industrial projects in cities of the Ferghana Valley: Namangan, Andizhan, Ferghana, Kokand, and Leninsk.

6. A. Etamberdyev, Vosproizvodstvo trudovykh resursov sel'skoi mestnosti Uzbekistana, Tashkent, 1972, p. 211.

7. Materialy XXV s"ezda KPSS, Moscow, 1976, p. 217.

8. The survey was conducted at light industry enterprises in the Uzbek and Tadzhik SSRs.

9. Materialy XXV s"ezda KPSS, p. 85.

8

Protection of Female Labor

N. N. Sheptulina

The basic norms and regulations regarding women's working
and living conditions were adopted during the first years of
Soviet power: equal right to work, prohibition of employment
underground and in some other jobs, at night, and on overtime,
a ban on carrying loads, paid pregnancy and maternity leave,
and so on. They embodied the demands of the first Program
of the Russian Social-Democratic Labor Party (August 1903).
The second Program of the Russian Communist Party (Bolshe-
viks) (March 1919) set a new task: "The Party does not restrict
itself to formal equality for women; it seeks to rid them of the
material burdens of the outdated household by replacing it with
housing communes, public dining rooms, centralized laundries,
day nurseries, etc."[1]

Some departures from the norms governing women's work
were permitted due to economic difficulties. For example, to
prevent replacement of women at factories during the unem-
ployment of the twenties, they were permitted to work night
shifts in industries where this was especially necessary. Due
to the shortage of workers in the thirties, women were allowed
to work underground. However, the general guidelines of the

Russian text © 1978 by "Nauka" Publishers. "Otrazheno v zakonakh," *Ekonomika i
organizatsiia promyshlennogo proizvodstva*, 1978, no. 3, pp. 30-35.

party's policy regarding legislation on women's working and living conditions remained unchanged.

In 1928 committees for improving women's working and living conditions were set up under the presidium of the Central Executive Committee of the USSR, the presidiums of the executive committees of the union and autonomous republics, and under krai, oblast, city, and district executive committees. In 1929 sections for everyday life were set up under the soviets which did not function very long but played a positive role.

While these commissions, as well as the later Committee for Improving the Working and Living Conditions of Worker and Peasant Women, were functioning, a number of labor laws were promulgated. For example, on January 16, 1931, the RSFSR People's Commissariat of Employment for the first time in the history of labor legislation endorsed model lists of trades in individual industries (they have lost their significance by now), as well as lists of occupational titles in the government and administrative apparatus in which female labor should be exclusively or predominantly employed. The people's commissariats of employment of the autonomous republics and krai and oblast employment departments had the right to expand those lists taking into account local conditions and specific enterprises.

A decree of the USSR People's Commissariat of Employment of April 10, 1932, approved the "List of Especially Strenuous and Hazardous Jobs and Trades in Which Women Cannot be Employed," which is in force to this day. It prohibits women from performing specified jobs in the metallurgical, metalworking, chemical, leather, textile, and paper and printing industries and in transport, construction, and utilities.

On August 14, 1932, the USSR People's Commissariat of Employment passed a decree, "On Limiting Norms for Handling Loads by Adult Women," which is also still in force. According to these norms the maximum weight of a load transferred by hand over an even surface is twenty kilograms per person. In all jobs involving manual handling of loads, women should use, when the type of load permits, dollies with legs. The load together with the dollies must not exceed fifty kilograms for two

157

persons. Limits are also set on the weight of loads transported
in wheelbarrows, handcarts, and pushcarts.

The achievements in economic expansion during the years of
the first five-year plans made it possible to increase material
benefits for mothers and expand the system of children's preschool establishments on a national scale. Thus in its decree
of June 28, 1936, the Central Executive Committee and Council
of People's Commissars of the USSR increased benefits for
acquiring items of baby care and for baby feeding; it introduced benefits for large families and endorsed specific plans
for building children's establishments. For example, it provided for tripling the number of kindergartens (from 700,000
to 2.1 million) by January 1, 1939, in cities, industrial town-
ships, and railway transport.

The hard years of the Second World War to some extent held
up the development of legislation on women's working and living
conditions, but the state did not forget about them even in this
period. Thus in 1944 permission was granted to reduce work
quotas for women in many jobs in mines by 20 to 30%. A decree of the Presidium of the USSR Supreme Soviet of July 8,
1944, increased benefits for mothers of large families, introduced benefits for single mothers, and increased maternity
benefits on birth of a baby. Factory and office managers were
ordered to help pregnant women and nursing mothers by
issuing them additional food grown on subsidiary farms. Enterprises and offices which extensively employed female labor
were instructed to organize day nurseries, kindergartens, baby
feeding rooms, and personal hygiene rooms for women.

After the war, government and economic bodies stepped up
work aimed at improving working and living conditions for
women. In 1950 the USSR Council of Ministers forbade the
Ministry of Internal Waterways to employ women on a number
of jobs, for example, as stokers on ships using solid fuel. That
year bans were also issued on employing women in many jobs
in extracting, refining, transporting, and storing sulfurous oil,
sulfur-containing casing-head gas, and products from refining
them. The list of especially strenuous jobs in which women

could not be employed in the peat industry was expanded.

The Directives of the Twentieth CPSU Congress for the Sixth Five-Year Plan (1956-60) provided for further improving working and living conditions for women; notably, pregnancy and maternity leaves were increased. In 1956 the pregnancy and maternity leave was increased from 77 to 112 days, and women could take an additional three months' unpaid leave to look after their babies without interruption in their service record or jeopardy to their jobs.[2] Factory directors were advised to issue pregnant women free vouchers for sanatoriums and rest homes to be covered from factory funds. Ministries and departments were charged with improving sanitary and personal services for women.

In 1957 the Soviet government issued an ordinance ending the use of female labor in underground jobs in the mining industry and the construction of underground structures, with the exception of nonphysical jobs and sanitary and service jobs. In 1960 a ban was issued on employing women on board commercial, research, and transport vessels of the fishing fleet (with the exception of floating crab and fish canneries, fish-packing and whale-packing vessels, etc.).

The CPSU Program adopted by the Twenty-second Party Congress laid down basic guidelines for improving the position of women: "All remnants of women's unequal position in daily life must be completely removed, social-living conditions must be created for combining happy motherhood with ever more active and creative participation of women in social labor and public activity, in scientific and artistic occupations. Women must be given relatively lighter, but at the same time sufficiently well-paid, jobs. Pregnancy leaves will be extended."[3]

Subsequent legislation, notably the Principles of Labor Legislation of the USSR and the Union Republics (1970) and the labor codes of the union republics (1971-72), provided for additional benefits and guarantees for women.

Under Article 69 of the Principles of Labor Legislation, women may not be employed in night work, except in industries where this is a special necessity, and it is permitted only as a temporary measure. Enterprises are already enforcing measures aimed at limiting women's night work. However, there are still many enterprises at which women's night work will apparently continue as a temporary measure. In its resolution of November 22, 1974, the Presidium of the All-Union Central Council of Trade Unions (AUCCTU) supported provisions granting higher annual premiums for night shift workers, as well as preferential treatment of night workers in obtaining vouchers to sanatoriums, preventive health centers, tourist stations, rest homes, and nursery and kindergarten accommodations for their children. The national economic guidelines for 1976-80 provide for higher bonuses for night work.

Special labor protection provisions are in force for pregnant women, nursing mothers and mothers of babies up to one year old. Article 69 of the Principles prohibits their employment in night and overtime jobs or sending them on business trips.

In accordance with the decree of the AUCCTU of April 2, 1954, "On Duty Hours at Enterprises and Offices," pregnant women and mothers of children up to twelve years old cannot be assigned to work after the end of the working day, at night, or on off-days and holidays.

Following a doctor's statement, pregnant women are transfered to lighter jobs for the duration of pregnancy while retaining their average pay for the preceding six months.

If it is impossible for nursing mothers or mothers of children up to one year old to perform their former jobs, they are given other jobs, without detriment to their previous earnings, for the duration of nursing time or until the child is one year old (Article 70 of the Principles).

Benefits for mothers of infants with regard to length of pregnancy and maternity leaves and payment for them, service records, additional vacation time, etc., are listed in Articles 71 and 72 of the Principles. It should be specifically noted that Article 73 provides for employment guarantees and prohibits discharging pregnant women, nursing mothers, and mothers of children up to one year old. It is also prohibited to refuse employment or reduce pay for reasons associated with pregnancy or nursing a baby. The management of an enterprise cannot discharge pregnant women or mothers of babies up to one year old, except in cases in which the office, enterprise, or organization is going out of business (discharge with provisions for re-employment).

Violation of the listed guarantees is a criminal offense.

Among the norms that enable women to combine work with motherhood are those which establish a procedure for granting paid leave in case of sickness of children. In accordance with the decree of the USSR Council of Ministers of July 26, 1973, "On Improving Pregnancy, Maternity, and Sick-Child-Care Benefits," leave to care for a sick child has been extended.

An important part in improving working conditions for women is played by specially empowered local administrative bodies that supervise observance of labor legislation regarding working women. On July 7, 1975, the Presidium of the USSR Supreme Soviet passed the decree, "On Practical Application of Legislation Regarding Labor Protection for Women," which recommends that the Council of Ministers, the presidiums of the supreme soviets of the union republics, USSR ministries and departments, the AUCCTU, and the Prosecutor General of the USSR intensify supervision and control of the observation of legislation regarding labor protection for women by all ministries and departments, enterprises, offices, organizations, and executive and administrative personnel.

As Deputy V. V. Nikolaeva-Tereshkova stressed in her speech at the Seventh Special Session of the USSR Supreme Soviet, ministries, departments, and economic organizations must advance to a qualitatively new level of activity in handling all questions connected with improving working and living conditions and provisions for rest, recreation, and medical services for women. An important part in this must be played by the respective Standing Committees of the USSR Supreme Soviet.

At its Fifth Session the Ninth USSR Supreme Soviet (1976) set up standing committees of the Soviet of the Union and the Soviet of Nationalities on questions of women's working and living conditions and maternity and child care (thirty-five deputies in each).

N. N. Sheptulina

They elaborate proposals on working and living conditions for consideration by the respective chambers of the USSR Supreme Soviet or its Presidium, help government bodies and organizations as well as deputies of the USSR Supreme Soviet implement decisions of the Supreme Soviet and its Presidium on questions of women's working and living conditions and maternity and child care, and monitor the implementation of legislation on the protection of labor rights.

Similar standing committees are also being set up by the supreme soviets of the union and autonomous republics as well as by the soviets of people's deputies. Article 35 of the new Constitution of the USSR defines ways to further develop and improve legislation on working and living conditions for women.

Notes

1. See KPSS v rezoliutsiiakh i resheniiakh s"ezdov, konferentsii i plenumov TsK, seventh ed., part 1, Moscow, Gospolitizdat, 1954, p. 415.
2. In 1968 the length of unpaid leave to look after a baby was extended to the baby's first birthday.
3. Programma KPSS, Moscow, Politizdat, 1964, p. 97.

PART TWO
THE IMPACT OF FEMALE
EMPLOYMENT ON THE FAMILY

9

Women's Work and the Family

E. E. Novikova, V. S. Iazykova,
and Z. A. Iankova

Women's Domestic Work

The effects of a working woman's occupational activities on
her family are varied and diverse. On the one hand they help
raise her family's living standards and expand its social contacts. On the other they promote the development of the woman's personality and thereby raise her social status, enrich her
intellectual and cultural life, and sharply enhance her role in
family and daily life. This, in turn, promotes equality in the
family and the rational division and sharing of domestic work.

At the same time, as sociological studies convincingly demonstrate, solving the problems of working women entails overcoming a number of contradictions.

Most prominent among them is the "dual" employment of
women who combine their job duties with those of mother
and wife. In his greetings to the women delegates of
the Sixteenth Congress of the Soviet Trade Unions, L. I.
Brezhnev said: "We have still certainly not done enough to alleviate the dual burden they bear at home and at work. But this
is all the more reason to express our gratitude to our mothers,
wives, and sisters for their selfless work."[1]

The difficulties stemming from combining work and family

Russian text © 1978 by Profizdat. *Zhenshchin, trud, sem'ia (Sotsiologicheskii ocherk)*
(Moscow: Profizdat, 1978), pp. 53-78.

E. E. Novikova, V. S. Iazykova, and Z. A. Iankova

duties often have a negative effect on women workers' participation in employment and social activities; they do not participate enough in campaigns to promote innovation and efficiency
and in the work of public organizations. The same difficulties
often give rise to tensions and conflicts in the family.

These contradictions can be resolved only by creating conditions for the optimal combination of the occupational and family
roles of both women and men. To do so it is necessary to study
more thoroughly the sphere of human activity associated with
the concepts of "domestic work" and "family and domestic relations." This is also important because in recent years skep-
tical, and even negative, attitudes have been emerging, especially among young people, toward domestic work as an activity
supposedly devoid of social meaning.

Such attitudes are, it seems, largely explained by the fact that
domestic work still remains largely mechanical and nonproductive. Furthermore it still takes a great deal of a woman's energy and time. Women workers spend an average of three to
three and a half hours a day doing domestic chores. This undoubtedly prevents the well-rounded cultural development of
women and reduces their social activity.

The negative attitude toward domestic work has been fostered
to some degree by the absence of a clear-cut definition of it in
the scholarly literature. Concrete sociological studies are
usually restricted to analyses of the structure of the time a
person must devote to the household and family. Such an approach often reduces domestic work to doing household duties, and
then the one-sided conclusion is drawn that this work will inevitably vanish as the family loses its function as an economic
unit. Domestic work is accordingly viewed as a survival from
the past, with emphasis laid on its low productivity and extra-
social orientation. The inevitable conclusion from such reason-
ing is that since domestic work is nonproductive, not directly
socialized, and it creates no consumer value, it has no prospects for further development.

Such a narrow assessment of all domestic work is erroneous.
Under the conditions of the developing scientific and technolog-

166

ical revolution, the development of the individual and his capacities for creativity is of direct practical significance; therefore domestic work, which is associated, among other things,
with the upbringing of children and the mutual social education
of spouses, cannot be classified as wholly nonproductive labor.

At the same time, domestic work cannot be unequivocally
described as productive and therefore treated as a category
that will persist in the future as an independent sphere of application of labor despite the development of public forms of
meeting the everyday needs of the population.

Solving this problem requires a differentiated approach to
different aspects of domestic work and a profound analysis of
its character and content and of the correlation between its reproductive (mechanical) and productive (creative) functions.

It is useful to distinguish between work in the home aimed
primarily at meeting the needs of family members, house cleaning, laundry, and so on, and domestic work as a whole, which
also includes educational, organizational, aesthetic, and other
essentially creative functions that can be compared to types of
activity Engels classified as "lofty" functions. It should also
be borne in mind that although work in the home is aimed at
meeting the needs of a separate family or individual, it is socially useful since it contributes to the increased material and
spiritual wealth of our society as well as to the upbringing and
molding of the individual. Political-economic analysis alone is
not enough for an evaluation of domestic work; also necessary
is a profound sociological analysis of its character and content,
which can provide a deeper understanding of changing trends in
it at present and in the future.

With the development of material production and the service
sphere, the changing character of domestic work is seen primarily
in the transfer of some of its functions to public institutions for
everyday services and in the transformation of other functions.
The evolution of socialist production relations into communist
ones is breaking down the relative economic isolation of domestic work.

These processes are indicative of a convergence of the domestic sphere with the production sphere. Of course, their optimal convergence remains a more or less remote prospect, and no complete convergence will, apparently, ever occur; but it is already obvious that as the content of domestic work changes, it acquires a different character.

This trend can be seen in analyses of both objective data and the subjective aspirations of the members of our society. For example, in the course of a poll conducted by the Institute of Sociological Research of the USSR Academy of Sciences, the following replies were offered to the question "Why is domestic work necessary?": the desire to reduce family expenditures, create domestic comfort, organize family meals and recreation and thereby bring the family closer, and increase the amount of spare time of other members of the family.

Some 82% of those polled chose the last two responses, which confirms the apparent change in the purposes of the economic activity of the family.

The further development of the service sector and improvement in its quality will lead to changes in the content of domestic work: at first, an improvement in its least productive and reproductive functions (washing floors, cleaning rooms, doing laundry, etc.) and, subsequently, their gradual transfer to public establishments for everyday services.

"It is my conviction," wrote F. Engels, "that true equality of men and women will be achieved only when the exploitation of both by capital is eliminated, and when running the household, which is now a private occupation, becomes a branch of social production."[2]

The Communist Party regards as one of the most essential tasks of economic development the transformation of public domestic services into a highly developed branch of modern industry, the expansion of the system of domestic service establishments, a considerable increase in the number of persons employed by them, and the improvement of their occupational skills.

A sociological analysis of the process of socialization of everyday life leads, however, to the conclusion that this process is erratic. The development of the sphere of everyday

services has been characterized by contradictions of both a
subjective and objective nature.

It has been shown that the more a woman is satisfied with
the content and character of her occupational activity, the more
she tends to rely on domestic services, and the more she seeks
to mechanize household chores to free time for developing her
occupational knowledge, general culture, and public activities.
Conversely, the less a woman is satisfied with the content of
her work and the lower her education, the more she ignores
household appliances and relies on her own hands to keep her
house in order.

Some women, moreover, prefer so-called minor mechanization, that is, equipping the house with household appliances, attaching less importance to the industrialization of everyday life,
which they see as mainly supplementary. There are several
reasons for this. Domestic service establishments are often
located far from the home; they cannot meet all demands, which
causes lines and substantial losses of time. Many of their services are in low demand because of their poor quality. The
greatest demand is for services that cannot be done at home or
by oneself, especially dry cleaning, tailoring, shoe and home
repairs, and the like.

A poll of women workers in Leningrad revealed the frequency
with which they seek the help of domestic service establishments and the types of services they prefer (see Table 1).

It can be seen from the table that more than half of the
polled women use the services of dry cleaners, but few use
laundries. The reasons stated for rejecting laundry service
included poor quality, long waiting time for return of laundry,
and distance from home.

Most of the polled women said they would like to see more
public services and of better quality. In their view eating out
costs more than eating at home (over 50% of those polled), does
not save time, and meals are of low quality ("They don't taste
good" — 30% of those polled). Besides, menus at cafeterias
are not designed for family meals: they offer no children's
food, no dietary food for old people, and so on. The premises

169

E. E. Novikova, V. S. Iazykova, and Z. A. Iankova

Table 1

Regular Use of Services Provided by Public
Service Establishments*

Public service establishment	Number of families using their services	% of total polled
Dry cleaner	248	54.6
Rental store	145	20.0
Laundry	94	13.0
Cafeteria	23	3.0
Take-out restaurant	59	8.2
Others	15	2.0

*A. G. Kharchev and S. I. Golod, Professional'naia rabota
zhenshchin i sem'ia, Leningrad, "Nauka" Publishers, 1971,
p. 82.

and working hours of cafeterias are also unsuitable for family
meals. Only 0.8% of the polled women said they did not go to
cafeterias because they liked to cook for themselves. 3

This gives special significance to the problem of rational
division and sharing of domestic work.

The revolutionary transformation of society, by eliminating
the exploitation of man by man and man's "alienation" from society, is leading to the gradual overcoming of a distorted attitude toward reality. One of these "distortions" is the view that
domestic work is specifically "woman's work."

Sociological studies carried out in our country reveal the
relative persistence of this old, patriarchal point of view on
the distribution of family duties.

The proportion of families in which full sharing of domestic
work has been achieved is now around 35-55%. In other families there is either partial sharing of duties, or the woman
continues to do most of the work at home.

The inequalities in the distribution of house work between

Table 2

Time Spent on Domestic Duties
(hours and minutes)*

Type of house work	Married women		Married men	
	on weekdays	on off-days	on weekdays	on off-days
Preparing food, washing dishes, heating stoves	1.15	2.10	0.14	0.18
House cleaning	0.40	1.00	0.11	0.24
Shopping	0.55	1.30	0.21	0.29
Looking after children	0.25	0.50	0.09	0.14
Domestic work as a whole	3.15	5.30	0.55	1.25

*B. M. Levin, Motivatsiia zhenskogo truda i semeino-bytovye otnosheniia, Moscow, 1970, p. 7. (ISI AN USSR).

171

wives and husbands are shown in Table 2.

Moreover, numerous sociological surveys show that a fair distribution of household duties is increasingly a factor in women's evaluations of the happiness of their marriage. In families where the wife performed all or most of the household chores, only 21.6% rated their marriage as happy, and more than 40% declared it unhappy; in families where husband and wife shared household duties equally 60.8% said they were happy in marriage, and only 5.6% were dissatisfied.[4]

Women are increasingly prone to reject the conventional stereotype whereby the wife alone is responsible for household duties. Only 15% of working women felt that the husband should not share in them. These are usually older women with relatively low occupational and general cultural standards.

Fair distribution of household duties is more typical of young families where the couple is 24 or 25 years old, as well as of families with a secondary or higher education.

Furthermore, the degree of cooperation also depends on the structure and type of family and the stage of its development. The more optimal the family structure and the closer its members are bound by common needs and attitudes, the greater the sharing of household duties. In small families with only a married couple, the sharing of duties is more consistent than in large families that include representatives of several generations; here the traditional domestic way of life usually persists. Sharing of duties is also more common in the early stages of family life.

In evaluating domestic work, sociologists from socialist countries increasingly proceed from the principle of the shaping of the woman's personality. Those functions of household work that create scope for the woman's self-expression and help shape her as an individual (bringing up children, organization of free time) are seen as activities organically inherent in the modern family that should be encouraged and developed. Those functions of domestic work which, on the contrary, retard the development of the personality (serving the family) are viewed negatively. They should be gradually transferred

172

to highly mechanized and automated domestic service establishments in line with the development of the scientific and
technological revolution. Therefore the processes of sharing
and dividing household duties among family members —
primarily between husband and wife — will in the future affect
mainly functions of a creative nature. Such are the trends in
the future development of domestic work generated by the scientific and technological revolution and directly linked with the
overall objectives of communist society.

Bringing Up Children

Among the freedoms, rights, and duties of Soviet citizens
listed in the new Constitution of the USSR there is, for the
first time in history, the obligation "to be concerned with
bringing up children, preparing them for socially useful labor,
and rearing them to be worthy members of socialist society." [5]
The appearance of this article in the Constitution is the result of the socioeconomic and cultural changes that have taken
place in the life of our society. The constitutional right of
every Soviet person to education and work in accordance with
his or her abilities, requirements, and knowledge has contributed to his or her educational opportunities. Upbringing has
become a prime function of the Soviet family, and the harmonious blending of public and family forms of upbringing has become a characteristic trait of the Soviet way of life.
The growth in the number of children's establishments and
the diversity of forms of their work are indications that the
social education of children and adolescents is gaining in popularity and recognition. However, the educational influence
of the family on children, far from decreasing, is also growing, enriched by the experience earned in joint educational efforts.
The family influences the emerging personality of the child
first through the direct, purposeful efforts of its adult members, primarily the mother and father, and second, through

173

the whole tenor and way of life, which are determined not so much by the family's well-being as by its social mores, the structure of its material and spiritual needs, and its means of satisfying them.

The content and forms of parents' influence on the child's personality depend in large measure on the extent to which their moral attitudes correspond to the political, ethical, and aesthetic mores of society, the extent to which family interests integrate with public interests. The nature of this influence depends in many ways on the educational background of the parents, on their knowledge of the psychological features of child development, and on their ability to correlate family and public influences, the influence of school, the mass media, etc.

The educational impact of family influence is much greater when the child takes an active part in family life and decision-making, and when he or she strives for self-education and self-perfection. This is especially important in the upbringing of adolescents.

Family upbringing thus includes both objective conditions and subjective activity, spontaneous and conscious elements. These components are all interrelated and constitute a continuous chain of complex cause-and-effect relationships.

The nature and extent of a woman's participation in public life is the basis for the optimum performance of her organizational and educational functions in the family. As A. S. Makarenko rightly noted, "Only a mother who herself lives a real, full-blooded life as a person and a citizen can be a real mother who educates, serves as an example, and elicits love, admiration, and the desire to emulate her."[6]   In this case the contradictions between work and home and between the new and old functions of woman in the family lose their antagonistic character and are gradually overcome.

By relieving women of a part of the burden of child care, society provides them with greater opportunities for spiritual growth and thereby creates better conditions in the family for bringing up children and adolescents. The pedagogical sophistication of both fathers and mothers is steadily rising. Thus a study conducted at the Kharkov Palace of the Newborn showed that the level of pedagogical awareness of polled mothers was fairly high (Table 3).

Table 3

Knowledgeability of Parents in Pedagogy, Medicine, and Psychology before Childbirth*

	Fathers (%)	Mothers (%)
Read pedagogical and medical literature	70.7	87.0
Attended talks by doctors	12.3	93.9
Consulted doctors and teachers	11.0	59.7
Attended lectures or listened to radio talks for parents	6.6	10.3
Did not prepare for birth of child	7.7	—

*Proizvodstvennaia deiatel'nost' zhenshchiny i sem'ia, Minsk, 1972, p. 200.

The general education received by Soviet women also helps them make correct educational decisions and overcome many difficulties in bringing up children and adolescents. It is not only that an educated, cultured woman penetrates deeper into her child's psychological world and has a better understanding of the specific features of its character and behavior; a high standard of spiritual requirements and expectations on the part of the parents sets the atmosphere in the family, and its influence is especially great during the period of character formation.

An atmosphere of spiritual and intellectual life in the family is indispensable for the correct shaping of the child's personality. The content of conversations, the way free time is spent, the choice of books for reading and discussion, the ability to respond to all sorts of requests from the child — all this contributes to the prestige in which the mother is held in the family

and enhances her educational potential. Children are receptive
to the interest she shows in her work and other fields, and to
her public activity.

Of interest in this respect are the data from a sociological
study of the sharing of educational duties by husband and wife
in the family. Both father and mother usually accompany children out of doors, visit cultural establishments, and check their
homework. The mother, however, more frequently has discussions with them about family affairs (in our research 75.4% of
the women and 67.2% of the men), books read or plays seen
(56.7 and 48.9%), political and public events (45.5 and 25%),
work and public activities (60.4 and 36.4%).[7] All this is indicative not only of the mother's authority in the eyes of her
children but also of her great educational potential.

The common educational effort of husband and wife depends
on the degree to which they share common interests. In the
survey mentioned above, 71.5% of the couples often discussed
family affairs, 52.3% discussed books they had read or shows,
films, or TV programs they had seen, 37% discussed political
and public events, 50.2% discussed work, public activities, or
studies, and finally, 32% of the couples shared common hobbies
and interests.

Community of interests, naturally, has a direct effect on
both children's education and the self-education and mutual education of the parents, that is, on the most important functions
of the family in socialist society. Reflecting the new structure
of family relations, community of interests is also an illustration of the community of family and public goals characteristic
of socialism.

The development of new family cooperation, with its fair
distribution of all household duties, strengthens relations in
the family. However, the findings of many studies show that the
father often lags behind the mother in both the time he devotes
to the children and the forms in which he takes part in their
upbringing. This often has a negative effect on relations both
between the parents and between them and the children. Sociologists at Tartu State University have, in particular, estab-

lished that in most cases relations between children and mother develop more favorably than with the father. Boys and girls tend to heed the mother's advice and demands more, they associate more and are on friendlier terms with her, and her influence on them is accordingly greater.

The greater authority of the mother is a reflection of the activity of women in both the public and family spheres. Women extensively use the opportunities provided by society to enrich their lives and imbue family contacts with new content. This does not detract from the importance of the father's authority or his role in bringing up children. A father's influence cannot be replaced by the mother's or that of children's institutions. Numerous studies show that the greatest effect is achieved in combining the educational efforts of mother and father and of public and family forms of education.

This is clearly perceived in families where household duties are consistently shared and where understanding between the parents is greater. We recall that such sharing is more frequent in young families with fairly high educational standards of both husband and wife. Insofar as the cultural standards of the population will grow with the introduction of universal secondary education, this trend will develop and expand in both town and country, in urban and rural communities.

The educational process in the family has grown much more complex under scientific-technological modern conditions. The revolution has brought about substantial changes in the home, communications, and family recreation. Urbanization, migratory processes, improvements in transportation and the growing volume of cultural information obtained through the radio, television, and films have expanded the domestic world of the family, expanded its contacts, made it possible to sense one's participation in events taking place far beyond the family circle, and widened the horizon of both the old and young generations. But these same factors have resulted in a weakening of the social control exerted by those closest to children (family, neighbors, relatives, friends).

The separation of employment and household work has

E. E. Novikova, V. S. Iazykova, and Z. A. Iankova

sharply restricted opportunities for labor education through
the participation of children in productive labor shared with
other members of the household. In the modern family labor
education occupies an insignificant place and is primarily associated with noncreative, routine forms of household work.
It does not introduce children to work requiring extensive concentration of will and effort or associated with psychological
and physical strain. At the same time, the family continues to
play a decisive part in shaping young people's attitudes toward
work and their motivation to work; it remains the principal
counselor in the choice of occupation and way of life. Accordingly, family labor education cannot be treated as an isolated
process; joint efforts by the family, school, and work collective
are necessary.

Today trade union organizations provide considerable help
to the family and school in bringing up adolescents. The social
development plans of industrial enterprises provide for extensive construction of preschool establishments, summer camps,
children's arts and hobbies houses, etc.

More and more trade union organizations are contributing to
the labor education of schoolchildren by helping families in the
occupational orientation of young people, encouraging creative
interests, and molding genuinely communist attitudes toward
work.

Thus, for example, for several years now an occupational
orientation system covering "school — vocational-technical
school — factory" has been functioning at the "Stankoliniia"
automatic line factory in Moscow. A special council headed
by the director of the factory was set up. It includes representatives of public organizations, educators from local schools,
teachers from the vocational-technical school, workers and
engineers from the enterprise, and parents. The best workers
at the enterprise speak before pupils from schools No. 71 and
459 of Moscow's Zhdanov Raion, over which the factory has assumed patronage. Classes in various worker trades have been
introduced into the school curriculum. The factory's Komsomol
organization also takes part in the social education of the school-

children. Science, technology, and production days are organized for the children, as well as visits to the factory, where
they can see the worker collective at work and in everyday life.
In the classes where young people from the factory meet with
the children, progress has improved, and interest in the factory and the work collective has grown.

A new and socially significant form of labor education in
rural communities is the so-called student production team.
Work on the team is not a game, it is the real thing, an actual
form of participation by pupils in the implementation of state
farm production plans. It fosters a sense of responsibility in
the children, stimulates independence and initiative, develops
the urge to acquire new knowledge and work habits, and promotes thoughtful vocational orientation. [8]

Every year new forms and methods of work with children
in residential blocks appear. This is of great assistance to
the family, and of course primarily to the woman, in bringing up
children. Various do-it-yourself, housekeeping, sewing, botany,
aircraft modeling, and other groups organized by clubs help
deepen the knowledge acquired in school, develop creative
thinking, and provide the children with interesting pastimes.

Hundreds of thousands of people in our country gladly donate
their talents and free time to children. They include technology
enthusiasts and nature lovers, musicians, handicraftsmen and
collectors, young people and old, men and women. The local
soviets of working people's deputies and party, Komsomol, and
trade union organizations strive to channel their surging energy, knowledge, and great imagination into work with children
at clubs, Young Pioneer Palaces, amateur interest groups in
neighborhoods, at facilities for young technicians, etc.

By assisting the family in bringing up children, the state
and society promote the process of molding the new man.
At the same time, by improving in every way the content
and forms of social education in children's establishments
and striving for scientific organization of the education and
physical and spiritual development of children, the state re-
lieves women of a substantial part of the burden of caring for

children, organizing their recreation, keeping track of their studies, etc.

An important factor affecting family upbringing and the woman's educational functions is the trend toward smaller families.

On the one hand, with fewer children parents would appear to be able to devote more attention to their upbringing, provide better conditions for them, and give them more material and spiritual benefits. On the other hand, however, age-old experience and the latest findings in education and psychology show that raising a single child is a very complex and contradictory process. The child constantly feels itself the focus of attention of the older members of the family, the object of their love and admiration, which often leads to egocentrism, inflated self-image, and the mentality of a parasite. An only child lacks the chance to enter into comparatively equal relations with other children, care for younger children, and feel a sense of responsibility for them. The mother is burdened with the added need to compensate for the lack of such contacts herself. But even then the development of such character traits as collectivism, independence, and responsibility for a task is restricted by the special nature of mother-child relations.

Most women understand the negative consequences of an only child in theory, but in practice they continue to prefer a small family. A survey conducted by the Central Statistical Administration of the USSR, which covered more than 33,000 women in all the union republics, revealed that 1.5% wanted to have one child, 42% wanted two, 39.4% wanted three, 11.7% wanted four, and 6% wanted five or more. The ideal number of children in a family on average for the USSR is 2.9.[9] Figures approaching this were found in a poll of women workers at eleven Moscow enterprises. Most of the women (60%) felt that two children made the best family, 36% were for three, and only 3% thought that one child was best. The actual figures, though, were 17% with no children (but planning to have one soon), 64% with one child, and 18% with two.

In a sample survey of 70 Moscow families with an average

married life of 11.2 years, 61% of the families had one child, 30% two, 8.5% three, and only 0.5% had four children. The average number of children per family was thus 1.4. [10]

The moral and educational need to increase the number of children in families insistently requires not only material encouragement of the birth of the second and successive children (including housing, children's establishments, etc.) but also meeting a complex of women's spiritual needs that both directly and indirectly affect her desire to have children (more free time, changes in its structure, etc.).

The greater "autonomy" of the rising generation, the loss of the family's monopoly of influence over children, and their precociousness first of all pose the problem of parental authority in a new light and, second, entitle the child to greater participation in family affairs.

The example of parents and relatives and contact with them is of tremendous importance in bringing up children in the family. "Your own behaviour," wrote A. S. Makarenko, addressing himself to parents, "is the most decisive thing. Do not imagine that you are bringing up your child only when you speak to him, lecture him, or tell him to do something. You are bringing up the child every moment of your life, even when you are not at home. How you dress, how you speak with, and about, other people, how you rejoice or grieve, the way you behave with friends and enemies, how you laugh or read the newspaper — all this is of great significance to the child. The child sees or senses the slightest change in tone of voice, all the convolutions of your thoughts reach it in invisible ways you do not even notice. And if at home you are rude or boastful, if you drink, or even worse, if you insult the mother, you needn't think of education: you are already bringing up your children, bringing them up badly, and the best advice and methods will not help you." [11]

In other words, the parents' system of values and norms of behavior has a special impact on the molding of the child's personality in the family. In a Soviet family the stronger links between family and society have a dominant im-

181

pact on the mind and character of children, on their behavior and way of life.

A cohesive family with a high level of social interaction fosters an adolescent's ability to easily join in the life of the student community at school and make friends with his or her contemporaries. Such children have a developed sense of personal dignity and collectivism; they can stand up for themselves and their comrades.

There is a direct link between the system of social values of parents and, the level of cognitive needs of the child. Parents oriented toward lofty, socially meaningful goals and ethical ideals devote much more attention to their child than parents who place consumer interests in the forefront. Children growing up in families with lofty social ideals usually strive for real achievement in studies and in work, not for the formal symbols of success. In families with low levels of social and emotional activity, especially in so-called "difficult" and "problem" families, there are more chances for the development of a morally deficient personality. The possibility of negative influences on such a child is especially great in the transitional period, during puberty. The transitional age in itself often breeds various excesses because the child is incapable of independently solving many difficult moral problems. The situation is aggravated when the parents are unable to suggest a correct solution through their own example or advice.

Bringing up children at home is most effective in families oriented toward meaningful work, active participation in public affairs, harmonious integration of family and public forms of cultural and domestic services and recreation, and a distribution of family duties in which the main purpose is the shaping and development of the personality of all its members. These families promote genuine equality and rational division of and cooperation in work, which, we repeat, is directly mirrored in the nature and content of the roles and functions of the woman in the family and the household, especially her function of bringing up children, which should be considered the prime criterion of progress in the family and in society.

Free Time and the Development of
Women's Personality

The changes taking place in social production and the life of Soviet society give working women more and more free time and radically affect its structure. It is estimated that over the last thirty or forty years, time spent on household duties has decreased by some 20%, giving men 2.5 and women 6.8 more hours of free time a week. [12]

The amount and structure of time spent on household duties by men and women is being shared more and more evenly, an indication of the growing real equality between them. In cities, for example, the difference in time spent on household duties by working men and women has decreased 1.3-1.5 times.

Free time is a powerful factor and a condition of the social progress and spiritual growth of every working person. It has been figuratively called "space for development of the personality." As that "space" expands, so do the opportunities for personal development. "It goes without saying," wrote Marx, "that free time, which is both time for recreation and time for more lofty activity, changes the individual who possesses it into a different subject, and it is as a different subject that he enters the immediate process of production." [13]

It is hard to overestimate the importance of free time for a person. At the same time, it is also hard to overestimate its importance for society as a whole. Society is interested in the most effective utilization of free time. Obviously, much depends on the person himself: the scope and direction of his requirements, interests, and creative activity. Of decisive importance, however, are the social guarantees, the conditions society creates for the development of the individual.

How a modern woman spends her time is convincing proof of the development of her spiritual needs, interests, and values.

The convergence of the cultural standards of women and men, the formation of the personality of the socialist type of woman, whose spiritual requirements and ways of meeting them differ little from those of men, can be illustrated with the results of numerous sociological surveys carried out over the last few years in our country. These surveys also include studies of time budgets. They show that the greatest increases have taken place in the share of time spent by women on public activity and studies. At present more than two thirds of the population, both men and women, engage in civic work. The only exceptions are housewives and pensioners, whose public activity decreases. But even they devote more of their free time to it than before. Whereas in 1922 only 4.4% of housewives were publicly active, and then in only one form (participation in demonstrations), today 22.3% of the nonworking women do educational and organizational work at their place of residence.

The time spent in public work has on the whole increased five- or sixfold in the years of socialist construction, and the range of such activity has increased by six to ten units. [14]

Women devote more and more of their free time to activities that raise the level of their general and specialized knowledge: regular reading, visits to museums, clubs, attendance at lectures, cultural enlightenment, studying foreign languages, etc.

Time devoted to studies and education has increased three- or fourfold over the last thirty years. In the 1920s, according to Academician S. G. Strumilin, only 6.9% of the members of working-class families, and only those in large cities, devoted their spare time to educational improvement by attending clubs, schools, or courses. According to a nationwide poll, at present 46.9% of all men and 36.8% of all women in large, medium-sized, and small towns go in for political education, and 41% of the men and 32.9% of the women take self-education. [15]

Studies of spare time carried out in the midtwenties showed that women spent one quarter the time men did reading newspapers, and half as much time reading books.

According to a study done in the sixties by the Soviet sociologist B. A. Grushin, 86.8% of men and 77.2% of women read newspapers regularly. Among housewives the percentage regularly reading newspapers reached 71%. Grushin also found that 73.8% of men and 65.9% of women read books several times a week.[16]

Studies show that women still read newspapers and magazines less regularly. However, they show as much interest as men in events in economic, political, and public life, both in the country and abroad, reported over the radio and television (Table 4).

Table 4

Interest in Politics among Men and Women*
(% of total)

Degree of interest	In events in the USSR		In events abroad	
	men	women	men	women
Interested and follow with great interest	70.0	61.8	73.5	71.1
Not always interested	9.6	18.1	7.9	18.1
Not interested	5.9	5.6	3.6	3.0
No answer	14.5	14.1	15.0	7.8

*S. N. Ikonnikova and V. E. Lisovskii, Molodezh' o sebe, o svoikh sverstnikakh, Leningrad, Lenizdat, 1969, p. 58.

The cultural revolution has drawn women into a new world of awareness, quest, public activity, and creativity.

The very scale of demands on the spiritual culture of women has changed. Whereas thirty-five or forty years ago the Soviet state was concerned with drawing women into production and public activity, with teaching the bulk of the female population to read and write, today the issue is the harmonious development of all her spiritual potentialities, satisfying the highest requirements for creative work, education, various forms of contact according to interests, bringing up and educating children, and spiritual activity in free time.

One of the main ways of solving this problem is through raising the ecucational standards of women. As they rise, the

E. E. Novikova, V. S. Iazykova, and Z. A. Iankova

amount and structure of utilization of free time by men and women draw closer together. According to a study carried out in Krasnoiarsk Krai, for example, among workers with an education up to the fourth grade, men had 74% more spare time than women, 37% more in the group with grades 5 to 9, and only 27% more in the group with secondary and incomplete higher education. In the first group men spent 2.8 times more than women reading newspapers, magazines, and books, and 1.8 times more in the second group. In the group with secondary and incomplete higher education there is little difference between the structures of free time of men and women. True, men less frequently attend educational establishments (women 8.2 hours a week, men, 7.6 hours), but they devote more time to self-education (8.3 hours a week, as against 5.3 for women). [17]

The introduction of compulsory ten-year education creates the conditions for further improvement of the structure of free time in all sociodemographic groups in all regions, cities, villages, and communities.

Studies have established the dependence of the structure of women's free time on such factors as the nature and content of work, marital status, stage in the development of the family, and its composition.

Sociological studies lead, in particular, to the conclusion that the more meaningful a working woman's job, the more creative the nature of her public and occupational activity, the greater her spiritual needs in her free time (she reads more books relating to her work, listens to radio and television broadcasts on science and technology, goes to exhibitions, engages in industrial rationalization, etc.). These studies also show a direct link between both the scope and type of a woman's activity in her free time and the existence or absence of small children and the degree of duty sharing in the family. In one case a woman inevitably devotes all her free time to the home, serving her children, husband, and other members of the family; in the other she harmoniously combines functions of serving and bringing up children with recreation and creativity.

The relation between spiritual requirements and the content

of work can readily be traced in an analysis of the reading interests of men and women. For this, 840 readership cards were analyzed at the library of the First State Bearings Plant in Moscow. The analysis showed that the reading interests of men and women depended less on sex than on the content of their work and their cultural standards. The results of the study also showed convincingly that scientific and technological progress stimulates the interest of women from all social groups in scientific matters.

Improvement in the system of information also has a marked effect on the way spare time is used. An important role here belongs to people's universities. Such institutions in the most diverse fields (literature, music, art, science, technological progress, atheism, law, family-household culture) are equally accessible to the engineer and the worker, to men and women, to old people and young. The students of these distinctive educational institutes are offered information in different spheres of human culture in vivid and popular form. There are 38,000 people's universities throughout the country. They are attended by more than four million people, over half of them women.

The gradual convergence of the spiritual interests of all sections of the population is an objective trend in the development of socialist society. This trend is apparent in an analysis of the frequency of visits to movies, theaters, and clubs. Unlike reading matter, interest in which appeared among the overwhelming majority of the population only with the elimination of illiteracy and semiliteracy, movies immediately attracted a mass audience. At present all groups of the population also avail themselves of many other information media.

A comparison of the recreation of men and women shows that there is no difference at all in the types of activity, and very little in its structure. Women tend to spend less time in front of the TV set, but they go to the theater, movies, or museums more frequently; they read fewer newspapers but more books.

Thus a high level of recreation is characteristic of the overwhelming majority of workers, enginers, and employees, men as well as women.[18]

As a result of the cultural revolution, participation, not only in consumption but in the creation of cultural values as well, has become an essential element in the life of all Soviet people. Numerous studies show that working women in major cities devote much of their free time to the satisfaction of cultural needs. And those forms of activity that are associated with the mastery and creation of new spiritual values, which are so important in the development of the human personality, are becoming ever more widespread.

Suffice it to note that today some four million women participate in amateur art groups. Many of them have attained high professional standards. Among them are People's Artists of the USSR, Lenin Prize Laureates, Liudmila Zykina, Aleksandra Strelchenko, Evgeniia Miroshnichenko, and many other famous masters of Soviet art.

People's theaters, studios, and groups play a special part in the development of people's creative potentialities. Soviet trade unions alone sponsor some 3,000 amateur film studios and art circles attended by people of both sexes and with different educations and occupations. Tens of thousands of women take part in amateur art festivals and contests sponsored by the Central Council of Trade Unions together with unions of creative workers.

All these facts are indicative of the successful solution of the task of bringing art to the people, as first posed by Lenin.

At the same time, sociological studies indicate that there still remain differences in the degree to which men and women are able to satisfy their spiritual demands. This is especially true of married women with small children.

A study carried out in Estonia, in the course of which 100 men and women between the ages of 26 and 40 were polled, showed a marked difference between the opportunities for cultural advancement of women with at least one child and those with no children (Table 5).

It can be seen from Table 5 that childless women are greater consumers of culture than women with children. For men the

Table 5

Frequency of Attendance at Cultural Events
in Families with and without Children*
(per 100 persons)

Type of event	Times attended			
	men		women	
	childless	having children	childless	having children
Movies	96	107	117	90
Theatrical productions	82	110	127	89
Recitations	89	104	126	89
Total	93	109	122	89

*Dinamika izmeneniia polozheniia zhenshchiny i sem'ia,
Moscow, 1972, p. 16 (ISI AN SSSR).

presence of children in the family is no obstacle to satisfying
their cultural needs. On the contrary, these needs continue to
develop and are met to an even greater extent.

The fact that women with children attend cultural events less
frequently is by no means due to their indifference or lack of
interest in spiritual values. The reason is the lack of spare
time. These conclusions were confirmed in a poll of visitors
to the A. S. Pushkin Museum of Fine Arts, where women account for 56% of the total. The largest group is young women
up to 25 years of age. Between 25-30 the number of male and
female visitors is the same, and in the 31-40 age group the
number of women is smaller. Apparently at some stage household concerns and bringing up children begin to take more and
more of a woman's free time, and she is no longer able to visit
cultural institutions as frequently as before. However, surveys
show that when the children have grown up, women again resume more active involvement in cultural values. More free

E. E. Novikova, V. S. Iazykova, and Z. A. Iankova

time and improvements in its structure and better working and domestic conditions for Soviet women are a prime resource for the development of her personality and the achievement of de facto equality with men.

Notes

1. Materialy XVI s''ezda professional'nykh soiuzov SSSR, Moscow, Profizdat, 1977, p. 10.
2. K. Marx and F. Engels, Sochineniia, vol. 36, p. 294.
3. A. G. Kharchev and S. I. Golod, Professional'naia rabota zhenshchin i sem'ia, Leningrad, "Nauka" Publishers, 1971, p. 85.
4. N. G. Iurkevich, "Rabota zhenshchiny na promyshlennom predpriiatii i stabil'nost' sem'i," in Materialy XII Mezhdunarodnogo seminara po issledovaniiu sem'i, Moscow, ISI AN SSSR, 1972.
5. Konstitutsiia (Osnovnoi Zakon) Soiuz Sovetskikh Sotsialisticheskikh Respublik, p. 66.
6. A. S. Makarenko, Sochineniia, vol. 4, Moscow, "Akedemiia pedagogicheskikh nauk" Publishers, 1951, p. 441.
7. Sotsiologicheskie issledovaniia, 1974, no. 1, p. 104.
8. B. S. Arkhipov, "Problemy trudovogo vospitaniia molodezhi," in Vospitanie molodezhi v razvitom sotsialisticheskom obshchestve, issue 1, Moscow, ISI AN SSSR, 1973.
9. Literaturnaia gazeta, July 4, 1973.
10. Sotsiologicheskie issledovaniia, 1974, no. 1, p. 101.
11. Makarenko, Sochineniia, vol. 4, p. 347.
12. B. Grushin, Svobodnoe vremia (Aktual'nye problemy), Moscow, "Mysl'" Publishers, 1967, p. 51.
13. K. Marx, "Iz neopublikovannykh rukopisei," Bol'shevik, 1939, no. 11-12, p. 65.
14. V. I. Bolgov, Biudzhet vremeni pri sotsializme, Moscow, "Nauka" Publishers, 1973, p. 194.
15. Ibid.
16. Grushin, Svobodnoe vremia, pp. 80-82.
17. Bolgov, Biudzhet vremeni, p. 239.
18. Dinamika izmeneniia polozheniia zhenshchiny i sem'i, Moscow, ISI AN SSSR, 1972.

10

Changing Family Roles
and Marital Instability

A. G. Kharchev and M. S. Matskovskii

The Problem of Evaluating Divorce
and Its Social Consequences

Under socialism divorce plays a dual role in relation to marriage. If it is directed against survivals of the past in marital relations, against the exploitation and moral humiliation of one of the spouses, it can be a means of morally elevating matrimony, an assertion of the equality of men and women; but it can also be the antithesis of matrimony if it is a result of those survivals, the ethical immaturity of the spouses, and a rejection by them in their behavior of what underlies the social requirement for the institutionalization of marital relations: mutual obligations, duty, responsibility for children. Socialist society upholds the former function of divorce and places no obstacles to the dissolution of marriage when it is really necessary, but it tries to prevent divorces that are destructive with respect to the very institution of the family and its social role.

Obviously the nature of divorce, its causes and social consequences, vary widely from one case to another. It is a quite complex matter, which is why Soviet marriage and family law

Russian text © 1978 by "Statistika" Publishers. *Sovremennaia sem'ia i ee problemy* (Moscow: "Statistika" Publishers, 1978), pp. 106-15, 119-21, 134-43.

provides that divorce cases be handled either by civil registrar's offices or in court, when the interests of one of the spouses or children are involved.

The efforts of socialist society to prevent morally unjustified divorces concentrate on the educational rather than the legal or judicial level, through improving the systems of preparing young people for marriage and cultivating appropriate attitudes and orientations among them.

An objective analysis of the problems of divorce is impossible without studying families at various stages of trouble. Accordingly, in this section we would like to pay special attention to the problem of family stability, regarding the concept of stability as a kind of continuum, the extreme point of which is destabilization. We also think that the factors affecting family stability should be taken into account at the very earliest stages in the establishment of marital relations. Hence the problems of divorce are inseparable from problems of premarital relations, marriage, and the mutual adaptation of the spouses.

It is a well-known fact that in recent years in the USSR (as in other developed countries) divorces are on the rise (see Table 1).

Divorce statistics have been analyzed in a number of interesting sociodemographic studies. [1] We therefore believe our main task is to examine the socioethical aspects of this problem and determine ways society can most effectively counteract negative trends in marriage and family relations. Such an approach makes it possible to focus attention on those aspects of premarital relations and family building that are statistically the most frequent causes of unhappy marriages.

Unfortunately, in the USSR we still have too little sociological information about the causes and consequences of divorce and must therefore rely on foreign as well as Soviet empirical data. The former can serve as one of the sources for developing hypotheses aimed at explaining various aspects of sexual behavior that are relatively independent of the social system and can be explained either by biopsychological factors or by the direct influence of scientific and technological development, urbanization, and so on.

Table 1

Number of Divorces in the USSR*

Year	Number of divorces per 1,000 people
1940	1.1
1950	0.4
1955	0.6
1960	1.3
1965	1.6
1966	2.8
1967	2.7
1968	2.7
1969	2.6
1970	2.6
1971	2.6
1972	2.6
1973	2.7
1974	2.9
1975	3.1

*Narodnoe khoziaistvo SSSR v 1975 g., Moscow, 1976, p. 44.

At the same time, it should be borne in mind that under the conditions of capitalism, the main trends in the impact of the consequences of the scientific and technological revolution on relations between the sexes are epitomized in the socioeconomic structure and dominant system of values and cannot serve as a standard for modeling corresponding correlations when studying the socialist family.

The works of K. Marx and F. Engels[2] showed that the domination of private property restricts the development of the personality in both the ruling and exploited classes (though the nature of such restrictions differs widely for both groups). Private ownership also breeds antagonism not only in relations be-

tween classes but between public and private interests as well.
Under such circumstances the development of the personality
also has a contradictory character, which is reflected directly
even in the family and its structure, value orientations, and
functions.

Thus industrialization has already led to the massive involvement of women in professional activity. One of the results of
the scientific and technological revolution has been a further
intensification of this process. As a series of studies has established, women's work in production helps expand the scope of
their social contacts, develops an interest in raising their occupational and cultural standards, and breeds a sense of independence and personal worth, that is, enriches and develops
their personalities.[3]

All of this results in the enhancement of the role of personal-
subjective and psychological aspects in both the sexual behavior
of women and marital and family relations. The family evolves
from a community in which the elements of a social institution
predominate into a community in which features of a sociopsychological group predominate.

Under capitalism, however, all these natural and progressive
processes are distorted insofar as the development of a woman's
personality takes place under conditions that perpetuate, both
in the economy and in culture, traditional, age-old attitudes
toward her as representing a "secondary," subordinate sex.
The scientific and technological revolution inevitably aggravates
this contradiction, creating a basis for numerous conflictual
situations both in women's occupational activities and their personal lives. This has a number of important social consequences:

1. There appear more and more symptoms of women's dissatisfaction with their socioeconomic status; prominent among
these symptoms is the upsurge in feminist movements in capitalist countries.

2. One consequence of the development and enrichment of the
personality of women in those countries has been the emergence
not of more progressive norms of sexual behavior (as might
have been expected) but of women's acceptance of norms for-

merly restricted to men, such as norms permitting premarital sex and presupposing weaker, often purely formal sanctions for marital infidelity. These changes, which began back in the '20s and became known in the West as the "sexual revolution," were also facilitated by such effects of the scientific and technological revolution as urbanization and its accompanying weakening of the traditional system of social control, the growing intensity and anonymity of social intercourse, and the concentration of large numbers of young people in educational and tourist centers, which stimulated the appearance of the so-called youth "subculture," with its emphasis on "sexual freedom."

A large share of the responsibility for the epidemic of extramarital sex belongs to the mass media in bourgeois societies, which did a great deal to reduce the vast richness and diversity of emotions associated with human sexual love to a purely instinctual level.

3. Since the development of the family from a social institution into a social and psychological group makes its stability dependent on the durability of moral bonds between the spouses, the moral crisis of contemporary capitalist society must be reflected in marital-family relations.

To be sure, some family conflicts, especially divorce cases initiated by women, can be explained by their greater demands on marriage and, in particular, on the personalities and behavior of their husbands. Many Western sociologists note that today romantic love and expectations of happiness play a greater part in the motivations for marriage than in the recent past. Even if such motivations (especially in an atmosphere where utilitarian considerations predominate) are a reflection of the romantic worldview characteristic of youth, they substantially increase what is expected of marriage and thereby the possibility of disappointment.

Thus under the conditions of capitalism, the changes in marital-family relations promoted by the scientific and technological revolution are very contradictory. Progressive trends created by the development of science and technology and the growth of public wealth are restricted or distorted when they come into contact with obsolete economic, sociopolitical, and cultural forms of human life and existence. We certainly do not view the scientific and technological revolution as either solely a panacea for or solely a threat to the family. The development of science and technology creates a wide range of diverse opportunities, and the question of which of them are realized, and to what extent, in the development of marital-family relations depends on a variety of factors, primary among which, as noted before, are the socioeconomic system and the system of cultural values based on it.

However, a change in the socioeconomic system and, correspondingly, in the social essence of relations between the sexes does not automatically result in greater family solidity and stability. For there are different ways of assuring stability: by strengthening interpersonal ties within the family, as well as by strengthening the family group through external "pressure," without consideration of the wills or desires of its members. If family solidity is understood to mean just a minimum of divorces (as is often the case), the difference between these two approaches to ensuring that stability (and it is a difference of principle, in essence a difference between humanism and antihumanism, between communist and proprietary morality) recedes to the background and is often quite blurred. Moreover, in that case the family of a serf may prove more progressive than any contemporary family form.

As regards stability as a result of external force, the socialist revolution is in effect directed against it insofar as socialism strives for the freedom and equality of women, repeals the old exploitative jurisprudence, and rejects religion and proprietary morality.

The external "bond" that assured family unity and stability in the old society was destroyed by the objective logic of socialist transformation. However, the strengthening of ties between family members, as a function of moral consciousness and the moral maturity of the society as a whole, proceeded at a slower rate. In other words, the process of destroying the old outstripped the process of creating and developing the new.

196

The situation was further aggravated by destructive wars and the disproportions between the male and female population caused by them, as well as by the economic difficulties and housing shortages during the initial stages of development of the new society — that is, factors not associated with the essence of socialism as a social system but engendered by the complex historical circumstances in which it appeared and developed.

By now many of the factors that had disrupted marital-family relations have receded into the past, but the emotions, views, and attitudes bred by them continue to exert some influence.

Strengthening the economic independence and social equality of women greatly enhances the "specific gravity" of psychological harmony, on the one hand, and of psychological collisions and conflicts in marital-family relations, on the other. These conflicts, which in the old family were settled relatively easily primarily because the woman's interests were little esteemed and little considered, acquired great significance in the new socialist family. It is not accidental that the claim of "incompatibility of temperaments" has become a major reason for divorce, and the phrases "there is no spiritual closeness between us" or "we don't understand each other" have become a kind of moral indictment of a marriage.

As mentioned before, the basic expectations of marriage in contemporary socialist society are oriented toward personal happiness, that is, primarily toward mutual love. Surveys carried out in different cities, among different strata of society, all revealed a remarkably similar picture (1968-73 data): for 80 to 90% of Soviet people love is the main factor in the choice of a future mate.[4]

At the same time, unfortunately, there is no simple relationship between love and marital solidity. The latter is influenced by the complexity of love itself, by greater demands on a partner chosen for love, by various difficulties that can lie in wait for a family, especially in the first years of married life, and even by the fact that the duration of sexual love is very different for individuals. However, the very fact that love is a prime

197

factor in marriage is a major achievement of socialism.

In any society, including socialism, the emotional ties between spouses undergo substantial changes in the course of living together: the role of such moral values as spiritual closeness and mutual gratitude for all the good things experienced in married life grows. Consequently the problem of strengthening marriage becomes an issue of moral upbringing, maturity, and proper organization of family life. It is true that not every divorce is immoral; but it is also true that the less developed a person's sense of duty, the more lightly he decides on divorce. A study of divorce hearings in the socialist countries shows that the most frequent reason for the collapse of a family is not the replacement of an old love by a new one but an old love being sacrificed for a casual liaison.

To formulate a scientifically well grounded position for society to take on divorce, it is first necessary to clearly analyze its various consequences. They can, in our view, be correlated with the effectiveness of the functioning of the social institution of marriage, with the fates of the separating spouses and their lives following the divorce, with the kind of upbringing and psychological characteristics of the children of divorced parents, and with the effects of divorces on the reproductive processes of the society.

Let us examine each of these consequences in greater detail.

We mentioned earlier that in the contemporary Soviet family, divorces are associated mainly with the disintegration of individual family groups and do not mean the disintegration of marriage as a social institution. However, the growing number of divorces has had a serious impact on the effectiveness with which the institution of marriage functions.

First of all, there has been a change in attitudes toward divorce, which is no longer exceptional and has become an ordinary, normal event. This has led to lower demands in choosing a mate.

Of course, the question of the effect the attitude "If worst comes to worst, we can get a divorce" has on this choice requires empirical evidence. But the fact that "one third of all divorces take place in families less than one year old, another third in

families one to five years old," and that divorce has become
a "problem of young families"[5] to some extent confirms the
conclusion.

There is another way in which divorce influences the effectiveness with which the institution of marriage functions. The
prospect of divorce, or rather the fear that the husband (wife)
will take advantage of the right to divorce in the very first
more or less serious conflict, reflects in one way or another
on the behavior of each spouse and their attitudes toward their
family roles, on their mutual evaluations and self-evaluations,
and on family planning, at least until both husband and wife acquire a sense of family stability and consequently some sense
not only of the present and immediate future but the relatively
long-term future as well.

The effects of assessments of prospects for the marriage by
each spouse on their behavior and on the moral and psychological atmosphere of family life have also not been studied because social psychology does not deal much with problems of
the family. However, some surveys of reasons for marriage
and divorce and also empirical observations of the behavior
of specific families indicate probable confirmation of this hypothesis. "Since 1966 some 650,000 divorces have taken place
each year. In addition more than 100,000 men are widowed each
year at a relatively early age (before 50). But the number of
remarriages has been decreasing and in recent years averaged
just over 300,000 a year. No more than 12% of divorced men
marry again each year."[6]

This is why we think the hypothesis that divorces increase
the number of people who do not remarry and, most important,
do not want to, at least in the next few years, is largely correct.
Any increase in the number of people who do not want to remarry has a negative effect on the prestige of marriage, reduces the number of people who can have children, and under-
mines the social norms of marriage as an institution. It is
well known that there is a strongly negative correlation between
the number of children in the family and the number of divorces.
It is undoubtedly connected with general ethnic and cultural tra-

A. G. Kharchev and M. S. Matskovskii

ditions and with general attitudes toward the family, the household, women's work, etc., which vary greatly in different republics. But these explanations in no way contradict the hypothesis
of the effect of the trend toward higher divorce rates on the stability and functioning of the family.

Divorces increase the number of incomplete families. Within
such families a specific system of relations between mother and
child is created, and behavior patterns develop that in some
respects represent an alternative to the norms and values on
which the institution of marriage is based.

Divorce also has a wide-ranging impact on the separating
spouses themselves. This problem has not yet been studied
empirically in Marxist sociology, and we must therefore rely
only on foreign sources in examining it. The well-known
American family sociologist W. Goode[7] surveyed 425 divorced
mothers in Detroit. Most of them stated that they had not lost
their social status or acquaintances as a result of divorce (as
was the case with women of older generations). Many of the
respondents thought divorce was better for their children, that
it would have been much worse for them to be involved in
their parents' squabbles. Other American sociologists —
H. Christensen and K. Johnsen[8] — analyzed a number of empirical works and on that basis established the following types
of reaction to divorce. One fairly frequent reaction is a kind
of shock mixed with shame and self-pity. The divorced spouses attempt to rationalize the situation and to prove that they are indifferent to the ensuing problems. Another widespread reaction
is a sense of anxiety and impatience resulting from the disrup-
tion of habits and loss of accustomed roles. They often seek
to increase their social activity. Friends and relatives usually
help them meet new people. Often following a divorce a person
begins to behave contrary to conventional norms, seeking solace
in drink or making up for the loss of family with more frequent
sexual encounters. One sometimes finds mutually exclusive attitudes toward the former spouse, alternating outbursts of hate
and love. That is why sexual intimacy between the former husband and wife sometimes continues for some time after the di-

vorce. In some cases they even remarry.

American specialists estimate that in the early '70s "a little more than one out of every five marriages was a remarriage, and one out of every eight married persons had been married before." [9] In the view of P. Glick [10] there are indications that the number of remarriages in the United States is increasing, and that each year up to 3% of the partners marry for the third time or more. [11] This phenomenon has been called "sequential polygamy" in American sociological literature.

Empirical studies carried out in the United States show that the percentage of remarriages among divorced people is higher than among widowed spouses. One of the reasons is that some people resort to divorce to legally formalize a new de facto marriage. Also, divorced people are usually eager to get rid of the past and show by remarrying that nothing serious has happened. Finally, divorce usually occurs at an earlier age than widowhood, and this provides greater opportunities for remarrying.

A number of foreign works examine the psychological, psychopathological, and psychophysiological consequences of divorce. J. Bernard, who has analyzed such works, finds that "a study of people in the state of divorce at any interval of time produces an impressive list of pathologies. Life expectancy is relatively low; mortality and illness rates, including alcoholism, are very high, as is the percentage of mental disorders and suicides. It should be borne in mind that these indices are also above average among widows and widowers, but they are much lower than among the divorced." [12]

Also meriting attention are the results of empirical studies by foreign sociologists on the consequences of divorce for children. One such study [13] compares three groups of children: from happy, unhappy, and divorced families. Children from happy families had a better lot all across the board. In the other two groups, though, it was found that children from divorced families had fewer mental disorders, fewer brushes with the law, and better relations with at least one of the parents.

In other indicators (attitude toward school, tendency toward bad company) the children in these latter two groups did not differ a great deal, but they differed substantially from children living in happy families. Comparisons were also made of a number of social and psychological characteristics of children in families where the mother had remarried and of children living with the mother alone. It was found that mother-child relations were better in families where they lived alone.

According to another study [14] fewer children have a high self-image in divorced families than in complete families or in single-parent families resulting from death or separation. Also, children of divorced families have a higher incidence of mental disorders. According to these data the unfavorable consequences of divorce are greater for children of those social groups which attach greater significance to social mores and sanctions against divorce. A child's self-image depends to a considerable degree on the mother's age at the time of divorce. In the case of mothers under 24 at the time of divorce, only 22% of the children had a high self-image by the time they were 12 to 14, while the children of mothers who had divorced later had a high self-image in 42 cases out of 100 (the proportion of children with a high self-image in nondivorced families is 45%). A number of studies also note that the longer the mother and child lived together between divorce and remarriage, the more destructive for the child is the displacement of the mother's attention to the new partner or new child.

According to J. Landis [15] the impact of divorce on a child's mental state depends on a number of factors:

the child's subjective notions of family happiness immediately prior to the divorce;

the age of child and mother;

the degree of expression of negative attitudes toward divorce in the family's social group;

the parent's ability to help the child cope with its anxieties and assure a safe environment.

Along with conclusions of some interest, works by bourgeois sociologists contain quite a few assertions at the level of elementary empirical experience which, clothed in pseudoscientific form, often sound rather banal. For example, divorce has a lesser impact on children up to the age of three than on older children; the probability of remarriage of a divorced partner is in inverse proportion to the number of children remaining with him or her, etc. Moreover, the scientific information contained in these works should be judged (and hence used) with due regard for the fact that it was obtained from aggregates of persons whose social and class characteristics were virtually ignored in the study or were deduced according to methodological principles diametrically opposed to the principles of Marxist-Leninist sociology. Many aspects of the generalizations from empirical material by bourgeois sociologists reflect the specific traits of the bourgeois way of life and cannot be extrapolated to socialist society arbitrarily, without certain reservations. This is true, in particular, of the characterizations of the behavior of divorced women, which, as we know, depend in many ways on the woman's position in society and the dominant system of ideological values.

Does this mean that the results of studies by foreign sociologists can in no way be applied in our scholarship and practice? If that were so, there would be no need for scholarly contacts. The point is that not all facets of human behavior, especially in relations between the sexes, are regulated by social and class factors. Moreover, some components of these relations are of a biopsychic nature and common to all members of the human race. Academician P. N. Fedoseev notes: "It has become a truism for us that man is created by society, that man is a social creature, that his social conditions determine his development, behavior, etc. But we are also opposed to simplistic notions that there are no natural determinants of human existence. Man is a social creature; but as part of nature, he is also a biological creature." [16] And to the extent that a person's behavior goes beyond the limits of social and class regulation, he can display traits defined in social psychology as common to all mankind. Clearly, to the extent to which these traits are more or less faithfully reflected in foreign studies, their results can be useful to Soviet science, first, as a source of theoretical hypotheses in the respective fields of learning, and second, as practical, experimental knowledge. This, in particular, is true of a number of observations by foreign sociologists concerning the reactions of former partners to divorce, the effects of divorce on children, and some other problems. It goes without saying that when Marxist studies are done in this field, the need for foreign data will decline substantially. They will, however, remain important as material for comparison and for verifying data obtained by Soviet scholars, insofar as human behavior associated with marriage, divorce, and the birth and upbringing of children is so complex, and often contradictory, that it requires a very large number of all sorts of empirical facts to be sure of the scientific veracity of their theoretical interpretation.

Let us cite a simple example in this connection.

Findings by both Soviet and foreign scholars show that the upbringing and psychological traumas of children are affected not so much by divorce itself as by the atmosphere that preceded it or, even worse, a highly unfavorable family atmosphere for a long time. According to A. B. Sakharov, nine tenths of all juvenile delinquents grew up in just such an atmosphere. Only in 10% of the cases did juveniles commit crimes despite countervailing family conditions.[17] Many sociologists list so-called fatherlessness among the factors highly detrimental to upbringing. As one work notes, "60% of the pedagogically neglected school children were children with no father."[18]   At the same time, according to other sources, "in studying the living conditions of juvenile delinquents (1965-66, Taganrog and Vladimir), it was found that in the surveyed group, 22% (Taganrog) and 16% (Vladimir) of the youngsters lived with only one parent. In a control group of youngsters with no criminal records, the percentage was almost the same: 21% (Taganrog) and 18% (Vladimir)."[19]

These highly contradictory conclusions can be verified only by taking into account a much larger range of factors characterizing the family's situation, from the qualitative as well as quantitative aspect, and comparing the data thus obtained with the findings of other studies, including, possibly, foreign ones.

Family Roles and Marital Instability

Socialist society is concerned with both family stability and the fullest satisfaction of both partners with their marriage, for one of the objectives of socialist policy is the personal happiness of man, with full observation of the norms of socialist ethics and morality.

Divorce and remarriage may enhance the chances of greater satisfaction in marriage, at least for one of the partners. However, as a mass phenomenon divorces play a largely negative part both in the changing birthrate and in the upbringing of children. First, divorces reduce the reproductive period of a woman's life; second, an unsuccessful first marriage may postpone a first baby for a long time (which is undesirable from the medical point of view); third, as mentioned before, unfavorable relations in the family preceding divorce may have an adverse effect on the woman's reproductive attitudes, although in some cases this may be neutralized by her desire to create and strengthen a new family. Along with optimization of fertility processes, Soviet society views one of its main tasks to be rearing new generations in accordance with the norms and ideals of socialist morality, so that all children in our country grow up physically and mentally healthy. That is why divorce can be regarded as beneficial only if it changes the conditions for molding the child's personality for the better and puts an end to the negative impact of family squabbles on the child's mental state. A family can live even though it performs poorly or even fails to perform any function except parenthood. A family dies if it ceases to do that for which society creates and supports it — raise children. It dies even before the marriage — the basis of the family — is actually dissolved. Therefore the main goal of our society is not to reduce the number of divorces in general but to prevent the dissolution of families that are still intact and capable of functioning socially, but that have encountered apparently insurmountable difficulties....

*　　*　　*

[The study of marital and family relations] should reflect the

A. G. Kharchev and M. S. Matskovskii

real, not ideal, roles and duties of husband and wife in their attitudes to the values and mores of our society. Such an approach will
make it possible to reflect both the achievements of socialist society in changing marital-family relations on the basis of genuine
humanism and equality and the actual forms in which the practical
behavior of individuals and practical activity of individual families
still fail to correspond, first, to social requirements, and second, perhaps, to their own theoretical standards. We speak of
individuals and individual families because the unity of personal,
group, and public interests inherent in socialism in principle
precludes the transformation of this lack of correspondence into
a mass phenomenon.

It should also be borne in mind that the socialist way of life
and communist upbringing increasingly promote family roles
among the members of our society which are a direct continuation of socialist social relations. They include, in particular,
forms of regular mutual assistance to neighboring families,
parental participation in the work of schools, Pioneer organizations, neighborhood youth clubs, family contacts with work
collectives, and so on.

In other words, under socialism role conflicts do not always
necessarily develop on a "traditional" basis. They may
reflect progressive trends in the development of the socialist
family.

The weakness of Western sociological approaches is that
they are restricted to the individual-psychological, rather than
the social-psychological, level, and they enumerate roles stat-
ically rather than dynamically and in isolation from existing
socioeconomic structures and the development of society. This is
all the more erroneous because divorce is in fact influenced not
only by the way the spouses perform their respective roles but
by the failure of role behavior to correspond to role expectation.

The significance of the social and psychological aspects
of intrafamily relations in assuring the stability of the
family has been discussed in a study by V. Mathews and
C. Mihanovich, who investigated differences between families
that considered themselves happy and families on the way to

divorce. [20]   They drew up a questionnaire of 400 questions
derived from a review of literature on marital conflicts. They
studied ten main areas of possible sources of tension between
spouses: (1) basic human needs; (2) financial problems; (3) conflicts over domestic affairs and children; (4) employment problems; (5) problems of relations with the in-laws; (6) problems
involving religion; (7) sexual conflicts; (8) problems of interaction, especially decision-making; (9) personality problems;
(10) problems of social relations. Each area included forty
problems: twenty associated with the person questioned and
twenty with his or her partner.

The main result of this study of marital relations was a refu-
tation of the oft-repeated speculative assertion that happy families have the same problems as unhappy ones. Unhappy families have many more problems, substantially differing from
those of happy families. The study also helped show that most
problems are not resolved and remain latent throughout the
whole life cycle. Table 2 presents ten problems that most
clearly distinguish happy and unhappy couples.

Despite the importance of psychological conflicts between
the partners, objective contradictions related to the family have
a much greater impact on marital relations and, hence, family
stability.

Besides the contradictions pointed out in his time by
F. Engels (the contradiction between the male oppressor and
the oppressed female, the business character of marriage and
selectivity of human feelings), [21] the bourgeois family today
suffers from the conflict bred by the woman's desire to escape its
confines in her daily activities and assert herself not only in
the family roles assigned to her from ancient times but in occupational activity as well.

According to the findings of H. Christensen and H. Johnsen,
for example, in the United States 53% of married men and 21%
of married women believe that most women should be satisfied
with household work as their basic activity, and 56% of the
married men and 28% of the married women agreed with the
view that family instability was a result of the fact that women

Table 2

Points of Difference between
Happy and Unhappy Families

Problem	Happy families (% of 630 polled families)	Unhappy families (% of 354 polled families)
Partners do not share views on many problems	10.95	50.28
One partner has poor empathy with feelings of the other	6.03	40.39
One partner uses words that irritate the other	12.38	45.19
Partner often feels unloved	3.33	35.31
Partner pays no attention to the other	8.57	38.70
Partner feels need to be confided in	5.55	33.89
Partner feels need for person to confide in	5.55	33.89
Partner rarely compliments other partner	13.33	41.52
Partner concedes more frequently than other partner	10.47	38.13
Desire more love and affection	11.92	38.41

did not want to stay at home.

Under the conditions of socialist society, the work and public activities of women do not contradict prevailing norms and values, which, based on the unity of public and personal interests, are also increasingly becoming the norms and values of every individual.

This highly important feature of the socialist way of life

lends a fundamentally different, nonantagonistic character to both the conflict between the roles of the man and the woman in the family and the contradiction between the professional employment and family duties of the woman. Under socialism the acuteness of these contradictions depends in the first place on the cultural and moral level of the partners and their immediate environment.

The cultural and moral maturity of family members in many ways determines the ways in which the woman's work affects the moral-psychological atmosphere of family life and the stability of family relations.

A woman's work can adversely affect the family's performance of reproductive, educational, domestic, spiritual, and emotional functions. In this case, however, the issue should not be reducing the number of working women but finding ways to more rationally combine woman's occupational work with the performance of certain family functions and the full and harmonious development of her personality. The search for such ways should, in our view, be pursued in two directions.

First, it is obvious that there are some functions, notably reproductive and to a certain extent educational, that a woman cannot transfer either to other members of the family or to public institutions. Therefore her participation in work and the general development of her personality on a par with men are possible only if at certain stages in her life (the birth of a baby and the first years of its life) society can provide the opportunity to concentrate on those functions by relieving her of employment either completely and temporarily or partially.

Second, a change is needed in some of the traditional notions still held by certain groups and reflected in the expectations and structure of the performance of family functions. The point is that ideas about the duties of husband and wife evolved long ago, under entirely different economic and social conditions. Yet even now, when most women are employed on an equal footing with men, and many types of household duties traditionally performed by men have become irrelevant (like chopping wood in an urban family or some types of work in rural families), conventional consciousness often continues to impose the same demands on women as before. It follows that any transfer of a substantial share of domestic duties to the man and the equal and fair sharing of family responsibilities, which are a prerequisite for rationally balancing a woman's duties as a worker and a housewife, are possible only with a total change in traditional notions regarding women's family duties, the division of household work, and what is typically man's or typically woman's work.

In discussing the quest for ways to rationally combine women's employment with the performance of household functions, we would like to note the negative effects of certain obsolete truths often propagated in scholarly and popular publications.

The first such truism declares that the time used to satisfy household requirements is indispensable, and any change in time budgets is possible only at the expense of free time not related to domestic activities. Yet sociological studies show that people with equal incomes and equal living conditions (and living within the same territorial community, in a particular town or village) spend different amounts of time on meeting domestic needs. The problem is that there exist different attitudes toward using public everyday services. Unfortunately there are no special studies in our country of the rational organization of domestic work, and no optimum models for such organization have been developed. Yet such models could help point families more rapidly toward use of the new types of services offered by the developing socialist service industry and could overcome the stereotyped negative attitudes toward service institutions held by many people in the past.

A second outdated truism is that domestic activities are a priori regarded as the antithesis of useful, creative work in industry. Our purpose is not to refute this assertion as a whole but to show that it is far from always correct. First of all, it should be noted that as yet not all jobs provide opportunities for the full development of a person's creative abilities. That is why some forms of domestic work (sewing or cooking for women, odd jobs at home for men) retain their significance

210

for personal self-affirmation.

On the other hand, joint household activities by husband and wife based on reasonable sharing of domestic duties can help improve relations between them. A man's participation in household work helps him gain a better sense of his role and enhances his responsibility for the family.

The sharing of family and household duties can be of beneficial influence on children, helping to foster proper work habits and countering the development of egoistic and parasitic propensities.

We thus think it necessary to work out scientifically founded views on the problems of domestic needs and their satisfaction in the Soviet family.

It should be noted in this connection that household work should not be identified or confused (from the point of view of evaluations) with bringing up children. The latter involves even more important social functions, requires much greater personal creative abilities, spiritual strength, etc.

Sociological studies note a steady trend in the transformation of family power structures from traditional to democratic and a consequent change in the roles of husband and wife. This process is apparently irreversible, insofar as it is dictated by specific socioeconomic conditions, on the one hand, and by the norms of socialist morality, on the other. In our view, however, this objective trend often comes into conflict with the insufficient readiness of some families to support democratic relationships. The main conditions for overcoming this contradiction are equal participation of both partners in decision-making, personal responsibility for maintaining stable relations in the family, the desire to contribute equally to family activities, and the ability to take each other's interests into account.

These conditions do not, of course, in themselves guarantee the solution of all family conflicts within the family framework, but they can substantially blunt them.

One of the most important conditions for obtaining sufficiently reliable data about divorces is to distinguish the motivations for divorce from its causes. By motivation Marxist

211

literature means "the basis of a decision to satisfy or not satisfy a (certain) need in a given subjective and objective environment." [22] As applied to divorce this means the basis of a decision that the requirements of marriage cannot be satisfied in the given marital union. Depending on the cultural level of their previous relationship, the particular behavior of each of the partners will lead them to advance different grounds for their decision to break up the marriage. Obviously, ordinary consciousness is incapable of evaluating the totality of causes leading to divorce and often concentrates on the most obvious ("drunkenness"), sidesteps the explanation of causes ("incompatibility of character"), or offers generally erroneous explanations ("bad living conditions," which could hardly have worsened since marriage). An idea of the results of studies of motivations in Soviet literature can be gained from an analysis of Table 3, which covers the results of the five most representative studies (approximately half the studies on the subject in our country).

An analysis of Table 3 makes it possible to draw some very important and characteristic conclusions concerning the state of empirical work on family sociology. The studies cannot, obviously, achieve all the goals facing scholarship and practice: the accumulation and systematization of knowledge and help in drawing up scientifically grounded recommendations. Neither are they of much help in establishing patterns or discovering regional differences or differences between city and countryside. There are several reasons for this, principal among them being:

1) the author usually lacks a conceptual model for examining the causes and motivations of divorces;

2) the causes are defined in extremely vague and ambiguous terms, such as "frivolous attitude toward marital responsibilities," "absence of common views and interests," "incompatibility of characters." The respondents can invest such terms with the most diverse meanings and can understand and interpret them differently, which reduces the scientific value of the results;

3) the variety and incompatibility of many of the enumerations and motivations offered by researchers make it difficult to generalize and interpret the data obtained. The dashes in the table denote the absence of the given motivations in the lists presented in the study;

4) the procedures for obtaining information are very diverse. For example, the questionnaires are accompanied by instructions permitting the selection of one or several answers to questions, which makes it hard to compare the information obtained;

5) different methods (primarily analysis of divorce cases and court hearings) are used, although there are no special works showing which method is the most reliable;

6) an extremely important finding by V. T. Kolokol'nikov and S. M. Pelevin is the sharply differing views on the motivations of divorce expressed by husband and wife, by the court and each divorcing spouse, and finally, by the plaintiff and the defendant. Yet most authors do not separate the motivations of the husband and wife or of the initiator of the divorce and the other partner, which makes the picture of divorce motivations highly ambiguous.

Finally, the last circumstance we would like to note stems from the fact that the literature offers very few indications of the differentiation of motivations and causes of divorce depending on the sociodemographic characteristics of the divorcing spouse. Obviously the reasons must differ depending on the duration of the marriage, the age of the partners, their education, and so on.

We know of no sufficiently serious works that discuss the problem of the correspondence between the motivations and causes of divorce, and we can only indicate the fact of their coincidence or noncoincidence in various specific cases. In particular, an analysis of responses to questionnaires shows that people speak in much greater detail about events that immediately preceded the questionnaire and have much greater difficulty recalling more distant events. It is also obvious that most people can offer objective information regarding facts, but they are highly subjective in interpreting them. This is because so many people are basically incapable of comprehensive

Table 3

Study of Motivations of Divorce in Soviet Literature
(in %)

Motivations / Study	A	B	C husband	C wife	D husband	D wife	D court	E plaintiff	E defendant	F
Absence of common views and interests (including religious differences)	33.9	—	—	—	—	—	—	6.7	3.5	6.5
Incompatibility of characters	28.2	16	63	27	22.2	6.7	15.1	9.2	7.2	13
Infidelity	24.4	29	51	28	15.3	12.6	9.4	11.3	36.0	17.5
Absence or loss of love	23.5	—	—	—	12.3	8.6	5.3	8.1	7.7	—
In love with another person	—	—	—	—	—	—	—	—	—	7.5
Frivolous attitude to marital responsibilities	23.3	—	—	—	—	—	—	4.6	4.6	—
Bad relations with parents (interference of parents or other relatives)	22.0	6	—	—	11.3	4.4	1.5	1.6	5.5	3
Drunkenness (alcoholism)	21.5	39	11	111	10.6	44.3	38.7	24.2	11.8	14.2
Beatings, cruelty, rows, fights	16.6	—	—	—	0.6	5.6	3.6	17.2	5.8	3.8

214

Reason for divorce	A	B	C	D	E	F	G	H	I	J
Abnormal living conditions	14.4	—	—	—	0.5	0.3	0.3	1.4	2.9	—
Sexual dissatisfaction or physiological incompatibility	6.0	—	—	—	—	—	—	1.7	2.4	—
Impossibility of having children (infertility)	5.4	—	—	—	1.0	0.7	0.8	0.8	0.7	2.5
Refusal to have children	5.0	—	—	—	—	—	—	1.1	2.1	—
Sickness of partner	3.7	—	6	3	2.6	1.7	2.1	0.4	1.6	2.8
Married without love or frivolously	—	4	—	—	4.5	2.0	8.5	—	—	—
Partner imprisoned for 3 or more years	—	6	—	—	2.1	2.6	3.3	—	—	—
Long separation for objective reasons	—	—	—	—	3.1	3.8	5.4	—	—	7.7
Stepchildren	—	—	—	—	—	—	—	—	—	0.5
Existence of another family	—	—	—	—	—	—	—	—	—	21

A. D. M. Chechot, Sotsiologiia braka i razvoda, Leningrad, "Znanie" Publishers, 1973.

B. N. G. Iurkevich, Sovetskaia sem'ia. Funktsii i usloviia stabil'nosti, Minsk, Belorussian State University Press, 1970.

C. L. V. Chuiko, Braki i razvody, Moscow, "Statistika" Publishers, 1975.

D. V. T. Kokol'nikov, "Brachno-semeinye otnosheniia kolkhoznogo krest'ianstva (na materialakh zapadnykh oblastei Belorusskoi SSR)," author's abstract of candidate dissertation, Minsk, 1972.

E. S. M. Pelevin, "Voprosy effektivnosti pravovogo regulirovaniia razvodov v SSSR," author's abstract of candidate dissertation, Leningrad, 1972.

F. N. Ia. Solov'ev, Brak i sem'ia segodnia, Vilnius, 1977.

A. G. Kharchev and M. S. Matskovskii

and objective analysis of their personal lives and suffer from lapses of memory, to say nothing of the inclination of most to forget past events. The high degree of selectivity of memory must also be taken into account, i.e., the things that are remembered are those that are consistent with the views a person holds at the given moment. At the time of divorce people will naturally more readily remember the negative events in their former married lives than the positive events, which were probably more frequent in the earlier stages of their marriages. Certain psychological barriers that lead to a distortion of information are also an important source of confusion.

It seems that the overwhelming majority of these barriers play a definite role in answering questions about the reasons for divorce. We have already analyzed the barrier to consciousness in discussing the fact that many people find it impossible to objectively evaluate events in their personal lives. The barrier of rationalization can play an important role in a person's evaluation of the reasons for divorce. The person being questioned may try to rationalize his or her behavior and present reasons for divorce that are obvious and socially acceptable, or at least commonplace and encountered in the press.

Thus to increase the scientific and practical effectiveness of research on the reasons for divorce, it is necessary to eliminate a number of shortcomings in the methods used that prevent us from getting objective and comparable information.

Notes

1. See, for example, S. M. Pelevin, "Voprosy effektivnosti pravovogo regulirovaniia razvodov v SSSR," author's abstract of candidate dissertation, Leningrad, 1972; L. Iu Perchik, "Voprosy brachnosti i razvodimosti v SSSR," in Naselenie i narodnoe blagosostoianie, Trudy moskovskogo instituta ekonomicheskoi statistiki, vol. 3, Moscow, 1972, pp. 153-58; D. M. Chechot, Sotsiologiia braka i razvoda, Leningrad, "Znanie" Publishers, 1973; L. V. Chuiko, Braki i razvody, Moscow, "Statistika" Publishers, 1975; and N. G. Iurkevich, Sovetskaia sem'ia. Funktsii i usloviia stabil'nosti, Minsk, Belorussian State University Press, 1970.
2. See K. Marx and F. Engels, Ekonomichesko-filosofskie rukopisi 1844 goda, in Iz rannikh proizvedenii, Moscow, 1956, pp. 560, 602.
3. See, for example, A. G. Kharchev and S. N. Golod, Professional'naia rabota zhenshchin i sem'ia, Leningrad, 1971; F. Nye and L. W. Hoffman, The

<u>Employed Mother in America</u>, Chicago, 1965.

4. See A. G. Kharchev, "Sovremennaia sem'ia i ee problemy," <u>Zhurnalist</u>, 1972, no. 11, p. 59.

5. V. I. Perevedentsev, "Neobkhodimo stimulirovat' rost naseleniia v nashei strane," <u>Voprosy filosofii</u>, 1974, no. 11, p. 91.

6. Ibid., p. 91.

7. W. Goode, <u>After Divorce</u>, New York, 1956, p. 123.

8. H. Cristensen and K. Johnsen, <u>Marriage and the Family</u>, New York, 1971, p. 484.

9. P. Glick, <u>American Families</u>, New York, 1957, p. 213 [retranslated from the Russian].

10. Ibid., p. 226.

11. H. Christensen and K. Johnsen, op. cit., p. 485.

12. J. Bernard, "No News, but New Ideas," in <u>Divorce and After</u>, P. Bohannan, ed., New York, 1970 [retranslated from the Russian].

13. F. Nye, "Child Adjustment in Broken and in Unhappy Unbroken Homes," <u>Marriage and Family Living</u>, 1957, no. 19, pp. 356-61.

14. M. Rosenberg, <u>Society and the Adolescent Self-Image</u>, New York, 1965, pp. 85-106.

15. J. Landis, "The Trauma of Children When Parents Divorce," <u>Marriage and Family Living</u>, 1960, no. 22, pp. 7-13.

16. P. N. Fedoseev, "Problema sotsial'nogo i biologicheskogo v filosofii i sotsiologii," in <u>Biologicheskoe i sotsial'noe v razvitii cheloveka</u>, Moscow, 1977, p. 19.

17. D. M. Chechot, op. cit., pp. 29-30.

18. N. Ia. Solov'iev, <u>Brak i sem'ia segodnia</u>, Vilnius, 1977, p. 129.

19. D. M. Chechot, op. cit., p. 29.

20. V. Mathews and C. Mihanovich, "New Orientations on Marital Maladjustment," in <u>Dating and Marriage</u>, A. Kline and M. Medeey, eds., pp. 322, 332.

21. See Marx and Engels, <u>Sochineniia</u>, vol. 21, pp. 61, 65-70.

22. D. A. Kiknadze, <u>Potrebnosti. Povedenie. Vospitanie</u>, Moscow, 1968, p. 51.

11

Changes in the Status of Women and the Demographic Development of the Family

A. G. Volkov

Changes in the social status of women have a varied impact on the structure, functions, and social role of the family. Especially important here is the impact of the new status of women on the process of formation of the family, its development, and its breakup.

Reproduction of the population is, in the final analysis, reproduction of families, and social development affects population growth through their demographic development. The demographic development of the family (number of children, when they appear, how long they remain in their family of origin) influences the social structure and social functions of the family.

The purpose of this essay is to use materials of concrete sociodemographic surveys carried out in our country in the last few years to show how changes in the social status of women are reflected in the demographic characteristics and demographic development of the family.

In its demographic development the family passes through three stages: formation of the family, its growth with the birth of children, and its breakup, when the departure of grown children from the parental family marks the start of a new family.

Russian text © 1977 by "Nauka" Publishers. "Izmenenie polozheniia zhenshchiny i demograficheskoe razvitie sem'i," in *Izmenenie polozhenie zhenshchiny i sem'ia*, A. G. Kharchev, ed. (Moscow: "Nauka" Publishers, 1977), pp. 43-52.

The Demographic Development of the Family

It is especially interesting to study how changes in the status of women affect the time of family formation, notably the age at which women marry, the number of children and when they appear, divorce, and the splitting up of the family.

Comprehensive investigation of these problems is made difficult by inadequate data defining how these processes operate with different population groups and in different regions and how they relate to different features of the historical development of these groups, which is of special importance under the conditions of our multinational country.

The elimination of private ownership and women's inequality has done away with the proprietary nature of marriage and led to fundamental changes in the relationship between the sexes. Also, the illiteracy and occupational backwardness of women were overcome during the years of Soviet power, opening up broad opportunities for their participation in social production. All this significantly influenced the process of family formation. It is now usual for women to acquire their education and economic independence before marriage. In 1939, 90 of every thousand women had a higher, incomplete higher, or secondary (full or incomplete) education; in 1970 this number had reached 452. In those years, respectively, 104 and 651 women were employed in socialized production.[1]

The main growth in the number of women having an education is in the young age groups. This process is continuing. As of the beginning of the 1970/71 academic year, women accounted for 49% of the students at institutions of higher learning and 54% of the students in specialized educational institutions.[2] In cities families are formed later on the average than in rural communities (see the table on page 220).

The prevalent view that raising the educational level of the population usually leads to the postponement of marriage until after education is completed has not been confirmed by direct findings. Indirect testimony to this, however, can be seen in the very low percentage of married women in the younger age groups when they are still studying. Later marriages in cities, especially the larger ones, are evidently due not only to the fact

Proportion of Married Women (%)
among Women of Given Age Group

Age group	Cities		Villages	
	1959	1970	1959	1970
16-17	2.0	2.0	3.7	3.5
18-19	12.6	14.9	22.1	26.9
20-24	46.1	51.9	55.0	65.1
25-29	76.2	80.9	75.6	85.9

Itogi vsesoiuznoi perepisi naseleniia 1970 goda, Moscow, 1972, vol. 2, p. 263.

that cities have so many institutes of higher learning and specialized secondary educational establishments, but also to the fact that more young people live outside the parental family; for them it is relatively more important to gain economic independence and create other preconditions for setting up a family.

The figures in the table refer to the USSR as a whole. There are, however, substantial differences between marriage ages in different regions. Even though the traditions of early and very early marriages among the indigenous peoples of the Central Asian union republics have been considerably weakened, early marriages there still remain fairly frequent. Thus, according to L. F. Darskii, in 1949-59 the probability of a woman marrying at 17 in rural areas of regions with a high birthrate (the Central Asian union republics, Azerbaidzhan, and others) was twice as high as in cities of the same regions, and more than five times greater than in rural areas of regions with a low birthrate (the Ukraine, Latvia, Estonia, and others).[3]

In 1970 more than half the women in our country entered their first marriage between the ages of 20 to 24.

A number of recent demographic works note a rise in the average age at marriage. However, this age depends to a great extent on the age composition of the potentially marriageable population, and hence on the number of marriages, and the age at marriage,

in preceding years. The table on page 220 indicates rather
the reverse: a decline in the marrying age of women; and judging by the percentage of married women in each group, it is
more rapid in rural localities.

As for urban women, two circumstances are evidently of importance. On the one hand, the conditions of urban life, notably
the earlier socialization of young people, especially in big cities,
contribute to the transformation of social norms regulating sexual relations outside of marriage. "Weakening of the traditional
ban on premarital sexual relations," writes L. E. Darskii,
"has resulted in more premarital liaisons, which are often just an
extended form of marriage in which the initiation of sexual
relations precedes the formal and actual conclusion of marriage."[4]

On the other hand, the trend toward earlier marriages appears also to be a result of the fact that with family planning so
common, marriage is not necessarily associated with the immediate appearance of children.

The changing status of women has had a profound effect not
only on the timing of family formation but also on the character
and pace of demographic development of the family. The first
thing to be noted here is the tendency to limit the number of
children.

The changing character of women's work, now usually performed outside the home, and often at a considerable distance
from it, has resulted in shifting the center of social intercourse to
the place of work, on the one hand, and in a change in the structure of the time budget, on the other. Women's participation in
social production has not only assured them economic independence but also expanded the scope of social intercourse. All
this has resulted in a fundamental change in the structure of
needs.

The growth of occupational knowledge expands the need
for work in occupations that provide income and social
status and increase the need for new and more varied forms
of recreation. As well-being rises, so do material requirements.

Development of the mass media and concentration of the population in big cities increases contacts between people and results in the dissemination of new concepts of desired or preferred family life styles.

Radical changes in the structure of needs, as well as the transformation of social values in general and the value of the family in particular, have primarily affected attitudes toward children. With the loss of the family's production function, children are no longer "insurance" against old age: old age security is now provided by society. The need to accumulate a service record and the desire to keep abreast of professional knowledge are an inducement to women to avoid lengthy interruptions in work caused by the birth and rearing of children.

The value of education for both parents and children has increased. In the absence of privileges based on property or class, education and professional and occupational training have become one of the basic criteria of social status.

Finally, family expectations have also risen with regard to the content of the children's education and the conditions under which they are brought up. Even with the general improvement in families' material circumstances, and even though the society assumes a considerable share of the care for children, the fewer children in the family, the more attention and resources, all other things being equal, the parents can devote to them. Socialized child care and education help the mother combine employment with child rearing. However, the contradiction between a woman's professional work and her social role as wife and mother still remains. When a mother spends her whole workday outside the home, she naturally devotes less time to bringing up children, although she gives it greater meaning.

All the above circumstances have resulted in the wide spread of so-called family planning. A planned family is a small family.

According to an extensive survey of 33,000 women from blue-collar and white-collar families carried out by the Demography Laboratory of the Scientific Research Institute of the Central Statistical Administration of the USSR, answers to the question

222

"How many children do you intend to have?" were distributed as follows.[5]

Expected number of children	% of women giving this number
0	1.0
1	15.4
2	52.6
3	19.5
4 or more	11.5

The average number of children the women expected to have was 2.42. The proportion of women planning to remain childless was very small, only 1.0%. Most women who responded to the questionnaire (69.0%) intended to have no more than two children. Only 5% of those polled gave no definite answer.

A similar picture is revealed by similar local surveys. For example, a poll of some 14,000 women in Latvia who had married in 1959 revealed that 90% of those with two children had no intention of having any more.[6]

Special studies indicate, however, that the desire for a small family should not be seen solely in terms of the contradiction between a woman's work and her social role as a wife and mother, or as a result of the fact that the growth of material and spiritual needs runs ahead of possibilities for satisfying them.

The changing status of women has led to a transformation of the whole range of their needs and interests, including the realm of family and marital relations. The "natural" function of bearing children is increasingly influenced by social factors, and the demographic function of the family is influenced by such functions as specialization, social intercourse, consumption, and so forth.

Evolving living conditions and fundamental changes in social status have led women to develop specific notions regarding the number of children a family should have; a clear demographic ideal of the family has taken shape. This is indicated by the responses to a question in the aforementioned survey, "How many children do you think a family should generally have?" It is significant that only 3.4% of the women gave no definite answer to this question.

The nature of this ideal is indicated by the following figures: [7]

"Ideal" number of children	% of women giving this number
0	0.4
1	1.5
2	41.0
3	39.4
4 or more	17.7

The average "best" number of children per family was 2.89. The overwhelming majority of women (80.4%) thought two or three children made the ideal family. Moreover, their views were only marginally affected by the number of children they already had. Whereas the average optimum family size as seen by childless women was 2.7 children, it was 2.5 for women with one child, 2.8 for women with two children, and 3.3 for women with three children. All the polled women were still of childbearing age. In regions with high birthrates a fairly high proportion of women considered the best family to be one with fewer children than they actually had.

The new attitudes on the number of children in a family have also been influenced by the decline in infant mortality, which has dropped over the last sixty years to less than one tenth of what it had been, and now stands at 26 per 1,000 newly born.

One factor somewhat influencing the number of children may be the parents' desire to have another child of a particular sex. A third child most frequently appears in families where the first two are of the same sex. The effect of such factors, however, is considerably less than that of the social factors mentioned before.

The Demographic Development of the Family

We will not consider the specifically demographic problem
of the dependence of the number of children in a family on the
age at marriage. We will note only that the later a woman marries, the lower, under otherwise equal circumstances, the fertility of that marriage. This dependence, however, varies widely
according to social and ethnic group and is less apparent in
planned families and more apparent among population groups
that do not practice family planning. It is therefore possible
that both marriage age and the number of children in a family
are influenced by the same social and sociopsychological factors.

The second significant feature in the demographic development of the family is not only a reduction in the total number
of children but a change in their timing and the intervals between births. The proportion of women having children early,
especially between 20 and 24, is growing. The trend is for the
first child to appear earlier and earlier in married life. The
mean interval between marriage and the first baby declined
from 2.3 years for women who had first married in 1920-24 to
1.7 years for women first married in 1945-49. [8] At the same
time, mothers of large families tend to have their first child
on average later than mothers of small families. According
to some studies, a decrease in the number of children is accompanied by an increase in the intervals between births. Also,
on average, childbearing is ending earlier and earlier, as indicated by the reduction in the average age of women at birth
of their last child from the older to younger generations. Thus
according to a survey conducted in 1960, women in the 70-74
year age group had had their last baby on average when they
were 39.1 years old, while women in the 50-54 group had last
had a baby at 34.2 years. [9]

The demographic development of the family is influenced by
the stability of marriage. The stability of marriage has to some
extent been eroded by the legal and economic independence of
women, the focus on the personal qualities of the future spouse
in choosing one's mate, and the elimination of the former per-
manence of marriage. Another cause may be earlier marriages,
when young women have not yet achieved social and psychologi-

cal maturity: it is a known fact that divorces are greater among early and short marriages. The number of children also influences marital stability. With only one child (or even two children) the spouse's sense of responsibility for the family's fate is reduced. And if one of the spouses was an only child, he or she is relatively worse prepared to perform the role of spouse. Moreover, with an extensive network of preschool educational establishments, a woman is in a position to bring up a child alone. (We will not mention the comparatively rare cases when divorce is due to childlessness of the spouses.) The independence of women in the realm of marital and family relations is confirmed by the fact that in a substantial number of cases, it is the woman who seeks to dissolve the marriage.

From the point of view of the demographic development of the family, it should be noted that divorce leads either to the formation of an incomplete, stunted family, when the mother remains with the child alone, or to the enlargement of a family if she returns to her parents. In either case the negative effect of this on the reproduction of the population is indubitable (if a new marriage does not take place). It should be added that divorce is most frequent among young people, which on the average slows family growth.

In the third stage of development of the family (the stage of breakup), the grown-up children marry and either leave the parental family or live with their parents until the latters' death. In the former case we have a breakup of the old family and formation of a new one; in the latter we have first a growth, then a reduction in size — but in either case there is a change in the family's demographic structure.

Of great importance in the demographic development of the family is the departure of the grown children from the parental family. Unfortunately, due to certain methodological difficulties, this process and its effects on the structure of the family have not been adequately studied. Grown children leave the family at different times and different ages. If they go on to form families of their own, this means a change in the composition of the family of both wife and husband. In view of the need to take into

226

account the age characteristics of family members and the diversity of demographic events, traditional methods of studying demographic processes are not applicable. One can study the views of families of different composition regarding the time of such separation; but in judging the actual rate of separation, this information should be used with great caution (as in all cases of evaluating opinions about facts).

Furthermore, the splitting up of the new family takes place gradually. Frequently the young family first separates from the paternal family economically, and only later territorially. Sometimes, on the contrary, material ties remain after territorial division. Marriage may either prevent or follow division. Apparently both the point at which a couple marries and that at which an independent household appears should be taken as criteria of family division.

The rate of family division is also affected by the earlier socialization of young people and their achieving independent livelihood, both of which promote the economic independence of their parents. Surveys reveal that a significant proportion of newly married couples want to live apart from their parents, and it can be assumed that they leave as soon as circumstances permit. On the other hand, a young family in which both spouses work or study needs parental help in looking after the children and frequently in running the household, which results either in delaying division or in temporarily rejoining the mother's family when the daughter has a baby. Some role in this process can also be played by the death of one member of an elderly couple. Often the surviving spouse joins the family of an adult child.

The spread of small families is a factor in earlier division of the families of mother and daughter. In large families, even when the older children leave, the younger children remain with the mother until she reaches pension age. In small families, when the first or second child leaves, this means the complete breakup of the family. The process of "younger motherhood" noted before apparently also plays an important part in other respects. In many cases, when the first, or even second, child leaves the family, the mother may still be 40 or 45, that is, of working age, with an income of her own. In such circumstances the role of "grandmother" apparently does not appeal to her, and this also contributes to the breakup of families.

Under the conditions of the scientific and technological revolution, when the process of accumulation of knowledge is highly intensified, the difference in age between parents and children also implies some difference in needs and interests, a factor which, other things being equal, intensifies "centrifugal forces" within the family.

The earlier departure of grown children from the family is also facilitated by the general rise in material well-being, notably the steady improvement in housing conditions.

It is evident that the trend toward earlier division of families predominates. It is indicated indirectly by the considerable number of families in which only two generations are represented. The percentage of such families was 79.6% in Viriatino Village, Tambov Oblast, 70.8% in the Transcarpathian Ukraine, 78.9% in Lithuania,[10] and 82.4% in Bolotnoe District, Novosibirsk Oblast. [11] The majority of families are simple, consisting of one couple, with or without children. According to the 1970 census, of a total of 58.7 million families, 37.3 million, or 64%, were families consisting of one married couple, with or without children; 9.4 million families included one of the spouses' parents or other relatives.[12] This confirms A. G. Kharchev's hypothesis that the family is moving toward a common structure: a group based on monogamous marriage and reduced to its "natural size" — parents and their children. [13]

Examination of the aforementioned processes leads to the conclusion that the profound changes in the social status of women that have taken place in our country over the past half-century have had a broad and multifaceted effect on the demographic development of the family, and thereby on the overall course of the reproduction of the population. Investigation of this influence helps not only to forecast further developments in the family structure of the population but also to develop necessary measures for bringing social influence to bear on these processes.

The Demographic Development of the Family

Notes

1. Itogi Vsesoiuznoi perepisi naseleniia 1970 goda, Moscow, 1972, vol. 3, pp. 364, 365, 559.

2. Vestnik statistiki, 1972, no. 1, p. 90.

3. L. E. Darskii, "Tablitsy brachnosti zhenshchin SSSR (po vyborochnym dannym)," in Izuchenie vosproizvodstva naseleniia, Moscow, 1968, p. 97.

4. Ibid., pp. 84-85.

5. V. A. Belova, "Obsledovanie mnenii o nailuchshem i ozhidaemom chisle detei v sem'e," Vestnik statistiki, 1971, no. 6, p. 30.

6. P. P. Zvin'drish, "Dinamika i demograficheskie faktory rozhdaemosti v Latvii," in Voprosy demografii (issledovaniia, problemy, metody), Moscow, 1970, pp. 253, 254.

7. Belova, op. cit., p. 26.

8. R. I. Sifman, "Intervaly mezhdu rozhdeniiami i mezhdu vstupleniem v brak i pervym rozhdeniem," in Izuchenie vosproizvodstva naseleniia, p. 115.

9. R. I. Sifman, "Dinamika plodovitosti kogort zhenshchin v SSSR," in Voprosy demografii (issledovaniia, problemy, metody), p. 151.

10. A. G. Kharchev, Brak i sem'ia v SSSR, Moscow, 1964, p. 231.

11. A. G. Volkov, "Analiz struktury sem'i dlia prognoza chisla semei i ikh sostava," in Problemy demograficheskoi statistiki, Moscow, 1966, p. 32.

12. Itogi Vsesoiuznoi perepisi naseleniia 1970 goda, Moscow, 1974, vol. 7, pp. 238-239.

13. A. G. Kharchev, "Byt i sem'ia kak kategorii istoricheskogo materializma," in Problemy byta, braka i sem'i, Vilnius, 1970, p. 16.

12

Maternal Care of Infants

I. Katkova

In recent years specialists in various fields have been devoting considerable attention to studying the factors which impede the birth of the desired number of children in families.

An analysis of the findings of such studies reveals that among the reasons noted by women, along with material and housing conditions, were others, such as the difficulty of raising children of preschool age and the difficulty of combining participation in social production with maternal functions.

It is well known that families experience particular difficulties in arranging care for children during the first years of their lives. Investigation of some of these difficulties was the purpose of a survey of young families carried out in the city of Tambov by the Department of Social Hygiene and the Organization of Public Health of the I. M. Sechenov First Moscow Medical Institute.[1] Data were gathered on the length of time a woman spent on nonpaid leave after the birth of a child. In addition, case histories of the development of children from the surveyed families were analyzed in children's clinics. Information was obtained on the incidence of illness, its frequency

Russian text © 1978 by "Statistika" Publishers. "Materinskii ukhod za novorozhdennym," in *Zhenshchiny na rabote i doma*, D. I. Valentei et al., eds. (Moscow: "Statistika" Publishers, 1978), pp. 38-46.

and duration in the first three years of life of 565 first-born children; data were also obtained on the temporary inability of mothers to work because they had to look after sick children during this three-year period.[2]   Data from a questionnaire (survey) of the socioeconomic status of the family during the first years of marriage were also drawn into the analysis.

According to the labor legislation of the Soviet Union and the union republics,[3] women are entitled, in addition to pregnancy and maternity leave, to leave of absence without pay until the child is one year old. According to the findings of the Tambov survey of 565 young families with children, 32% of the women did not take advantage of the leave after the birth of the first child (14.3% of them were studying), 37.3% did not work during the first six months of the baby's life, 24.4% did not work during the first year, and 6.3% did not work for over a year. An analysis of the causes connected with women's remaining home showed that 42.8% of the women were obliged to do so because of the absence of space in nurseries, 19.3% because of the illness of the baby, and 37.1% declared they wanted to look after and raise the child themselves during the first year of its life. It is interesting to note that irrespective of the length of the interruption of work, only 6% of the women said they would like to continue looking after the child for three years without working.

Women's desire to care for infants only during the first year was also noted in the research by V. N. Shcherbakov.[4] According to his findings 60% of the working women in Moscow and 40% in Kaluga went back to work one year after the baby's birth. But, the author notes, of the women who returned to work earlier, only 20.6% used the services of the day nurseries. He also found that the higher their mother's educational level, the greater the number of mothers who raised their children themselves during the first year. In our study we found an inverse relationship on this issue. This contradiction can be explained by differences in the composition of the surveyed groups of women according to length of employment, length of marriage, type of work, and level of material and living conditions of the family.

According to the survey conducted in Tambov, 64.9% of the
women with higher, incomplete higher, or secondary specialized
education went back to work before the child reached the age of
one, but only 54.3% of the women with general secondary or
lower education did so. Obviously, for women with higher, incomplete higher, or specialized secondary education, two factors play a definite role here: on the one hand, their greater
material interest in work, since, having studied longer than
women who completed only secondary school and hence began
work earlier, they are faced with greater material problems,
while their demands and expectations are higher; on the other
hand, their need for interesting, creative work and their unwillingness to lose their high qualifications by staying away
from work too long.

Among a cohort of women residents in Alma-Ata, the average
duration of unpaid leave during the period was 115.5 days for
women of the first group, as compared with 215.8 days for
women of the second group.[5] In our view this is connected with
the fact that women with higher, incomplete higher, or secondary education have a greater interest in their professional activity and want to return to work sooner after the birth of a
child than women with lower levels of education.

The Tambov survey showed that the longer the spouses'
working careers, the more likely is the wife to take advantage
of the opportunity to interrupt work to look after the child for
a full year (32.2%), as compared with women with length of
employment of fewer than three years (13.5%). This is probably because these women have attained an adequate level of
qualification and social status and are not afraid of losing it
in one year, which new workers find much more difficult.

The surveys of families in Tambov and Alma-Ata,[6] as well
as data obtained by V. N. Shcherbakov and N. V. Trofimova,
reveal a direct relationship between the length of time a mother
remains away from work after having a baby and the family's
income. Thus in Tambov, among newlywed families with
monthly incomes of more than 100 rubles per family member,
31.2% of the women resumed work only when the child reached

the age of one, while in families with per capita incomes of up to 50 rubles, only 14.3% of the women stayed away from work this long.

In modern families, as we know, women's wages constitute a basic part of the family budget. According to the data of N. S. Lagutin and G. P. Sergeeva, of 100 couples, one sixth of the spouses have virtually the same wages, 25% of the women receive higher wages, and some 25% receive wages 30% lower than those of their husbands.[7]

The authors note that young spouses typically have more equal levels of pay. Consequently the mother's staying home during the baby's first year appreciably worsens the material situation of young couples during the early years of marriage. This can be illustrated with data from our family survey (see Table 1).

An analysis of Table 1 shows that, after subtracting from the general family budget resulting from the woman's staying home to look after the child until it is one year of age, the number of families with monthly incomes of less than 50 rubles per member increased fivefold where women had general secondary or less education, while the increase in families where the women had a higher level of education was ninefold. It should be noted that the average level of pay in the former group was 77 rubles, and in the latter, 83 rubles.[8]

The decision of the Twenty-fifth Congress of the CPSU to provide partial pay for working women who take leave to look after children until one year of age was an important step in improving the country's system of protection of maternity and infancy. Its significance as a medical and social measure is confirmed by actual sociohygienic studies of infant health in the first year of life. It is known that the duration of breast feeding and the start of formula feeding are important factors determining a baby's health. One of the reasons for early formula feeding is the mother's early return to work. Early return to work was found, in a number of cases, to lead to more frequent respiratory illness, including pneumonia (see Table 2).

We see from Table 2 that the incidence of pneumonia among

Table 1

Women's Education and Family Incomes

(per 100 women of corresponding level of education)

Income per family member (rubles)	Woman's education			
	general secondary or less		secondary or higher	
	family income			
	at marriage	minus loss due to woman's not working during first year of child's life	at marriage	minus loss due to woman's not working during first year of child's life
– 50	13.39	64.83	6.87	62.50
50– 70	16.54	28.87	16.25	29.37
71–100	55.11	4.70	50.63	6.25
100 +	14.96	1.6	26.25	1.88

Table 2

Disease Rate of First-Born in First Year of Life
(per 100 surveyed in Tambov)

Age of baby at which mother went back to work	Mother's education					
	general secondary or less			specialized secondary or higher		
	baby disease rate					
	pneumonia	acute respiratoral	total	pneumonia	acute respiratoral	total
Immediately after end of maternity leave	28.57	157.14	300.95	14.29	240.48	371.2
1.5 to 6 months	25.49	192.81	320.27	22.8	208.77	370.18
6 to 12 months	19.35	173.13	281.75	17.65	205.88	355.88
Total	24.01	174.93	304.22	18.8	218.04	366.92

babies whose mothers remained home only for the duration of maternity leave was lower by one half in the case of better educated mothers than for mothers with lower education.

However, the frequency of acute respiratoral diseases among babies whose mothers have a higher or specialized secondary education is somewhat greater than among those whose mothers have a lower level of education. A deeper study of this phenomenon reveals that it is due to earlier discharge of the babies after sickness, which contributes not only to more frequent respiratory diseases but also to more acute and lengthier bouts of pneumonia.

A similar relationship is noted in the work of G. V. Bespoludina, who shows that the risk of babies contracting chronic pneumonia increases with the parents' education. She also found that the course of acute pneumonia in first babies is most unfavorable.[9]

In V. N. Shcherbakov's study mentioned above, women workers who had no help at home in looking after children tended to take the child back to the nursery sooner after a disease. As a consequence, 25.6% of the babies of these working mothers had a recurrence of the disease within three days after returning to the nursery. According to N. V. Polunina,[10] in 51% of the cases in the first year of life, the interval between two cases of acute respiratoral disease was thirty days, and in half of them it was ten to twenty days.

How can the influence of children's illness on the mood, emotional states, relations between spouses, and a woman's maternal happiness be measured? Science has yet to offer an objective assessment of this.

The state, we know, assumes a substantial part of the costs of treating a sick child.[11] On December 1, 1975, additional benefits in temporary disability pay were introduced,[12] including benefits for caring for a sick member of the family. For families with three or more children under 16 years of age (18 for students), the allowance for time spent caring for a sick child is 100% of regular wages regardless of length of employment. It would be worthwhile to consider similar benefits for caring for a first child, especially during the first years of its life, which usually occur during the first years of married life, when couples more frequently experience material difficulties.

Beginning December 1, 1973, in accordance with the decisions of the Twenty-fourth Congress of the CPSU, all working women and collective farm members, regardless of length of employment, will receive full wages during pregnancy and maternity leave. This important decree was prompted by great concern for women as mothers and workers.

Despite the positive assessment of the role of primary maternal care for the newborn baby, in some cases in which a family experiences less favorable material or housing conditions, bringing up the baby at home may reinforce unfavorable effects on its health, and even breast feeding may not always compensate for this. Yet precisely in this group of women, as well as among women with the lowest educational or occupational levels, it is typical that the doctor is called in late or with some delay when the baby gets sick. This trend may not only continue but even grow, since thanks to maternity leave, women do not have to enroll their children in nurseries, where the children receive regular conditioning exercises.

Unfortunately, many parents make various mistakes in looking after their infants. That is why thorough and even greater medical control is essential to insure that mothers adhere to all sanitary and hygienic requirements of baby care.

The family plays a great part in performing daily preventive measures, and the fact that children get sick even under the most favorable conditions is a reflection of insufficient attention by the mother to her role in maintaining the baby's health and preventing illness and in caring for it during and after an illness.

Preventive medical observation of infants during the first year of life, in conjunction with primary maternal care of infants, must be strengthened, both by the family and by medical institutions.

The quality of maternal care plays so great a role that pains-

237

taking care, systematic and regular preventive observation, and adherence to all norms of hygienic upbringing of babies deserve to be encouraged, in our view, by higher rates of payment for partially paid maternal leave.

Works by social hygienists note that when children's clinics carefully prepare children to enter preschool institutions, the disease rate during the adaptation period at nurseries is reduced by more than half, mainly by cutting the number of acute respiratorial diseases.

In recent years it has been demonstrated that the health of parents, especially of the mother during pregnancy, influences the health of children.

In our country the high employment of women in social production has been noted. The Communist Party and Soviet state pay constant attention to improving working conditions for women by improving sanitary and hygienic conditions at work and promoting various preventive measures.

To assure the birth of healthy babies, the question of increasing prenatal leave for pregnant women depending on their health and type of work is on the agenda. This would considerably reduce the risk of adverse events during pregnancy and delivery and of premature births. Our estimates show that the cost of a premature birth is higher. It is therefore worthwhile to increase expenditures on sociomedical measures aimed at preventing premature births.

Speaking at the Twenty-fifth Congress of the CPSU, L. I. Brezhnev stressed that a great deal still needed to be done to improve the production of the health of mothers and children.[13]

An effective demographic policy in the future must help improve the health of these groups of the population, as prompted by the tremendous concern of the party and government for the destinies of future generations of the builders of communist society.

Questions of maternal and child protection are an important element in the implementation of a comprehensive demographic policy.

Maternal Care of Infants

Notes

1. For more on the study program, see A. F. Serenko, I. P. Katkova, N. A. Kravchenko, G. G. Grancharova, Kogortnyi metod v sotsial'no-gigienicheskom izuchenii rozhdaemosti v molodykh sem'iakh (Metodika issledovaniia), Moscow, 1971.
The study data are representative of families in cities in Tambov Oblast that are similar to the studied groups of families.

2. This article deals mainly with family problems associated with the birth and care for a child in its first year of life.

3. See Zakonodatel'stvo o pravakh zhenshchin v SSSR, Moscow, 1975, pp. 75-76.

4. See V. N. Shcherbakov, "Sotsial'no-gigienicheskoe znachenie i ekonomicheskaia effektivnost' iasel'nogo obsluzhivaniia detei rabotnits promyshlennykh predpriiatii," author's abstract of a candidate's dissertation, Moscow, 1972.

5. See I. P. Katkova and N. A. Kravchenko, "Nekotorye mediko-sotsial'nye problemy v sviazi s rozhdeniem pervogo rebenka (po dannym obsledovaniia molodykh semei v gorodakh Tambove i Alma-Ate)," in Kompleksnoe izuchenie sostoianiia zdorov'ia naseleniia Tambovskoi oblasti v sviazi so Vsesoiuznoi perepis'iu naseleniia 1970 g., Tambov, 1973, pp. 59-66.

6. See ibid.

7. See N. S. Lagutin and G. P. Sergeeva, Sotsial'no-ekonomicheskoe polozhenie zhenshchiny v SSSR, Moscow, 1975, p. 15.

8. In studying the effects of family income on demographic trends or disease rates, it is necessary to take into account changes in women's wages. Thus it is our impression that an investigation of the effect of family income on child mortality that takes into account the above recommendations would help establish more clear-cut relationships. In studying the effects of family income on the birthrate, finding that an increase in income is due to higher wages brought home by women may lead to the assumption that the increase is related to her being more busy, thus establishing a mechanism for the reverse effect.

9. See G. V. Bespoludina, "Dispansernoe nabliudenie za det'mi, stradaiushchimi khronicheskoi pneumoniei, i perspektivy ego uluchsheniia (po materialam spetsial'nogo issledovaniia)," author's abstract of a candidate's dissertation, Voroshilovgrad, 1975.

10. See N. V. Polunina, "Kompleksnoe sotsial'no-gigienicheskoe issledovanie sostoianiia zdorov'ia detei pervykh trekh let zhizni," author's abstract of a candidate's dissertation, Moscow, 1973.

11. See Decree of USSR Council of Ministers of July 26, 1973 (SP SSSR 1973 g., no. 18, p. 102). It provides for seven days of sick leave for the care of a sick child under 14, and ten days for single mothers, widows, and divorcees to care for a child under seven.

12. See G. S Simonenko, V interesakh materi i rebenka, Moscow, 1976, pp. 71-72.

13. See Materialy XXV s''ezda KPSS, p. 41.

13

Women with Large Families:
A Sociodemographic Analysis

O. Ata-Mirzaev

A great deal of demographic research is currently being conducted in our country. Significantly, it is based not only on official statistics but in large measure also on special sociological-demographic surveys. Each such survey is specifically targeted, making possible more profound analyses of the socioeconomic and sociopsychological mechanisms of demographic processes. Especially valuable from the methodological point of view have been the studies by R. I. Sifman, V. A. Belova, L. A. Darskii, and A. I. Antonov carried out over the last few years.

The purpose of this paper is to offer a sociodemographic analysis of large families based on a special sample survey of mothers of large families in Tashkent.[1]

We should note that in our opinion, demographers are not paying sufficient attention to studies of large families. Yet as a current sociodemographic phenomenon, large families continue and will continue to exert considerable influence on the dynamics of population growth in the USSR.

Given the well-known decline in the birthrate in most union republics and the country as a whole and the persistence of the tradition

Russian text © 1978 by "Statistika" Publishers. "Zhenshchina s mnogodetnoi sem'ei: Sotsiologicheskii analiz," in *Zhenshchiny na rabote i doma*, D. I. Valentei et al., eds. (Moscow: "Statistika" Publishers, 1978). pp. 28-37.

of large families among the Central Asian peoples, the dynamics of population growth in the USSR will apparently be largely determined by the high natural increase of the population in Central Asia.

Large families are more common in the Central Asian republics than in others. According to the 1970 Census, the proportion of children under 15 in the overall population was about 45% in the Central Asian republics, 24.2% in the Baltic republics, 26.5% in the RSFSR, and 28.9% nationwide. Moreover, for the USSR as a whole this index had declined by 3.9% since 1959, while in Central Asia it had increased by 6.8%.

In most union republics large families are the exception, but among the peoples of Central Asia they are typical. In the Uzbek SSR alone there are at present some 645,000 mothers of large families.

According to some data, native women want to have on average six or seven children; and in 1970 the actual fertility of women (average number of children per woman between 15 and 49 years of age) in Uzbekistan's rural communities was 7.3.[2]

Large families should be seen as a component of deliberate reproductive behavior expressed in meeting a woman's or couple's need to have children. At the family level, having many children stems from the traditions of a particular ethnic community and from the mores of the socioethnic environment in which the individual, the family, and their value orientations develop.

Family and marital traditions form within the framework of an ethnic community and are therefore very conservative. They change under the direct impact of socioeconomic conditions that strengthen some traditions and weaken or eliminate others. The favorable socioeconomic conditions of the Soviet period, especially the period of developed socialism, have created many opportunities for the Central Asian peoples to express their national traditions, including the tradition of large families.

In our survey Uzbek women and women of other indigenous peoples of Central Asia constituted the overwhelming majority

of mothers of large families — 93.1% — although the survey
covered city districts with great ethnic diversity as well as those
with a clearly preponderant nonindigenous population. The number of women with large families was negligible. The surveyed
group included 2.4% Russians and Ukrainians, 3% Tatars, and
1.5% other nationalities.

It is important to note that a large number of mothers of
large families of nonindigenous ethnic background were found
in mixed marriages.

More than half the surveyed women were under 40, and of
them 10% were 25-30 years old, that is, born after the war.
This is further confirmation of the persistence of the large-
family tradition and the increase in the birthrate among young
people from indigenous ethnic groups, which has been noted by
many researchers.

Many researchers think that education is a factor directly
influencing the birthrate. They note that the higher a woman's
education, the lower the birthrate and hence the number of children in the family. In particular, N. Tauber, analyzing the results of a survey of Moscow women, writes: "In analyzing the
connection between women's education and the average number
of children, our survey has again confirmed the inverse relationship: the highest number of children was found among women with
up to eighth-grade education: 1.19; then with increasing education the average number of children declines in each group,
down to a minimum of 0.89 for women with higher education."[3]

Our survey did not confirm this. We discovered no substantial differences in the average number of children among
mothers of large families with different educational levels.

Table 1 shows, first of all, that the percentage of women with
a higher, incomplete higher, or specialized secondary education among mothers of large families is fairly high: 19.2%.
Furthermore, mothers of large families with a higher education have a quite high average number of children, close to
the groups with no specialized education and the average number of children for the whole surveyed group.

It is thus our view that in the Uzbek SSR, education alone is

Table 1

Educational Level of Mothers of Large Families and
Average Number of Children in Family

Education	Number of women		Average number of children		
	persons	%	overall	working women	nonworking women
Higher	160	10.0	5.1	5.0	5.5
Incomplete higher	19	1.2	4.5	4.4	4.8
Specialized secondary	126	8.0	4.7	4.6	5.0
General secondary	243	15.0	5.1	4.7	5.5
Incomplete secondary	474	29.4	5.9	5.8	6.0
Primary	594	36.4	6.1	5.9	6.2
Total	1,616	100.0	5.6	5.4	6.0

243

no serious barrier to a woman's having many children. In analyzing the effect of education on the birthrate and the average number of children in a family, it is necessary to take into account a whole complex of socioeconomic and psychological preconditions affecting reproductive views and mores at the micro- and macrolevel.

However, it must be noted that women with a higher or a specialized secondary education who participate actively in social production and have a moral (not just a material) incentive to work are still more inclined to family planning. But here again, the question is not of a third or fourth child but of a fifth or more. It can consequently be assumed that women of the indigenous ethnic groups whose conscious reproductive behavior has formed or is forming at the present stage are oriented toward the "average" number of children typical of Central Asia.

Rural women of indigenous nationalities characteristically display an unconscious orientation toward large families, and the birthrate of the great majority approaches the physiological limit.

It seems that in an urban environment, especially in Tashkent, some categories of Uzbek women have begun to develop a conscious reproductive behavior oriented toward four or five children. Thus the survey revealed that the average number of children per mother of a large family was 5.6 in Tashkent, as compared with 7.3 for rural women.

It follows that in Tashkent, childbearing among women of the indigenous nationality is gradually declining as a consequence of family planning. The trend will apparently spread to the whole indigenous urban population, although at present there is no sharp tendency toward family planning among the indigenous urban population, even in larger Uzbek cities.

In Central Asia conscious reproductive attitudes are developing only among populations of highly urbanized regions, mainly in the capital cities of the union republics. While anticipating a reduction in the birthrate among women of the indigenous nationality in urbanized regions, we should keep in mind that its minimum will be higher than the current birthrate among women of European stock. It is, therefore, apparently premature to speak of any "gradual convergence of different ethnic communities with respect to their demographic and, notably, reproductive behavior."[4] It is all the more inappropriate, in our view, to proceed at the present time from this assumption in determining future birthrate trends, as G. A. Bondarskaia writes.

The reproductive level of the indigenous population of Central Asia will remain fairly high in the foreseeable and more distant future. At the same time, continued studies of apparent trends and features in the development of conscious reproductive behavior in Tashkent and other capital cities of the Central Asian republics are of great scientific and practical importance.

The results of our survey show that having many children is a basis of family stability. At the time of the survey, 92.5% of the mothers of large families were married; most of them were in their first marriage, and only very few were in their second. Widows accounted for 6.6%, and only 0.9% were divorced. This again confirms the low divorce rate typical of Central Asian peoples, a rate directly associated with large families. Among the indigenous peoples divorce is exceptional, especially if they have large families. Moreover, the main reason for divorce is usually the infertility of one of the spouses.

Most mothers of large families married at a fairly early age. Among the surveyed women some 40% had married before 20, and 81.1% before 25.

As Table 2 shows, during the Soviet years the average marrying age of mothers and fathers of large families has been consistently declining. As a result the difference between the mean marrying age of women born in 1915-19 and 1950-54 was 11 years, and among men born in 1915-19 and 1945-49 it was 6.3 years. The average marrying age of men is somewhat higher than of women in almost all age brackets.

In general, during the Soviet years a clear trend toward a drop in the marrying age of people of indigenous stock has become apparent. This is a reflection of profound socioeconomic changes accompanied by a steady rise in material well-being and a major consolidation of the family's economic base.

O. Ata-Mirzaev

Given the persistent traditions of large, cohesive families among people of indigenous ethnic groups, today's favorable socioeconomic conditions encourage relatively early marriages close to the legal marriage age. There are also traditional principles that strictly define the order by age of marriages in large families (see Table 2).

Table 2

Years of Birth and Marrying Ages of Mothers
and Fathers of Large Families

Years of birth	Age	Average age at marriage	
		women	men
1915-19	61-57	28.8	28.0
1920-24	56-52	22.6	26.6
1925-29	51-47	22.0	25.5
1930-34	46-42	21.1	25.2
1935-39	41-37	20.6	24.8
1940-44	36-32	20.1	24.3
1945-49	31-27	19.3	21.7
1950-54	26-22	17.8	*

*No figure because of negligible total number.

A mother of a large family is a "great toiler." In the surveyed group more than half the mothers of large families — 53% — were employed in social production. These women are, naturally, "doubly employed," with all the undesirable consequences thereof. It should be noted, however, that the burden of running a household is greatly reduced for the mother of a large family by the help she gets from both adult and younger members of the family.

As her children grow up, the mother of a large family has more and more opportunities to work, which is confirmed by the findings of our survey.

The proportion of young mothers who work is not high. The

employment rate increases steadily with the age of the woman and, consequently, her children. The employment rate among the women surveyed peaks at 37-41 years, reaching 68.3%. In later years the older children reach working age, and they are regarded as an important economic asset to the family. From this time on the employment of women declines sharply, and this is encouraged by the early retirement age, which is 50 years for mothers with many children.

The survey also showed that there is no clear-cut, direct relationship between female employment in social production and large families, although it could be noted that among nonworking women, the proportion with seven or more children was 30.7%, as compared with 19% among working women (see Table 3).

Table 3

Distribution of Women with Large Families
by Employment Status and Number of Children, %

	Number of children				
	4	5-6	7-9	10 or more	total
Working women	32.9	42.9	17.5	1.5	100
Nonworking women	22.5	46.8	25.8	4.9	100
Total	30.9	44.6	21.4	3.1	100

It can be seen from Table 3 that five or six children in the family is on the whole characteristic for women in both categories.

In urban conditions the mother of a large family is, of course, less inclined to seek work than the mother of a small family. However, when conditions are suitable, she too will readily go to work.[5]

The great majority of rural women in the Central Asian republics have large families, and at the same time, they are almost all employed in social production.

It is very important to note that mothers of large families
want to work. In our survey more than one third of the nonworking women expressed the desire to find a job at once.
Most also indicated that they needed to enroll their children at
a kindergarten or day nursery. Many mothers of large families
expressed the desire to work at home, part-time, or at enterprises close to home. And there were also those who wanted to
work under any conditions.

Of the surveyed women only 30.9% had never worked, but
even among them there were those who said they wanted to work.

At the same time, it must be recognized that at present a
large family greatly hinders a woman's increased public activity,
professional growth, and social mobility. The present level of
public services for the population is not sufficient to reduce the
burden of household chores for the mother of a large family
and draw her into social production. Most of the surveyed
women had no specialty and were employed in low-skilled or
unskilled jobs.

All this undoubtedly reflects on the "quality" of the present
population and future generations. On the other hand, under socialist conditions large families as a sociodemographic phenomenon possess a number of important positive aspects. Large
families foster such ethical ideals valued in socialist society
as industriousness, collectivism, mutual assistance, and so on.

We think that the "quality of the population" should not be
gauged solely from the standpoint of an educational level providing opportunities for occupational advance and social mobility.
There has not yet been a comprehensive elaboration of criteria
for evaluating "population quality" as applied to different socioeconomic conditions and social systems or differentiated
according to different occupational and social groups. We will
only note that in developed socialist society, exceptional importance is attached to moral values, particularly a person's
attitude toward work, toward other people, etc.

Thus the peoples of Central Asia have a tradition of large
families with strong economic and sociopsychological roots that
will continue to nourish the region's "demographic tree" for

many years to come. The mother of a large family will remain a "sociodemographic stereotype" here in the foreseeable future. Our aim is to create, under the conditions of developed socialism, more favorable conditions for running a household, raising children, and consistently involving mothers of large families in the active building of communism.

As L. I. Brezhnev noted in his answers to questions from the French newspaper Le Monde, we are not worried by the population growth in the republics of Central Asia as a result of the high birthrate. On the contrary, it is a phenomenon "which gratifies us, for, above all, it reflects the powerful upsurge in the economic level of our republics, the prodigious growth in the prosperity of the population in the former hinterlands of tsarist Russia, the tremendous progress they have achieved along the road of socialist transformation. All this, in the final analysis, consolidates that indivisible amalgam which we call a new historic community: the Soviet people."[6]

Notes

1. The survey was carried out in August 1976 and covered 1,616 mothers of four or more children. The Tashkent survey was the beginning of an integrated sociodemographic study of large families in the republics of Central Asia conducted by the Main Demographic Scientific Research Laboratory of the V. I. Lenin Tashkent State University.

2. See N. M. Aliakberova, "Sotsial'no-ekonomicheskii analiz pokazatelei vosproizvodstva naseleniia Uzbekistana," thesis abstract, Tashkent, 1976.

3. N. A. Tauber, "Usloviia zhizni sem'i i srednee chislo detei," in Demograficheskii analiz rozhdaemosti, Moscow, 1974, p. 15.

4. See G. A. Bondarskaia, "Etnicheskaia differentsiatsiia rozhdaemosti v SSSR i ee sushchnost'," in Rozhdaemost', Moscow, 1976, p. 120.

5. For more on this, see O. B. Ata-Mirzaev and I. Katanov, Vozmozhnosti i osnovnye puti vovlecheniia zhenshchin v promyshlennost' Uzbekistana i Srednei Azii, Tashkent, 1972.

6. L. I. Brezhnev, Otvety na voprosy frantsuzskoi gazety "Mond," Moscow, 1977, p. 15.

PART THREE
A POLICY AGENDA
FOR THE 1980s

14

The Quantity and Quality of Work: A Round Table

E. E. Novikova and B. P. Kutyrev

The USSR has the world's highest rate of employment of women. The last national census shows that in 1970, 92.5% of all women of working age were employed — just 6 percentage points lower than men. The following figures were cited at the Sixtieth Session of the International Labor Office: the share of women among workers in the USSR economy had reached 49.3% in 1975, while at the same time it was 42.2% in the socialist countries of Europe, 34.6% in Western Europe, 35.0% in North America, 30.9% in Africa, and 19.6% in Latin America. The number of working women among the total female population equaled 48% in the USSR, corresponding to 44.2% in the People's Republic of Poland, 31.6% in the Federal Republic of Germany, 29.0% in France and Great Britain, and 27.9% in the United States. The statistics demonstrate the high level of participation in social production by women of all age groups, especially those 20 to 39 years old.[1]

The average length of employment of Soviet women working in the national economy reached 37.4 years in 1970, or 5.3 years fewer than for men.[2]

The data we have cited characterize only one side of this

Russian text © 1978 by "Nauka" Publishers. "Kolichestvo i kachestvo truda," *Ekonomika i organizatsiia promyshlennogo proizvodstva*, 1978, no. 3, pp. 20-29.

issue — the quantitative. But there is another aspect: how efficiently female labor resources are used. In this connection one should recall V. I. Lenin's observation that for a socialist society, the decisive factor is not only the quantity of women who participate in social production but the character of their work. The government of proletarian dictatorship and socialist construction does not want nor can it desire women to work as an unqualified or poorly skilled work force or to vegetate in uninteresting, poorly paid jobs.[3]

The intensification of production, scientific-technological progress, the decline in rates of growth of labor resources, and the growing social activity of women are all objective factors that have created a need for special attention to questions posed at Lenin's behest. In recent years ever greater efforts have been directed toward improving working and living conditions for women. These problems were the subject of a "round table" that was organized by the research department of the Higher School of the Trade Union Movement of the All-Union Central Council of Trade Unions (AUCCTU) in Moscow, together with the editors of Ekonomika i organizatsiia promyshlennogo proizvodstva [EKO].

Scholars and specialists taking part in the "round table" (primarily women, since they constitute the overwhelming majority of those studying problems of female labor) included economists, sociologists, medical doctors, lawyers, and others.

*　　*　　*

Despite the great economic and demographic importance of problems of women's employment in our country, they remain insufficiently studied. Paradoxical as it might at first glance seem, one of the reasons for procrastination in scholarly examination of them is the apparent self-evidence of these issues. Indeed, superficially it seems obvious that it is hard to work and bring up children at the same time, that women workers are often behind men in job skills, and so forth.

Such conclusions, however, are at a merely commonsense level and are unsuitable for drawing scientifically substantiated conclusions and making practical recommendations. On the other hand, that the proportion of women feeling very tired by the end of a shift ranges from 48 to 70% of their total (depending on the number of children), and that in small towns in which industries employing mainly women predominate this proportion is as high as 60-90%, are scientific facts that can and must be used as a basis for specific proposals.

The need for a scientific approach to the problems of female labor was realized by all participants in the "round table" conference without exception, and we took the facts cited here from a book by one of the group members, Candidate in Economics S. Ia. Turchaninova (Moscow).[4]

The extent of the sphere of action for science and scientific studies in this field can be illustrated by citing several unsolved questions, notably with respect to the high employment of women in the national economy. Views on this important socioeconomic fact have been rather contradictory. Positive assessments have relied on industry's demand for manpower, the positive influence of the work collective on the general development of the woman worker, and economic independence for women. Negative assessments have cited the heavy work load borne by women on the job and at home and hence their lack of free time to develop their personalities. Another important argument, presented as an example, is that the existence of low-skilled female labor does not stimulate the replacement of manual jobs by machines.

Obviously the question can be answered only after a thorough study of the work of women in the economy, taking into account all factors, including structural relationships, the nature and conditions of work, and others. A scientifically based solution of the existing dilemma is needed, as pointed out in her presentation by Candidate in Economics V. B. Mikhailiuk (Odessa).[5]

Another illustration of the need for a scientific approach is the search for ways to reduce the burden of women's domestic and private subsidiary farming chores. Time budget studies show

that women do 2.5 times more household work than men. This
gap should, obviously, be closed, but how to do so is still a subject of protracted discussions. We feel that it can be done
through socialization of household chores, on the one hand, and
their more even distribution between men and women, on the
other. There can be no doubt that more extensive involvement
of men in work around the home will yield positive results.
Facts disprove the notion that men are ill adapted to this kind
of work: men, in fact, make the best cooks in the world. And
under the Fundamental Law of the USSR, "spouses are fully
equal in family relations" (authors' emphasis). This, however,
is not enough to make work at home easier. It is also necessary to mechanize and automate household chores. Science,
notably economics and sociology, must establish the optimum
degree of socialization of household work and participation by
men in it.

Another topic of debate meriting scholarly investigation is
the work and rest schedules of women. Let us first quote the
conclusions of the paper by S. Ia. Turchaninova, one of the or-
ganizers of a poll conducted by the Central Labor Resources
Laboratory. The poll revealed, in particular, that the degree
of satisfaction with a work schedule mainly depends on how
schedules and shifts correspond to the individual dynamic
diurnal stereotype. On the whole, however, women workers
are more sensitive to work schedules, since, with their "dual
employment," they are more dissatisfied with night shifts, as
well as with the lack of coincidence of their off-days with the
off-days of other members of the family. Men are much less
sensitive to schedule differences. Their assessments range
from 92% satisfied with a two-shift, six-day week, to 70% accepting a three-shift six-day working week. This comparative
tolerance of men to work schedules indicates that the task of
raising the shift coefficient in industry can be comparatively
painlessly resolved by using male labor.

This conclusion is undoubtedly justified, but probably only to
a certain extent. It is hard to imagine women weavers who
work night shifts ever being replaced by men. The conclusion

256

is that as in the case of household work, the objective is to draw more men into multishift work; but we cannot forget the acute question of night shifts as such, their economic and social expedience and necessity.

After analyzing the "round table" discussion, we came to the conclusion that it is the duty of economics to provide managers with an integrated, systems approach to solving problems of women's work, taking into account its features and the long-term consequences of whatever decisions are made. It is no secret, for example, that as noted by some speakers, managers prefer to "compensate" for bad working conditions with additional pay instead of making the conditions better. Obviously a scientifically substantiated methodology for calculating social impact, and information on the long-term consequences of such "compensation," could produce some rational solutions. We feel that the growing shortage of manpower will make such studies even more necessary.

Today managers often claim to be short of the material means and money needed to improve the working and living conditions of women. More often than not, however, it is a question not of shortages but of the optimum distribution of available means and funds. For example, according to information supplied by L. S. Korovin, who works at the Institute of Economics and Organization of Industrial Production of the Siberian Branch of the USSR Academy of Sciences, the lion's share of funds allocated for labor safety techniques and practices at industrial establishments is spent on ventilation, while the main cause of sickness and occupational injuries may be the increased level of noise, vibration, etc. The irrational distribution of funds for labor safety was noted in the presentation by the well-known hygienist, Doctor of Medicine Z. A. Volkova (Moscow).[6]

That is why it is so important, as repeatedly emphasized by participants in the discussion, to affirm the following approach: every ruble additionally invested in improving working conditions today will more than pay off tomorrow in fewer sick leaves by women, higher and more stable fitness for work, and a better

257

E. E. Novikova and B. P. Kutyrev

moral and psychological climate in the worker collective. The required organizational efforts will also pay off.

It goes without saying that scientific grounds for a more correct, optimized approach to working conditions in general, and to women in particular, must be by the implementation in practice of legal statutes. Unfortunately, as Candidate in Law N. N. Sheptulina (Moscow) pointed out, managers sometimes show little concern for observing legislation regarding female labor and are rarely punished severely for their negligence.

The problem of the means needed to improve working conditions and raise the efficiency of women's work sparked extensive discussion at the "round table." We would like to note the optimistic conclusion that material funds are not always the main or decisive consideration in this field. Great opportunities lie in the "human factor" of production.

In this connection we note the contribution by Candidate in Philosophy E. Z. Danilova (Smolensk), who believes that changing current attitudes and fostering a new, genuinely communist attitude toward women on the part of men, in the work collective and at home, can be one way to raise production efficiency and thus create a reserve for improving working conditions for women.[7] Efficiency can be raised, in the first place, on the basis of a favorable atmosphere in the collective. A bad mood can reduce labor productivity by 10 to 20 percent. But a normal atmosphere in a collective is impossible without a highly moral attitude toward women, especially those who are easily wounded emotionally.

We note that in evaluating the qualities of a manager, women place his human qualities — sensitivity, attention, tact, etc. — in first place. That is why knowledge of basic elements of sociology, psychology, and pedagogy is so important for all managerial personnel without exception, especially in collectives where women predominate.

Unfortunately, certain prejudices or indifference still persist among managers. Thus in answer to the question of why toolmakers were men and odd-job workers were women, the superintendent of a toolmaking shop at a Smolensk factory (according to E. Z. Danilova) replied that the men's jobs were highly skilled and required brains. When the logical question followed, whether he really thought that men were cleverer than women, the shop superintendent shrugged his shoulders: "It's what people always say, and I never thought too much about it."

Prejudices form over the ages, but they can be shed, and the sooner the better. And the main part in this should be played not only by moral factors, which are also important, but by economic and legal levers.

*   *   *

The participants in the "round table" conference concentrated mainly on three aspects of the problem of raising the effectiveness of female labor in the USSR: economic, legal, and social. The economic aspect, naturally, came to the fore, but its connection with the others was also emphasized. The discussion, reflected in contributions by candidates in economics V. B. Mikhailiuk, N. M. Shishkan (Kishinev),[8] Z. M. Iuk (Minsk), N. I. Tatarinova, N. Ia. Tereshina (Moscow), and B. P. Kutyrev (Novosibirsk), centered around the topic "The Character and Conditions of Women's Work and Scientific and Technological Progress."[9]

The speakers pointed out that on the whole, scientific and technological progress has a positive effect on women's work because it eliminates hard physical labor. At the same time, in some cases new machines and technologies have been introduced without taking due account of the specific features of the female organism. Chemicalization of production, for example, results in more people employed in jobs with hazardous working conditions. Rapid developments in the radio, electronics, and automobile industries paradoxically call mainly for unskilled labor that is required to perform very monotonous, high-intensity jobs.

N. N. Sheptulina referred to an example described in Pravda: a production line was developed for brick works that made it possible to employ thirty women instead of 300. It was not put into operation, however, because it is more profitable to employ women workers of low skills, who are socially less mobile than men and whose demands regarding labor conditions are lower.[10]

Thus mechanization and automation as prime requisites for getting women out of hard physical jobs encounter some opposition. The mechanism of this opposition is, of course, not due to sex differences. The problem obviously lies in the general replacement of manual labor by machines and the introduction of the achievements of scientific and technological progress into industry as a whole. Thus it is not a "woman's" problem or, more exactly, not only a "woman's" problem.

The lag of women behind men in skill and wage ratings is one of the obstacles in the way of scientific and technological improvements in production, and it has remained firmly entrenched over the last few years. The reason, as stressed by S. Ia. Turchaninova, who noted the point, is not only, nor so much, the absence of special conditions for raising skills and qualifications, as the fact that higher ratings would require changes in the nature and organization of women's work and elimination of hard physical and unskilled jobs. This would create additional problems for management. Many speakers noted the need to overcome the tendency to keep women in manual and unskilled jobs. "Is it hard to automate the work of women in continuous production?" asks Z. M. Iuk, and she answers, "No it is not, but a manager feels it is too expensive."

One question requiring solution is differentiation of production quotas according to sex in some trades, for example, machine-tool operators. Since women are physically weaker than men, they can equal men's output only after gaining more experience. On the other hand, since women's household work, especially bringing up children, is economically essential for socialist society as a whole, these expenditures are an inalienable part of women's contribution to society. Differentiation of production quotas must also take these types of work into account. Such differentiation, moreover, would express public recognition not only of occupational functions but also of family-household functions.

The Quantity and Quality of Work

According to T. N. Sidorova, who works in the research department of the Higher School of the Trade Union Movement of the All-Union Central Council of Trade Unions (Moscow), male machine-tool operators are on average 30% better than their female counterparts in meeting production quotas, even though they take more "smoke breaks." Naturally, this affects wages, as well as the results of participation in the socialist competition movement. Thus at the Leningrad Machine-Building Association for the Light and Food Industries, out of twenty-seven award winners there were only four women, and not one of them was a machine-tool operator, although they account for 30% of the total. T. N. Sidorova cited examples from the Moscow Dynamo factory and the Ulianovsk heavy and unique machine-tools works, where the individual opportunities of the participants in socialist competition are taken into account.

As far as socialist competition is concerned, matters are simpler. It can be organized, for example, for women operators alone. Much more difficult is the question of how to differentiate production quotas. The participants in the "round table" discussion took a positive view of the reduction in output quotas for women tractor operators by 10% in comparison with men. At the same time, they stressed that pay should remain the same, despite the reduction of quotas. To prevent this from coming into contradiction with the law of socialist distribution according to labor, N. M. Shishkan, for example, suggested the difference be paid from public consumption funds. Not all, however, agreed with the principle of equal pay for different quotas. This question, we feel, deserves special consideration by economists.

Candidate in History E. E. Novikova, section chief in the research department of the Higher School of the Trade Union Movement, raised the question of the consequences of changes in the branch distribution of female labor, especially the growing proportion of women in the machine-building industry. Her studies indicate that the industry is not prepared for such changes. Unfortunately, even at the newest enterprises, which serve as models of technological equipment and production or-

261

ganization, there are many shortcomings: inadequate public
services, hard physical work, women lagging behind men in
skills and qualifications, etc.

Especially acute are problems of management of collectives
where women predominate. Whereas for the manager of a textile mill, for example, absence of women workers due to sickness, care for sick children, or pregnancy and maternity
leave is nothing out of the ordinary, the manager of a machine-
building plant finds such absence too high because he is used to
dealing with men. The time has come to take account of the
specific features of the present stage in recruiting personnel
in machine-building and certain other industries. On this in
many respects depends one of the prime social indicators: the
extent to which women workers are satisfied with their work.

*   *   *

Legal aspects of female labor were examined at the "round
table" discussions on two levels: first, the extent to which existing legal regulations, mainly restrictions on the use of female labor, correspond to the distinctive anatomical and
physiological characteristics of women workers, and second,
how they should be changed in line with scientific and technological progress and the penetration of female labor into new
branches of industry.

The lists of jobs closed to women were adopted back in
1932.[11] Much in them has, of course, become obsolete over
these forty-five years. On the one hand, the character of occupations has changed, and new ones have appeared; on the
other, socioeconomic requirements regarding the character of
work and working conditions have changed. A new list has now
been prepared, and it is passing through the approval process.
The "round table" participants spoke of the need to speed the
adoption of relevant legislation, taking into account that a rather
long time passes between its promulgation and full implementation. Thus, as N. N. Sheptulina noted, it took twenty years before women were finally taken off underground jobs, while the

Iron and Steel Ministry has still not carried out the 1957 decree of the USSR Council of Ministers. Few women have yet to be taken off night shifts and strenuous and hazardous jobs.

Z. A. Volkova dwelled specifically on rate-setting for the strenuous manual jobs in which many women are still employed. The maximum permissible load for them to carry, adopted in 1932, is twenty kilograms. This is a fairly high load. Fifteen kilogram would be acceptable, but an additional restriction should be introduced (it is currently being approved as a legal provision) with respect to the number of loads that can be lifted and carried during a shift. Thus it is recommended that a fifteen-kilogram load be lifted not more than ten times during a shift, and the total work done per shift should not exceed 30,000 kilogram-meters.

Doctors and lawyers also expressed their concern over the absence of scientific studies regarding the transfer of pregnant women to lighter jobs. Current provisions require a small but important qualification: a lighter job should also be a less hazardous one. There are quite a few examples, notes Z. A. Volkova, of pregnant women being transferred to "lighter" jobs without consideration of the hazardousness of the position and pregnancy complications resulting.[12]

The specific features of the female organism are still not sufficiently taken into account in regulating the work environment. In the view of doctors, hygienists, and physiologists, limits on permissible concentrations should be set regardless of sex, but they should include an adequate "safety factor" that would cover women as more susceptible workers.

As G. V. Morozov, section head of the All-Union Labor Protection Institute of the AUCCTU (Ivanovo), noted, legislative measures are needed to reinforce scientific recommendations for optimum work loads for women. Thus, given the high work load of textile workers (98% of the working time of a shift), there is apprehension about expanding the number of machines for which they are responsible.

Another topic of debate at the "round table," in which N. I. Tatarinova, N. Ia. Tereshina, and others took part, was whether,

in addition to the list of jobs in which female labor is prohibited, there should not also be a list of trades recommended
mainly for women. Opponents of such lists feared that they
could lead to the anchoring of women in certain trades and
thereby restrict the sphere of application of their work. Indeed, in practice such cases cannot be precluded, but they can
be avoided. What management needs are guidelines for worker
screening, selection, and placement on a scientific basis, taking
into account the specific features of the female organism. Such
lists are already being compiled in the USSR Ministry of Agriculture. The Code of Labor Legislation of the Lithuanian SSR
permits the management of enterprises, jointly with trade union
committees, to draw up lists of jobs in which it is recommended
to employ mainly women.

*   *   *

In conclusion, let us return to where we began: the need to
expand scientific studies of female labor. This is, so to speak,
a "secondary" task. The main thing is to halt the noticeable
trend toward winding down such studies. Thus, according to
G. V. Morozov, of 500 organizations surveyed by the Ivanovo
Labor Protection Institute, whose duty should be to study the
problem, 77% are not conducting any studies on the subject.
There are few such topics in the research plans of the re-
mainder.

The participants in the "round table" discussion were unani-
mous in their view that in studying the problems of working
women, it is necessary to pool the efforts of many specialists
and set up a coordinating center under a body capable of both
formulating recommendations and promoting practical measures. The absence of such a center does not facilitate the
development of uniform, scientifically substantiated views. In
a series of works one encounters what we see as utterly un-
founded proposals.

A coordinating center would make it possible to eliminate the negative consequences of the very popularity of the subject based on

the seeming simplicity of the problem. In fact it is an extremely multifaceted problem that can be solved only by the joint efforts of scholars representing many disciplines, working according to a unified program, and approaching investigation of the problems of female labor comprehensively and systematically, taking into account both short-term and long-term objectives.

In our view a planned approach would also help to enhance the effectiveness of scholarly studies. At present many conclusions of studies of women's working and living conditions are more like statements "for the record." Science should offer more recommendations for action to be taken by administrative bodies and managers.

As a practical measure the participants in the discussion recommended drawing up an integrated program, "Women in the USSR," that would be dovetailed with the five-year plans and long-term programs for national socioeconomic development. The results of some isolated measures are well known. Thus reduction of the working day by one hour did not result, as had been expected, in a corresponding increase in free time for working women. Instead the additional time went mainly into housework or work in private subsidiary agriculture. Obviously the objectives that have been set can be attained only on the basis of a comprehensive, planned approach.

Notes

1. Mezhdunarodnaia konferentsiia po trudu. 60-ia sessiia, 1975 g. Doklad VIII: Ravenstvo vozmozhnostei i odinakovyi podkhod k trudiashchimsia zhenshchinam, Geneva, n.d., pp. 4, 6, 8, 10 (in English).

2. Demograficheskie aspekty zaniatosti, Moscow, "Statistika" Publishers, 1975, p. 20.

3. K. Zetkin, Zavety Lenina zhenshchinam vsego mira, Moscow, 1958, p. 13.

4. See A. E. Kotliar, S. Ia. Turchaninova, Zaniatost' zhenshchin v proizvodstve, Moscow, "Statistika" Publishers, 1975, pp. 123-24.

5. For more on this, see V. B. Mikhailiuk, Ispol'zovanie zhenskogo truda v narodnom khoziaistve, Moscow, "Ekonomika" Publishers, 1970, p. 67.

6. For more on this, see I. G. Fridliand, Gigiena zhenskogo truda, Moscow, "Meditsina" Publishers, 1975.

7. For more on this, see E. Z. Danilova, Sotsial'nye problemy zhenshchiny-

rabotnitsy, Moscow, "Mysl'" Publishers, 1968.

8. N. M. Shishkan has prepared a highly informative work, Trud zhenshchin v usloviiakh razvitogo sotsializma, Kishinev, "Shtiintsa" Publishers, 1976.

9. A scientific conference on this question was held in 1975 (see Vliianie nauchno-tekhnicheskogo progressa na izmenenie kharaktera zhenskogo truda v usloviiakh sotsialisticheskogo obshchestva, Ivanovo, 1975).

10. Pravda, October 19, 1970.

11. See Zakonodatel'stvo o pravakh zhenshchin v SSSR, Moscow, "Iuridicheskaia literatura" Publishers, 1975.

12. For more on this, see Ozdorovlenie uslovii truda zhenshchin, Moscow, NII gigiyeny truda i profzabolevanii AMN SSSR, 1976.

15

How Working Women Combine Work and Household Duties

E. V. Porokhniuk and M. S. Shepeleva

Soviet scholars have studied various aspects of the ways women combine work with household duties.[1] The literature on the subject offers recommendations aimed at easing the load borne by working women: redistribution of family and household duties among all able-bodied members of the family, the use of household appliances, further expansion of the service sector and public catering, more favorable work schedules for women, and so on. Of special interest among all these recommendations is the suggestion that women be offered opportunities for working part-time.

The experience of Czechoslovakia, the German Democratic Republic, Bulgaria, and several Soviet enterprises testifies to the feasibility and usefulness of part-time work schedules. This is supported, in particular, by the positive results of an experiment conducted at the Vuit garment factory in Tallin, where several part-time work teams were organized in 1960. They included only mothers of small children or of children in poor health. After almost ten years the experience of these teams revealed that per worker, their results were not inferior to other teams in terms of productivity, cost, or quality,

Russian text © 1975 by "Nauka" Publishers. "O sovmeshchenii proizvodstvennykh i semeinykh funktsii zhenshchin-rabotnits," *Sotsiologicheskie issledovaniia*, 1975, no. 4, pp. 102-8.

and occasionally they were higher. In the women's view part-time work (a four-hour workday) appreciably helped them combine work with running a household and bringing up children.

The effects of part-time work on the performance of household and work duties were studied in a socioeconomic experiment carried out by a group of researchers from the Odessa Institute of the National Economy at one of the construction organizations in the city (Special Construction Administration 604 [OSU-604]).[2] The working time for women in this experiment was reduced by one hour. A series of studies was made to either confirm or refute the theory that shorter working hours would create more favorable conditions for enhancing the occupational knowledge of working women, their general cultural level and activity, and also have a favorable effect on the way they perform their household and family duties and bring up children.

The experiment was preceded by extensive preliminary work among the workers of the construction organization. Organizational and economic measures aimed at making up for any possible losses due to shorter working hours for women and assuring that production quotas and planned increases in productivity would be met were discussed in detail at a meeting, in which the women workers took part, of section chiefs and the trade union local. A special "Information Bulletin" was issued to explain the purposes and objectives of the experiment. Talks were held individually with the women selected for it. The establishment's women's council took an active part in the work.

"Provisional Regulations" were drawn up for the women transferred to the shorter working schedule, describing how the transfer would be done and explaining how wages would be computed and the indicators that would be used to judge the results of the experiment.

When some men in the work collective were asked about their attitude toward the experiment, 96.8% said they approved of it.

A socioeconomic argument for the experiment was devised. It involved an estimate of possible annual losses and a set of measures designed to make up for them. Financing was drawn from the material incentive fund.

The experiment covered eleven months. During that period no new women were hired, and none of the working women were discharged or moved to other positions. The reduction in the workday did not result in any changes in pay.

At first it had been decided to have all women at the enterprise work shorter hours, but a more thorough analysis showed that there was no point in involving unmarried young women (11% of all the women). Nor, at the request of the management, did the experiment involve cleaners or guards. And finally, an economic analysis of the consequences of a reduced working day for women engineers, technicians, and office employees showed that it would affect their material position (reducing their pay and vacation time).

Thus eventually only women working in the production sphere and having children of preschool and school age were transferred to a shorter workday. They included plasterers, concrete workers, motor workers, assemblers, and other trades. Women make up 24.2% of the personnel employed at OSU-604, 38.5% of them working in blue-collar jobs. Twenty-five percent of all the women workers were placed on shorter working hours.

Of the women involved in the experiment, 54% had one child, 39% had two, and 7% had three or more. The ages of the children were: 6% under one, 18% up to three, 26% up to 10, 24% up to 14, and 16% aged 15 to 18. Thus most women had one or two children aged three to 14.

In preparing for the experiment, objective data were studied (the work stations at which the women were employed, their service records, education, qualifications, family status, productive and sociopolitical activity); the women were also asked about their cultural-intellectual needs, plans for the future, relations with their fellow-workers, attitudes toward the experiment, and how they proposed to spend the additional free time.

Three months after the experiment started, the women involved were questioned again. This was done to determine the changes taking place in their work, studies, performance of household and child-rearing duties in the family, the structure of their free time, etc. Similar questions were studied in the course of two interviews, one six months after the start of the experiment, and the other in the concluding stage.

Men were also polled to compare the productivity and sociopolitical activity of women and men at the establishment and their participation in household and family duties. Finally, a special questionnaire was circulated toward the end of the experiment among experts[3] to determine their views on the effectiveness of reducing working hours for women of the enterprise. We should note one reservation: reduction of the workday by only one hour and the relatively short duration of the experiment justify only preliminary conclusions.

The first survey revealed that the level of sociopolitical activity of the women at work was lower than men: 36% of the men took part in the rationalizers' [work improvement] movement, but not one woman; 34.9% of the men and only 13.6% of the women took an active part in discussing questions at production meetings; 57.6% of the women declared they had no intention of improving their qualifications (even though half of them had the lowest job rating); 54.2% of the men and 12.6% of the women had regular public assignments, etc. Almost all the women cited two main reasons for this discrepancy: no spare time and fatigue.

Data on the contributions of women and men to household duties on the whole confirmed the general trend revealed in similar studies: 48.3% of the women questioned ran the household alone or almost alone, the others were helped by husbands or parents, and in only 8.6% of the families did the men share household duties with their wives approximately equally; the highest proportion of those performing household duties all alone were women with low education (57.6%) and women from peasant families (56%); the higher the education, the more inclined are women to acquire household appliances and make use of public services.

In the first survey 71.4% of the women said their husbands helped them in bringing up and looking after children (28.6% had no help). However, it was found that in many cases the

270

husband's contribution was restricted to taking the child to and
from kindergarten or nursery. A follow-up survey indicated
that only 28.4% of the fathers took a real part in bringing up
children.

The studies revealed a clear relationship between opportunities for a woman's personal development and the extent
to which her husband helps her around the house and in bringing
up the children. Thus more than half the women carrying the
burden of housework alone declared they had no time to read,
whereas 74% of those who received help from their husbands
read more or less regularly. Also, fatigue among the first
group of women was much higher. This reaffirmed our belief
that the redistribution of family functions among all able-bodied
members of the family is an important means of reducing the
contradictions between work and family duties and a prerequisite for women's personal development.

Different opportunities give rise to different inclinations in
the family-household and work areas. Indicative in this sense
are some of the responses to the first survey. When asked
what they valued most in their work, the majority of men replied: opportunities for improving skills and qualifications
(30.5%), prospects for advancement (28%), independence, opportunities for initiative and creativity (19.4%); among women
the leading responses were: proximity to place of residence
(34.4%) and convenient shift schedule (19.7%). Men and women
also replied differently when asked what they would do with
their additional free time if the working day was reduced. Most
of the women thought they would devote it to their children
(87%), work around the house (62%), or relax and enjoy themselves (50.8%). Men said they would devote the time to hobbies
(57%), children (26%), or some other part-time work (20%).

The data cited indicate that there is a serious need to create
more favorable conditions for the general development of
women and their performance of one of their prime duties:
looking after and bringing up children. This need is acutely
felt, and teachers, counselors, lawyers, and sociologists have
written about it. For example, the criminologist E. Stumbinia

has concluded, on the basis of surveys and other materials, that one of the major causes of juvenile crime and delinquency is the insufficient attention working mothers can give to their children.[4]

In the concluding stage of the experiment a quantitative and qualitative analysis was undertaken of the changes that occurred in the work, sociopolitical activities, and performance of family-household duties by the women working shorter hours. The overwhelming majority (87.2%) took advantage of the extra hour mainly for family and household duties and child-rearing.

In response to questions 77.4% said that the reduction of the workday had a favorable effect on child upbringing, 61.2% said it improved the moral-psychological atmosphere in the family, and 87.2% found it made running the household easier.

Furthermore 58.4% of the women noted that their children's progress at school had improved. An analysis of academic progress (in points on a five-point grade scale) revealed an improvement from an average 3.9 in the 1972/73 school year to 4.1 by the end of the first quarter of the 1973/74 year. The women noted that they tired less at work and could rest more on holidays (67.7%).

The fact that most women devoted the extra hour to family duties was apparently not satisfying to them, since in interviews they stressed that they had to do so not because they were eager to bury themselves in family concerns but because of the shortage of public services. By the middle of the experiment many women noted that they were reading more occupational literature and that they now had the opportunity to improve their qualifications, which they intended to do. Some of the women said they read more fiction than during the control period prior to the experiment or went to the movies or theater more frequently. Only 0.9% said that if the experiment were extended, they would use the additional free time to earn some extra cash.

Of the supervisory specialists and managerial personnel, 86% wholly endorsed the experiment,[5] 48% noted a rise in productivity among the women under the new schedule,[6] 76% noted an improvement in work discipline, and 67% pointed to better relations within the collective. On the question of wage payment for the reduced hour, 71% thought it should remain unchanged, and 24% felt it should be reduced somewhat; more than half (57%) were for reducing working time for women by one hour, and 38% suggested giving women the opportunity to opt for a reduction in working time up to 50%, with a corresponding adjustment of wages.

The conclusions from the experiment are not altogether unambiguous. Indeed, reducing the workday for women who combine production work with bringing up a family by even one hour creates more favorable conditions for looking after children and the family, reducing their physical load, and making some cultural advance. That is why we are convinced that a reduction of working hours for working women who really need it is an important and urgent task. It is in keeping with the humane principles of our society and the interests of strengthening the family and bringing up new generations. Furthermore such a step would help draw more nonworking women into the sphere of social production.

At the same time, there are some negative aspects. Some husbands viewed their wives' added free time as an opportunity to shift more household duties onto the women's shoulders (28% of the women interviewed mentioned this). The extra hour also had little effect on the involvement of the women in production and public activities. Despite previously voiced intentions, only 7-8% actually sought to improve their qualifications. There were still no women among the rationalizers, and the percentage having public assignments grew insignificantly (from 12.6 to 14.2%). This is rooted in our general circumstances, primarily the acute shortage of time for family and household needs. In addition, reduction of the working day became a definite obstacle to the promotion of some women to managerial positions.

Some researchers are against reducing working time for women. In the opinion of V. Tkachenko, for example, it could result in a reduction of the proportion of female labor in the national economy.[7] We think this view is erroneous. In speaking of the equality of men and women, V. I. Lenin, as we know, stressed: "The question is not of equalizing women in productivity, amount of work, its duration, working conditions, etc., but...that women should not be oppressed by their economic situation any more than men."[8]

It is common knowledge that the current problem can be radically solved by transferring the main forms of household work to the sphere of public production. Women will be rid of domestic "slavery" only when "household work, which is now a private affair, becomes a branch of social production."[9]

In the USSR, where the party is guided by the desire to create all the conditions for "Soviet women to receive new opportunities for bringing up children, as well as for greater participation in public life, rest, and studies, and for more extensive acquaintance with the fruits of culture,"[10] the service sector is regularly expanding (more and more service establishments, restaurants, etc., are opening, and their quality is improving), and household work is being mechanized. In practice, however, we can see that the restructuring of household work has been gradual and sporadic. There is an insistent need for operative measures that would make it easier for women to combine work with household duties, rid them of excessive workloads, and enable them to devote more attention to their own development and raising the new generations.

One can speak only of combining these duties, insofar as women's participation in the sphere of social production is an essential prerequisite for actual equality of the sexes. This was pointed out by V. I. Lenin: "For the complete emancipation of women and their genuine equality with men there must be a public economy, and women must participate in common productive labor."[11] On the other hand, performance of a woman's family duties is a necessary condition for the existence and development of family-marital relations. And as we know, the trend in socialist society in the sphere of family-marital relations is toward strengthening the family as a highly important factor in the socialization of the individual, as a specific microenvironment assuring the highest standards of child upbringing.[12]

Providing women with the opportunity to work part-time is a measure which, under present conditions (as long as the development of the service sphere still lags behind the requirements of the family) makes it easier for women to combine the difficult duties of a worker and the main performer of household and educational functions in the family. This measure can, of course, be treated as temporary, since it has its weak aspects.[13] But part-time work enables women to devote more attention to their families and children while at the same time preserving their work connections, their skills, service records, and all worker rights. The negative aspects can, to some degree, be neutralized by paying more attention to educating members of the family collective to redistribute family functions, by cultivating women's interest in raising their educational and occupational standards, and by setting up children's preschool establishments, social service facilities, and other facilities right at the enterprises.[14]

It is here that we see the obvious advantages of such a solution to the problem of women with children one to three years old, as compared with suggestions, aired in the press, to grant women three years leave to look after children (instead of building nurseries).[15] Not only because in three years the woman loses her qualifications, especially under the conditions of the scientific and technological revolution, but also because of the social damage to her as a person and counselor of her children as a result of her separation from the collective, as well as the economic damage to society.

In view of the fact that economic considerations are among the main incentives for women to work,[16] it would be expedient to introduce part-time work for women with children without reducing wages. Such a measure was suggested by the first and second all-union symposiums on working women and the family. The experiment at OSU-604 showed that, with intelligent utilization of available reserves and a serious approach to the organization of work, reducing working time for women without reducing wages does no harm to the establishment economically, while its social benefits are indubitable.[17]

E. V. Porokhniuk and M. S. Shepeleva

Insofar as the overburdening of married working women breeds, on the one hand, unfavorable conditions for their personal development as individuals and members of society and, on the other, makes it harder to bring up the new generations, the contradiction between women's family and production duties must be urgently resolved.

Notes

1. See A. G. Kharchev, "Zhenskii trud i sem'ia," in Sotsiologiia i sovremennost', Moscow, 1974; V. D. Patrushev, "Sotsial'no-ekonomicheskie problemy svobodnogo vremeni pri sotsializme," in Sotsial'nye problemy truda i proizvodstva, Moscow-Warsaw, 1969; Ia. Andriushkevichene, "Zhenskii trud i problema svobodnogo vremeni," in Problemy byta, braka i sem'ia, Vilnius, 1970; G. A. Slesarev and Z. A. Iankova, "Zhenshchina na promyshlennom predpriiatii i v sem'e," in Sotsial'nye problemy truda i proizvodstva, Moscow-Warsaw, 1969, and others.

2. The experiment was supervised by the authors of this article.

3. The experts were: the administration chief, department and section chiefs, and functionaries of the enterprise's party and public organizations.

4. See E. Stumbinia, "O prichinakh prestupnosti nesovershennoletnikh," in Kommunisticheskoe vospitanie podrastaiushchego pokoleniia, Riga, 1967, p. 54.

5. From the survey of experts.

6. All the women met their production quotas.

7. Kommunist Belorussii, 1963, no. 10, p. 58.

8. V. I. Lenin, Poln. sobr. soch., vol. 39, p. 201.

9. K. Marx and F. Engels, Sochineniia, vol. 36, p. 294.

10. Materialy XXIV s''ezda KPSS, Moscow, 1971, p. 75.

11. Lenin, ibid.

12. See Z. A. Iankova, Izmenenie struktury sotsial'nykh rolei zhenshchiny v razvitom sotsialisticheskom obshchestve i model' sem'i, Moscow, 1972, p. 12; A. G. Kharchev and S. I. Golod. Professional'naia rabota zhenshchin i sem'ia, Leningrad, 1971, pp. 161-70.

13. It can also, as mentioned before, be suggested as primary for women engaged in direct physical labor.

14. These questions require special consideration.

15. Literaturnaia gazeta, 1975, no. 22.

16. See Sotsial'nye problemy truda i proizvodstva, Moscow-Warsaw, 1969, pp. 413, 465, 483, and others.

17. In the nine months of work according to the experimental schedule, the overall construction and installation plan of OSU-604 was fulfilled 112.4%, and overall labor productivity rose 9.6% over the previous year, which was 1.4% higher than the planned increase.

16

Part-time Employment of Women

L. M. Kuleshova and T. I. Mamontova

The comprehensive improvement of working and living conditions for working women is one of the most important aspects of the social policies of the Communist Party and the Soviet state. The "Basic National Economic Development Guidelines for 1976-80" stipulate: "More extensive opportunities must be created for women with children to work a shorter workday or shorter workweek, and also to work at home." [1]

The question of part-time work for women was initially raised at the Twentieth CPSU Congress. In 1970 the Principles of USSR Labor Legislation (Article 26) affirmed the right of workers to work part-time by mutual agreement with factory management. However, this article was to some extent a program position drawn up with an eye to prospects for economic development. Part-time work has not become widespread to any great degree since then.

To provide an in-depth study of this problem, in 1977 the State Committee of the USSR for Labor and Social Questions sponsored a survey of part-time and full-time women workers and of managers at 120 enterprises in light industry, machine building, trade, passenger transport, local industry, and public

Russian text © 1979 by "Nauka" Publishers. "Zaniatost' zhenshchin na rezhimakh s nepolnym rabochim vremenem," *Sotsiologicheskie issledovaniia*, 1979, no. 2, pp. 90-93.

services in ten union republics: Russia, the Ukraine, Belorussia, Georgia, Azerbaidzhan, Moldavia, Latvia, Estonia, Kazakhstan, and Kirghizia. Its purpose was to define possible and actual motivations for women to work part-time, determine the preferred and actual length of part-time hours, and establish the factors that prevent more workers from working part-time.

Among the polled women, 76.1% of those working full time expressed the desire to work part-time, 51% of them opting for a shorter workday, and 25.1% for a shorter workweek. Only 23.9% of the women were fully satisfied with the established working time.

The main reasons why women would like to work part-time are: to bring up children, 62.3% (for 47.4%, only through preschool and the early school years); more free time, 14.2%; household work, 10.7%; and poor health, 6.8%. The last two reasons predominated among women over 35. Only 15.2% of the women who voiced a preference for part-time work would have liked four hours a day, 21.1% wanted five hours, and the majority (63.7%) spoke of six or seven hours.

The survey indicated that a shift to part-time work usually leads to higher quality of output, fewer rejects, and a greater number of workers whose output meets preliminary standards and need not be checked. Among women opting for part-time work there is a higher proportion taking on temporary assignments that do not require much time. As a result they are more extensively involved in sociopolitical work. In many cases part-time work makes it possible for them to continue their education while remaining on the job, without detriment to family duties.

What then prevents the spread of part-time work?

The views of top management on this score are presented in the table on page 279.

Experience with part-time schedules shows that the fewest difficulties in introducing them are encountered when it is possible to set up a team whose members all work the same hours and shifts. The experts, as we have seen, point out the lack of a sufficient number of persons wanting to work part-

Management Views on Factors Preventing the Spread of
Part-time Employment

Factors preventing the spread of part-time employment	Views of managers under whom part-time employment	
	is used, % (520 persons)	is not used, % (618 persons)
Difficult to apply because of team method of work	17.9	21.2
Labor shortage	14.8	11.9
Lower wages in proportion to shorter hours	13.1	20.4
No one wanting part-time work	11.0	7.5
Disruption of shift schedules	9.1	13.9
Financial accountability	—	8.0
No answer	34.1	17.1

time (although many managers are at the same time apprehen-
sive about a massive shift to part-time work). This difficulty
usually arises when teams are recruited only from workers of
a given establishment, without the cooperation of others. On the
other hand, the survey reveals that most people are unaware
of the possibility of part-time work, and thus too many think
that the only alternative to full-time work is no work at all.
A poll of nonworking women revealed that 57% would like to find
part-time work.

The economic losses caused by the shift of some women from
full- to part-time work are in part compensated by the fact
that the average hourly productivity of those employed four to
six hours a day is 15 to 30% higher than of those working a full
shift. This is because the work ends before there is a
sharp drop in productivity due to accumulated fatigue by the
end of a full shift.

Some managers think that the financial accountability of
women working in trade, catering, and social services makes

part-time work impossible. But at the Tallin House of Trade, for example, 80% of those working shorter hours are sales-persons and cashiers — more than 150 people in all.

As for "labor shortages" that could be caused by women transferring from full-time to part-time work, we found that 22.4% of the polled women would probably prefer to leave work completely if they could not transfer to more convenient work-ing hours. On average these women expected to work part-time for about four years, after which they would resume full-time work. It follows that a change to part-time work would pre-vent their dropping out of social production, would help pre-serve their occupational skills, and would reduce possible losses in output that would inevitably occur if they left work altogether. Characteristically, the average shift length for these women is 4.83 hours, while for those working full time it is 5.71 hours.

It is also economically advantageous to provide part-time jobs for older people. In our survey 4.3% of all part-time working women were from 55 to 77 years old, and their average work-ing day was 4.6 hours. It was estimated that each such woman had already worked an average of 4,000 hours part-time after reaching retirement age and planned to work another 2,500 hours. Some had been working part-time for ten years or more. Obviously they could not have worked normal hours. It thus follows that greater use of part-time work would help solve the problem of drawing able-bodied pensioners into so-cial production, thus contributing to a gradual transition for them from full employment to full retirement and easing the strain on the balance of labor resources.

Our survey also reveals that today the main obstacle to the more widespread introduction of part-time work is chiefly the negative attitude of factory and office managers. The reasons for this are their underestimation of social and psy-chological factors in production and the lack of experience in organizing part-time work and of incentives to introduce it. It is typical of many managers to attribute their unwilling-ness to introduce part-time jobs to a shortage of manpower;

however, their refusal to offer women convenient part-time work aggravates that shortage, since as a result many women simply leave work for family reasons.

Ministries and departments should thus pay more serious attention to the introduction at enterprises they control of part-time work schedules, especially for mothers of small children. Staff sociologists at factories, rate-setters, technologists, and factory line supervisors should determine in advance the sections, teams, and work stations where part-time work can be introduced. It is also necessary to include appropriate clauses in the social development plans of collectives. Public organizations, primarily the trade unions, particularly are also urged to assist in this work, which "is in accord with the line of the party and Soviet government aimed at consistently improving the position of women as workers, mothers, teachers of their children, and housewives."[2]

Notes

1. Materialy XXV s''ezda KPSS, Moscow, 1976, p. 217.
2. L. I. Brezhnev, O Konstitutsii SSSR, Moscow, 1977, p. 56.

17

The Position of Women and Demographic Policy

G. Kiseleva

It was noted at the Twenty-fifth Congress of the Communist Party of the Soviet Union that Soviet scientists should not lose sight of population problems, which have recently been growing more acute, and that the formulation of an effective demographic policy is an important task for the entire range of natural and social sciences.[1] This means that a very thorough and comprehensive study of demographic processes is necessary.

In speaking of the need to elaborate an effective demographic policy, we must bear in mind that demographic processes are a form of social processes that can be understood only when we analyze population changes in connection with the development of society as a whole. There are many aspects to the problems of population development and the dynamics and trends of demographic processes. We shall dwell on only one: the effect of women's social position on the dynamics of the birthrate and the possibilities of influencing it by means of demographic policies.

The birthrate is affected by a wide range of social and economic factors. Obviously, various factors influence it to different degrees. The most important ones, which in our view

Russian text © 1978 by "Statistika" Publishers. "Polozhenie zhenshchin i demograficheskaia politika," in *Zhenshchiny na rabote i doma*, D. I. Valentei et al., eds. (Moscow: "Statistika" Publishers, 1978), pp. 3-17.

have a determining effect on the dynamics of the birthrate, are
those associated with the changing social position of women and
the functions of the family. These changes are a result of the
social, economic, and cultural transformations effected by the
Soviet state since the socialist revolution which, within a short
historical period, have brought the birthrate down from a high,
virtually unrestricted level to a low, deliberately planned one.
The family is not only the primary nucleus of society; it is also the
primary nucleus for reproduction of the population. As the product
of a specific social system, it reflects that system's development.
It is through the family that all the socioeconomic and sociopsychological factors combine to influence human behavior,
including reproduction.[2]

Prerevolutionary Russia's economy was predominantly agricultural, and the large peasant family was the predominant
type of family. In the urban population there was a fairly large
stratum of small proprietors. The peasant's and handicraftsman's
family was at the same time the unit of production and consumption.
It also performed a basic demographic function: reproduction
of the population. Woman's productive labor was closely
linked, in both time and space, to her household duties of
providing for the family's consumption and looking after children. The level of the peasant and handicraft economy made
it possible to use child labor at a fairly early age, since work
operations were comparatively simple and usually required
no special training. Most children usually began to share in
various jobs at age 10 or 12. Under these circumstances the
family had a tangible, vested interest in children, especially
taking into account the high rate of infant mortality. Furthermore, in the absence of any state social security system for
old people, children were regarded as a form of old-age
security.

The most important features of demographic behavior typical of an agrarian society are rigid social control over that
behavior and strict adherence to social mores in marriage, childbearing, sexual behavior, and so on. All these norms were
prescribed by tradition or religion, and public opinion kept a

strict eye on adherence to them.[3] Social mores oriented woman toward the idea that her fundamental, primary destiny was motherhood. And the overwhelming majority of women saw the purpose of their life in being wife, mother, and housewife. Their social prestige was judged mainly by their achievements as mothers.

Thus economic conditions and the psychological premises set by them determined demographic behavior, which was oriented toward a high birthrate and large families. The demographic approach to mortality was largely fatalistic. It can succinctly be expressed in the words, "What the Lord giveth, the Lord taketh away."

The fundamental socioeconomic changes in our country as a result of the socialist revolution contributed to the economic, social, and cultural progress of society, which found expression in industrialization, urbanization, higher labor productivity, and the rising educational and cultural standards of the population.

In these conditions the family has ceased to be a production nucleus, especially under urban conditions. The consumer functions of the family are also changing substantially, growing narrower as its members and the family as a whole increasingly turn to public domestic services, public dining, etc.

At the same time, it is our opinion that the importance of the family's demographic function is substantially higher at our country's present stage of development. This claim may at first glance seem paradoxical given the preponderance of small families (one or two children) in the USSR today. However, in speaking of the family's demographic and reproductive function, we should bear in mind not only the quantitative but also the qualitative reproduction of generations; both aspects must be taken together. Let us dwell in greater detail on some aspects of reproduction of the population, the importance of which increases with social progress.

The current level of productive forces imposes great demands on education and skills in all spheres of production. This means that the training of highly qualified specialists takes more time and money. Whereas before the revolution, with an

agrarian economy, most children began to work at some job
or other from the age of 10 or 12, today they must study and
be supported almost completely by their parents until age 18 to
23. It follows that a family has to spend more money, and the
parents, especially women, must devote more time to bringing
up children and providing for their needs. Ever higher demands
and expectations are imposed on the mother as one of the child's
principal educators.

The quality of child-rearing depends in many ways on the
intelligence, the level of education, and cultural and intellectual
development of the mother. Whereas formerly the demographic
function of the family was basically reduced to producing
children and physically looking after them, today comprehensive upbringing, including cultural and intellectual development, is a prime, and very labor-consuming, element in the
family's demographic functions. Obviously these functions continue to include producing and looking after children. At the same
time, we would also like to stress that although we draw attention
to the mounting importance of the qualitative reproduction of
generations, this in no way implies any belittling of the need
for their numerical replacement.

The economic factors that once encouraged large families
are now gone. The country has a system of state pensions
coupled with free medical and nursing assistance for disabled
and old people. Hence from the economic point of view, today's
family has no interest in the birth of children.

The social changes in our country have affected not only the
functions of the family but also, and most radically, the position
of women.

These changes are reflected in law in the Constitution of
the USSR, Article 35 of which states, "Women and men in
the USSR enjoy equal rights." Implementation of these
rights is assured by a whole series of state measures, such
as providing women with the same opportunities as men in
receiving an education and vocational training, in work and
remuneration for it, in job promotion and in public, political, and cultural activities. The participation of women in

social production is one of the main prerequisites for social equality. "The first prerequisite for female emancipation," wrote F. Engels, "is the return of the entire female sex to social production; this, in turn, requires that the family cease to be an economic unit of society."[4]

The USSR today leads the world in level of employment of women in social production. According to the 1970 census, 82% of all women of working age (16 to 54 years) were employed in various branches of the economy.[5]

In 1975 women accounted for 51% of all workers and employees and 59% of the specialists with a higher or specialized secondary education.[6] Women's educational level is rising faster than men's. In our view this is due not only to the fact that in the USSR, all conditions needed to obtain a higher or specialized secondary education have been created for women, but also to the specific features of female employment in various industries. Most jobs require a higher or specialized secondary education.

While noting that mass involvement of women in social production is a progressive and legitimate development contributing to their economic and social independence, we must also bear in mind that women perform another social function: motherhood. This aspect of their life is no less important for the development of society than their participation in the production of material and cultural values. The sharing of activity between social production and household duties contains the seeds of a conflict between the social functions performed by women. This may appear in a shift in reproductive behavior toward smaller families, leading to a lower national birthrate.

In our view the birthrate is declining in the Soviet Union today not only because of the greater involvement of women in social production and the reduced free time at the disposal of a working woman. It is common knowledge that in all social formations women who did not belong to the ruling classes (that is, invariably the overwhelming majority) worked all their lives. Nor was their work any easier than that of our contemporaries in either physical effort or working hours. It would thus appear that the changes in the whole range of women's needs, including the desire to have children, are due not so much to women's involvement in social production itself as to changes in social status due to that involvement.

"Needs are the foundation on which the whole behavior and historical activity of man rests, including his thinking, emotions, and will. It is in the dynamics of needs, in their growing complexity, enrichment, and transformation, that the trend toward self-development is most directly manifest; it is the existence of needs that makes behavior active."[7] The system of human needs is shaped by objective conditions, with economic development, the nature of social relations, and the spiritual standards of the society foremost among them.

Human needs can be broadly classified into two groups: material and spiritual. To the material belong the needs for food, clothing, housing, etc.; spiritual needs include work, participation in public life, communication, acquisition and improvement of knowledge, aesthetic pleasure, harmonious development of one's personality, and the like.

All human needs are influenced by the social milieu and depend on the development of productive forces and relations. At the same time, the degree to which social conditions affect different types of needs varies. Thus, in our view, material needs, which also include physiological needs (food, sleep, rest, etc.) are less dependent on social factors than spiritual needs. Some physiological needs are basically the same for people irrespective of education or employment. Such needs as sleep and rest are more a factor of age, physiological characteristics of the organism, and the nature of one's work (physical or mental) than of a person's educational, cultural, or spiritual level. Of course, we have in mind the material needs of people living within the same socioeconomic formation.

Man's material, and especially natural, needs are, of course, limited by his physical capabilities, and they can be met to the point of saturation.

The second group of needs is an entirely different matter. These needs, which can be called spiritual, tend to grow indefinitely, change qualitatively, and breed new needs. Of course, they differ substantially in persons with different cultural and educational backgrounds, who are employed or not in social production, and who have different professional and occupational training.

"Under the conditions of developed socialism," writes V. G. Afanas'ev, "needs change radically, they become more diversified and refined, and material needs recede to the background. The need for creative endeavor, public activity, communication with other people and the collective advances in one's education and culture, and for comprehensive, reliable information about life in our country and abroad occupies an ever greater place among the factors of human behavior."[8] Spiritual needs demand more and more free time, and often money, to be satisfied. The more educated and intelligent a woman, the more active her participation in social production and extensive her range of spiritual needs.

Education, cultural background, and employment in social labor are key factors affecting one's scope of interest, system of values, and system of needs. The system of needs is a multitude of requirements of different degrees of value. "The need to have children is a sociopsychological trait of the individual; its manifestations are that, without children and the right number of them, the individual experiences difficulties as a personality."[9] The need for a first child is great. All or almost all families experience it. The need for a second, to say nothing of a third or more, child often comes into conflict with other family needs. It differs substantially in women with different levels of education, urban and rural dwellers, those belonging to different occupational groups, etc.

In our view, at the present stage of historical development, the need to have children among the people of our country is a spiritual need, insofar as today the family has no economic incentive to have children. Hence, in deciding whether to have children, people are motivated not by material considerations but by the desire to experience the totality of parental feelings. Contact with children, caring for them, and responsibility for their lives make people spiritually rich and mature and promote their harmonious development. In recent years, how-

288

ever, more and more families tend to satisfy this need with fewer and fewer children, often only one. At the same time, sample surveys carried out by Soviet scientists indicate that the majority of people consider two or more children to be preferable for a family.[10]

It is natural to ask why many women who think that it is best to have two or three children restrict themselves to having and bringing up only one.

There is probably no single answer to this question. Nevertheless special studies, the views of demographers, economists, sociologists, psychologists, and other experts, as well as hundreds of letters to magazines and newspapers provide some idea of the motivations of most women who restrict themselves to having and raising one child, or more rarely two.

A mother today usually finds herself in a poorer situation than men or childless women, notably with respect to the use she can make of her free time.

Academician S. G. Strumilin said in an interview: "Free time acquires added significance in connection with the resolutions of the Twenty-fourth Party Congress on raising the material and cultural standards of the people: it not only provides scope for the comprehensive development of man and worker but is an essential condition for attaining higher living standards. I long ago came to the conclusion that time is worth more than money; today this idea has found added confirmation."[11] The results of a number of sociological surveys of the time budgets of industrial workers and office employees show, however, that mothers with young children spend 30 to 40 hours a week on domestic work, leaving no more than 10 to 15 hours of free time.[12]

Women's wages depend on the quantity and quality of work, and social security depends solely on length of service and earned wages. Women without children or with only one child have greater opportunities to raise their occupational standards and consequently to receive higher pay and better pension benefits than mothers bringing up two or more children. The same is true of one's service record and its continuity. A working woman in our society enjoys considerable prestige in the eyes of both society and her family. Furthermore, employment in social production assures her both economic and social independence as well as the right to social security in old age.

These factors cultivate in the majority of the population, and especially among women, a reproductive behavior oriented toward small families. This was clearly revealed by a number of surveys. We find especially indicative in this respect a survey conducted in Moscow in 1970 by the Demographic Research Center and entitled "Causes of the Small-Family Mentality among Women in Moscow." [13]

One of the questions in the poll was: If your husband met all the family's material demands, would you agree not to work and devote yourself completely to bringing up children and housework? Seventy-seven percent responded that they would not want to give up work completely. On the question of vocation, 76% said they would prefer to combine household duties with work, only 19% said they would agree not to work and be only wife and mother, and 5% either gave no answer or said they preferred to devote themselves mainly to work and public activities.

Similar results were obtained in a sample poll of women in Moscow in 1974. [14] That survey showed that most women wanted to work in social production throughout their able-bodied years. Some 80% of the respondents objected to the idea of working until children began to appear and then resuming work after they had grown up, claiming that they would lose their occupational skills and knowledge, lose touch with the work collective, and forfeit their high earnings. About 70% of the women answered in the affirmative to the question: "Would you continue to work if your husband earned as much as you now do together?"

Judging by their answers, the family is ceasing to be the center that absorbs all a woman's efforts, energy, and concerns. Women need not only family life but also social communication and social activities. And it is mainly work in social production that provides social contact and a sense of self-worth.

As for reproductive behavior, in the 1970 survey the absolute majority of respondents were oriented toward small families, with 25% opting for one child and 60% for two. Actually the mean number of children among the surveyed women was 1.04, the average for the voiced preference was 1.81, while the mean for the ideal number was 2.48.[15]   One need not be an expert in demography to understand that if most families have one or two children, population growth will be negative, and the generation of children will be smaller than the generation of parents. In the view of B. Ts. Urlanis, simple reproduction of generations now requires that 10 couples have 25 children, with 26 or 27 for slightly expanded reproduction.[16]

We fully accept this view and would also like to stress that two or three children in a family is, in most cases, best not only in terms of quantity but also in terms of quality of reproduction. The negative consequences of the spread of one-child families (not only economic, but sociopsychological, moral, and genetic) have been noted by many scholars.[17]   On the other hand, of course, any appeal for very large families would at present hardly be in the best interests of the nation's social development. It would be contrary to the historically inevitable, socially determined transition from unrestricted childbirth to parental planning of how many children they will have and when to have them.

At the present stage of social development, not only women but society itself is interested in the massive participation of women in social production (which, furthermore, is today economically inevitable). It follows that it is unrealistic to raise the question of substantially reducing female employment. At the same time, the reproductive (and educational) functions of the family will retain their importance for many years to come. Nor can society remain indifferent to the way in which passing generations are replaced by new ones.

If we distinguish between people's individual needs and those of society as a whole, we must say that the need to have children is a requirement not only of the individual and the family but of society as a whole, insofar as "reproduction of life as

291

such" is one of the determining elements in the existence of
society. 18   But whereas the need of a family for children can
be satisfied with one or two offspring, even simple reproduction of
the population requires families with two or three children.
Attainment of a national birthrate that would be in keeping both
with the interests of social development and the interests of
the individual family is possible through an effective demographic policy that is a component of the socioeconomic policies
of the state. In our country, where all the levers for influencing
demographic processes (economic, administrative, sociopsychological) are in the hands of society, it is possible to pursue
successful demographic policies.

The prime prerequisite of a successful demographic policy
is its comprehensive character. It is necessary both to make
use of diverse measures and at the same time coordinate their
influence on all forms of population movement.

Demographic policies can be broadly classified in three
groups: economic, legal-administrative, and sociopsychological. Their common purpose is to promote the optimum type
of population reproduction.

Demographic policies have their specific character. For
example, demographic measures involving birthrates should
not legally regulate the number of children per family. This
would, in the first place, run contrary to the very essence of
the socialist system. Besides, compulsory measures often
arouse negative reactions and can have an opposite effect.

The purpose of demographic policy is not to influence birthrates directly, but rather to foster general opinions about the
desirable number of children a family should have.

This means that demographic policies concerning the birthrate should, on the one hand, aim at cultivating a healthy and
reasonable need for children in the family, and on the other,
take into account that having and raising children impose
substantial material and psychological burdens on parents and
take up much of their free time. Having and raising children
should be viewed not as parents' private concern but as their
performance of a major social task. Society should view the

effort to bring up children as socially useful and develop a
system of ways to evaluate and remunerate it.

We need greater public recognition of parenthood, which
would enhance the social status of motherhood and fatherhood;
this in turn would help develop a need to have children in keeping with the interests of both the family and society.

The attainment of a level of reproduction that corresponds
to the needs of our social and economic development presents
society with the task of drawing up and adopting a set of measures
to help women successfully combine work in social production with
motherhood. The Report of the Central Committee of the CPSU
to the Twenty-fifth Party Congress stated: "The party sees as
its duty constant concern for women, for improving their position as participants in the work process, as mothers and counselors for their children, and as housewives."[19] In drawing
up demographic policies one must be guided by this statement
as well as by the provision, recorded in Article 35 of the
Constitution of the USSR, that along with equal opportunities
with men in all spheres of public life, women must be
assured special measures in industrial safety and health protection; conditions must be created to enable women to combine
work and motherhood; and we must provide legal protection and
material and moral support for motherhood and childhood, including paid vacations and other benefits for pregnant women
and mothers and the gradual reduction of working hours for
women with small children.

One of the main tasks of demographic policy, which is an
essential component of the overall social and economic policies of the state, is to elaborate comprehensive measures
aimed at creating these conditions. In speaking of elaborating
demographic policies involving the birthrate, it should be
stressed that along with measures aimed at the population as a
whole, it is necessary to draw up separate, specific measures
that take into account the distinctive life styles and behavior
of separate local population groups. Demographic policies
are a direct function of the social system and the dominant
mode of production relations. Only in a socialist society, with

G. Kiseleva

its planned economy, is it possible to utilize in their most effective forms the most diverse methods of encouraging childbirth addressed to the whole population and to its separate
groups, from economic measures providing for substantial material assistance to families with children, to sociopsychological measures aimed at fostering notions about the desirability
of two- or three-child families instead of one-child families.
Developed socialist society possesses all the prerequisites for
successfully solving problems involving the elaboration and
implementation of an effective demographic policy.

Notes

1. See Materialy XXV s"ezda KPSS, Moscow, 1976, p. 73.
2. As defined by V. A. Borisov, "Reproductive behavior is the system of actions and relations affecting the birth, or nonbirth, of a child, in whatever order,
in or out of wedlock" (V. A. Borisov, Perspektivy rozhdaemosti, Moscow, 1976,
p. 16).
3. See A. G. Vishnevskii, Demograficheskaia revoliutsiia, Moscow, 1976,
pp. 126-30.
4. K. Marx and F. Engels, Sochineniia, vol. 21, p. 77.
5. See Naselenie SSSR, Moscow, 1974, p. 143.
6. See Narodnoe khoziaistvo SSSR v 1975 g., Moscow, 1976, pp. 541, 550.
7. P. V. Simonov, Vysshaia nervnaia deiatel'nost' cheloveka. Motivatsionno-
emotsional'nye aspekty, Moscow, 1975, p. 6.
8. V. G. Afanas'ev, "Chelovek: upravlenie samim soboi," in Nauchnoe upravlenie obshchestvom, Moscow, 1976, p. 262.
9. A. I. Antonov, "Problemy sotsiologicheskogo izucheniia reproduktivnogo
povedeniia sem'i," in Voprosy teorii i metodov sotsiologicheskikh issledovanii,
Moscow, 1974, p. 115.
10. See V. A. Belova, Chislo detei v sem'e, Moscow, 1975, pp. 46, 93.
11. S. G. Strumilin, "Akademiia nauk i zhizn'," Ekonomika i organizatsiia
promyshlennogo proizvodstva, 1974, no. 1, p. 19.
12. See L. A. Gordon, "Organizatsiia byta," Ekonomika i organizatsiia promyshlennogo proizvodstva, 1976, no. 6, p. 115.
13. The survey, in which the author took part, was conducted at 11 Moscow
enterprises and offices. A total of 5,226 married working women between the
ages of 18 and 45 were polled (see N. Tauber, "Usloviia zhizni sem'i i srednee
chislo detei," in Demograficheskii analiz rozhdaemosti, Moscow, 1974, p. 14;
G. Kiseleva, "Skol'ko u vas detei?" Nauka i zhizn', 1974, no. 6.
14. See Z. A. Iankova, "Razvitie lichnosti zhenshchiny v sovetskom obshchestve" Sotsiologicheskie issledovaniia, 1975, no. 4, p. 43.
15. Obviously, in analyzing the reproductive behavior of people in Moscow it

is necessary to take into account that as the capital and largest city of the USSR, Moscow has many specific features and, consequently, some distinctive aspects to the reproductive behavior of its inhabitants. At the same time, first the inhabitants of large cities, and then of other parts of the country, in large measure assimilate the basic mores and norms of behavior, demographic included, of the inhabitants of the capital.

16. See B. Ts. Urlanis, Problemy dinamiki naseleniia SSSR, Moscow, 1974, p. 288; B. Ts. Urlanis, "Skol'ko nado imet' detei?" in Narodonaselenie: issledovaniia, publitsistika, Moscow, 1976, p. 323.

17. See Osnovy teorii narodonaseleniia, D. I. Valentei, ed., Moscow, 1973, pp. 31-33; V. A. Borisov, Perspektivy rozhdaemosti, Moscow, 1976, pp. 229-31.

18. See Marx and Engels, Sochineniia, vol. 21, p. 25.

19. Materialy XXV s"ezda KPSS, p. 85.

APPENDIXES

Appendix A

From The Principles of Labor Legislation of The USSR
and The Union Republics

VIII. WOMEN'S LABOR

Art. 68. Work at Which Women May Not Be Employed. — It is forbidden to employ women in heavy work, in work with harmful working conditions, or in jobs underground except certain ones (non-manual labor and work in health and other services).

Art. 69. Restrictions on Assigning Women to Night Work, Overtime, or Business Trips. — It is not permitted to assign women to night work except in branches of the economy where this is called for by particular necessity, and then only as a temporary measure.

It is not permitted to assign pregnant women, nursing mothers or women with children under one year of age to night work, overtime, work on days off, or business trips.

It is not permitted to assign women with children aged one to eight to overtime work or to business trips, without their consent.

Art. 70. Transfer of Pregnant Women, Nursing Mothers and Women With Children Under One Year of Age to Lighter Work. — On the basis of a medical certificate, a pregnant woman is transferred to other, lighter work for the duration of pregnancy, with retention of her previous average earnings.

Nursing mothers and women with children under one year of age, if unable to perform their former work, are transferred to other work with retention of the previous average earnings until the infant is weaned or until the child reaches the age of one year.

Art. 71. Leaves for Pregnancy and Childbirth. — Women are granted leaves for pregnancy and childbirth, from 56 calendar days before childbirth until 56 calendar days following it, with payment of state social insurance benefits during this period. In the event of complications during childbirth or the birth of two or more children, a leave of 70 calendar days is granted following childbirth.

In addition to the leave for pregnancy and childbirth, a woman may, on request, be granted additional leave without pay until the child reaches the age of one year.

Art. 72. Breaks for Nursing an Infant. — Nursing mothers and women with

Pravda, July 17, 1970, pp. 2-4. Translation from _Current Digest of the Soviet Press_, vol. XXII, no. 34, p. 8.

children under one year of age are granted, apart from the common break for rest and meals, additional time for nursing the baby.

These breaks are granted at least every three hours, for at least 30 minutes each.

Breaks for nursing a child are included in working time and are paid at the mother's average rate of earnings.

Art. 73. Guarantees to Pregnant Women, Nursing Mothers and Women With Children Under One Year of Age Regarding Employment and Prohibition Against Discharging Them. — It is forbidden to refuse women employment or to reduce their earnings on account of pregnancy or nursing a child.

Dismissal of a pregnant woman, a nursing mother or a woman with a child under one year of age at the initiative of the administration is not permitted except in cases of complete dissolution of the enterprise, institution or organization, dismissal then being permitted with obligatory provision of another job.

Appendix B

Article 35 of Chapter 6 of the USSR Constitution of 1977

Article 35. Women and men have equal rights in the USSR. The exercise of these rights is insured by providing women with opportunities equal <u>to those of men</u>. In receiving an education and vocational training, in labor, remuneration and promotion and in social, political and cultural activity as well as by special measures to protect women's labor and health; <u>by the creation of conditions enabling women to combine labor and motherhood</u>; by legal protection and material and moral support for mother and child including the granting of paid leave and other benefits to pregnant women and mothers; and by the gradual reduction of working time for women with small children. [State aid to single mothers.]

Translation from *Current Digest of the Soviet Press*, vol. XXIX, no. 41, p. 5. Underlining indicates additions to the draft version; brackets indicate material dropped from the draft.

Appendix C

Excerpt from L. I. Brezhnev's Report of the CPSU Central Committee
to the Twenty-sixth Congress of the Communist Party, February 23, 1981

In accordance with the directives of the Twenty-fifth Party Congress, the Central Committee has given serious attention to the formulation and implementation of an effective demographic policy, since population problems have recently become more acute. The principal way to solve these problems is by increasing concern for the family, newlyweds, and above all, women. After all, it is clear to each of us how difficult it is at times to combine the responsibilities of a mother with active participation in production and public life.

During the Tenth Five-Year Plan, a series of measures was taken to improve working conditions for women, family recreation, and consumer and cultural services. It is necessary, however, to say frankly that as yet no appreciable change has taken place. Broader and more effective measures are needed. As is known, such measures are outlined in the Basic Guidelines. I am talking about the introduction of partially paid leaves of up to one year for mothers to care for a child, of shorter workdays for mothers of young children, and of expanding the network and improving the operation of children's preschool institutions, schools with extended-day groups, and all consumer services. The Guidelines provide for increased children's allowances, especially in connection with the birth of a second or third child. Clearly we cannot accomplish all that we would like to at once. But we will persistently search for ways to solve all these problems. In doing so, of course, we should give careful consideration to the special features of the situation in the various republics and regions.

Izvestia, February 24, 1981, pp. 2-9; translation by Gail W. Lapidus.

Appendix D

Excerpts from the Decree of the CPSU Central Committee
and the USSR Council of Ministers, "On Measures to Increase
State Assistance to Families with Children," January 22, 1981

The CPSU Central Committee and the USSR Council of Ministers, regarding assistance to families in the rearing of children as an important element of the social program for the development of our society, have deemed it advisable to carry out additional measures to increase state assistance to families with children, in order to ensure the sensible combination of the public and familial upbringing of children, to make things easier for working mothers, and to create favorable living conditions for young families. The resolution provides:

for working mothers who have total work records of at least one year and for women who are engaged in fulltime study, the introduction — to begin in 1981 and to be put into effect region by region — of partially paid leave to care for children until they reach the age of one year. The remuneration for this leave will be 50 rubles per month in the Far East, Siberia and the country's northern regions and 35 rubles per month in the remaining regions; and the granting to working women, simultaneously with the introduction of the aforementioned leave, of the right to additional leave without pay to care for children until they reach the age of 18 months, and subsequently the age of two years, preserving the woman's uninterrupted job record and her work record in her specialty.

The implementation of measures to increase the length of leave to care for newborn and young children and to raise the amount of remuneration for this leave will be continued during the 12th Five-Year Plan.

All-round development of the network of kindergartens and day-care centers, extended-day schools and groups, Young Pioneer camps and other children's institutions will be ensured in the 11th and 12th Five-Year Plans. The USSR State Planning Committee, the Union-republic Councils of Ministers and the USSR ministries and departments have been instructed to make provision in their draft plans for the fullest possible satisfaction of requirements for permanent and seasonal preschool institutions, with a view to eliminating, within the next few years, the shortage of such institutions in regions with a high level of female employment in social production.

When necessary, preschool institutions or groups for around-the-clock care of children, including on Sundays and holidays, are to be set up, and the exchange of places in district (borough) and departmental day-care centers

Translation from *Current Digest of the Soviet Press*, vol. XXXIII, no. 13, pp. 9-10.

and kindergartens is to be practiced more widely.

To improve the staffing of day-care centers and day-care groups at kindergarten-nursery schools and infants' homes [for children up to the age of three — Trans.] with qualified personnel, it has been decided that during the 11th Five-Year Plan the six-hour workday and the 36-day vacation established for kindergarten teachers will be extended to nurses working at these institutions.

The 11th Five-Year Plan makes provision for increasing the norms for food expenditures at preschool institutions by an average of 10% to 15%, and also for exempting families whose average income per family member does not exceed 60 rubles per month from making payments for the maintenance of children at day-care centers, kindergartens and boarding schools.

With a view to creating more favorable conditions for women that will enable them to combine work in social production with the rearing of children:

the Union-republic Councils of Ministers and the USSR ministries and departments have been instructed to work out and implement measures for the broad dissemination of the practice of employing women on schedules based on a short workday or short workweek, according to a sliding (flexible) schedule, or for homework;

for working women who have two or more children under the age of 12, to grant, beginning in 1981: an additional three-day paid leave (provided that total leave does not exceed 28 calendar days); a priority right to take annual leave during the summer or at another time that is convenient for them; and the right to as much as two weeks of additional unpaid leave to care for children, with the consent of management and at a time when production conditions permit; and,

during the 11th Five-Year Plan, to increase to 14 days the length of paid leave to care for a sick child, with additional days over and above the number specified by legislation currently in force to be paid at 50% of earnings.

The resolution provides for a number of measures to improve the material security of families with children, including:

to institute, during the 11th Five-Year Plan, the payment of lump-sum state allowances to working mothers and mothers who are full-time students, in amounts of 50 rubles for the birth of the first child and 100 rubles for the birth of second and third children, retaining the present sizes of the allowances paid for the birth of fourth and subsequent children; and

to increase in 1981 the size of the state allowance for single mothers to 20 rubles per month per child, with payments to be made until the child attains the age of 16 (or 18, for pupils who are not receiving stipends).

Provision has been made, beginning in 1981, to establish additional benefits in setting old-age pensions for women with less than a full work record who have raised five or more children or a disabled child.

A number of measures have been set to expand privileges for families with children and for newlyweds in obtaining state housing space and in individual and cooperative housing construction. It has been decided, during the 11th Five-Year Plan, to exempt newlyweds from payment of the tax on citizens with small families during the first year after their marriage is registered.

Appendix D

It has been deemed necessary to continue to pursue a policy of preferential state retail prices for children's goods. It is also necessary to increase the responsibility of ministries and enterprises that produce children's goods for satisfying the requirements for these goods of families with various income levels, without permitting a decrease in the production of inexpensive children's goods that are in public demand.

The resolution sets tasks involving serious improvements in the work of trade, public-catering and consumer-service enterprises, with a view to easing housework and reducing the time spent on housekeeping.

The implementation of a system of measures in the interests of protecting and enhancing the health of pregnant women and of children has been projected. The 11th Five-Year Plan envisages the introduction of additional benefits with respect to payment for accommodations in Young Pioneer camps, and it makes provision for the further development of the network of guest houses and other health-improvement institutions for family recreation.

The appropriate organizations have been instructed to increase the publication of literature on questions of demography, the family, marital hygiene, child-rearing, the enhancement of public health and the organization of worthwhile recreation and leisure-time activities and to intensify upbringing work with a view to strengthening the family as one of the highest moral values of socialist society.

Appendix E

Protection of Women

6. ON SUPPLEMENTARY MEASURES FOR IMPROVING THE CONDITIONS OF LABOR FOR WOMEN EMPLOYED IN THE NATIONAL ECONOMY

For the purpose of further improving the conditions of labor of women employed in the national economy and the protection of their health, the Council of Ministers of the USSR and the All-Union Central Council of Trade Unions decree:

1. To delegate to the State Committee of the Council of Ministers of the USSR on Labor and Social Questions together with the All-Union Central Council of Trade Unions and by Agreement with the USSR Ministry of Health, to approve, by July 1, 1978, a new List of production operations, occupations, and jobs with difficult and dangerous working conditions at which the application of the women's labor is forbidden, and also to establish the procedure and conditions for the application of this List.

2. For ministries and departments of the USSR, councils of ministers of union and autonomous republics, province, region, area, city, and district executive committees of soviets of people's deputies, for heads of enterprises and organizations, to ensure the job placement of women released from heavy work and work with dangerous conditions of labor, and where job placement is impossible in their occupations (or specialities), to ensure their respecialization or training in new skills.

3. To maintain for women released from difficult work and work with dangerous conditions of labor in accordance with this decree:

a) an uninterrupted period of work, if the interruption between the date of release from doing difficult work and work with dangerous conditions of labor and the date of starting other work or study does not exceed six months;

b) the average monthly wage at the previous place of work for the period of study or retraining, but not over six months;

c) the right to use departmental housing as well as children's preschool institutions at the previous place of work.

4. For the State Committee of the Council of Ministers of the USSR for Vocational and Technical Education, and the ministries and departments engaged in preparation of cadres for the national economy, to cease, starting in 1978, ac-

---

Decree of the Council of Ministers of the USSR and the All-Union Central Council of Trade Unions of April 25, 1978. Translation from *Soviet Statutes and Decisions*, Fall 1979, no. 1.

ceptance of women for training in the professions provided in the List indicated in Paragraph 1 of the present decree.

5. For the ministries and departments of the USSR and the councils of ministers of the union republics together with the central committees and republic councils of trade unions, by January 1, 1979, to prepare and approve plans of measures for 1979-85 for the mechanization of hand work and the further improvement of the health conditions of women's work.

6. To establish that changes in and additions to the List of production operations, occupations, and jobs with difficult and dangerous working conditions at which application of the labor of women is prohibited may be made by ministries, heads of departments of the USSR, and by the councils of ministers of the union republics by agreement with the State Committee of the Council of Ministers of the USSR on Labor and Social Questions, the USSR Ministry of Health, and the All-Union Central Council of Trade Unions.

7. Supervision of the fulfillment of measures provided by the present decree shall be exercised by the State Committee of the Council of Ministers of the USSR on Labor and Social Questions and the All-Union Central Council of Trade Unions.

8. For the USSR Central Statistical Administration to augment statistical reporting on labor with indicators of the number of women released from difficult work and work with dangerous conditions of labor by branches of industry and the national economy.

9. In connection with the present decree, to repeal as of July 1, 1978, decisions of the Government of the USSR in accordance with the attached List.

[List of repealed decisions not translated]

Appendix F

7. ON APPROVAL OF A LIST OF PRODUCTION OPERATIONS, OCCUPA-
TIONS, AND JOBS WITH DIFFICULT AND DANGEROUS WORKING CONDI-
TIONS AT WHICH APPLICATION OF THE LABOR OF WOMEN IS FOR-
BIDDEN

In fulfillment of the Decree of the Council of Ministers of the USSR and the
All-Union Central Council of Trade Unions of April 25, 1978, No. 320, "On Supplementary Measures for Improving the Conditions of Labor of Women Occupied
in the National Economy," the State Committee of the USSR on Labor and Social
Questions and the Presidium of the All-Union Central Council of Trade Unions
decree:

1. To approve, with the agreement of the USSR Ministry of Health, a new List
of production operations, occupations, and jobs with difficult and dangerous
working conditions at which the application of the labor of women is forbidden,
in accord with the Appendix.

For ministries and departments of the USSR and the councils of ministers of
the union republics, on the basis of the decree of the Council of Ministers of the
USSR and the All-Union Central Council of Trade Unions of April 25, 1978,
No. 320, to implement the release of women from the work provided by the
present list, on schedules developed jointly with the central committees and republic councils of trade unions during a period up to January 1, 1981.

2. Job placement of women released from difficult work and work with dangerous conditions of labor, and in case of impossibility of job placement in their
occupations (or specialities), respecialization or training in new occupations
shall be provided in accordance with the decree of the Council of Ministers of
the USSR and the All-Union Central Council of Trade Unions of April 25, 1978,
No. 320, by ministries and departments of the USSR, councils of ministers of
union and autonomous republics, province, region, area, city, and district executive committees of Councils of People's Deputies, heads of enterprises and organizations.

The discharging of women released from performance of difficult work and
work with dangerous conditions of labor, in case of their refusal of transfer to
other work, shall be made on the basis of the decree of the Council of Ministers
of the USSR and the All-Union Central Council of Trade Unions of April 25, 1978,
No. 320 with the payment of a termination allowance.

Decree of the State Committee of the USSR on Labor and Social Matters and the Presidium
of the All-Union Central Council of Trade Unions of July 25, 1978, No. 240/P10-3. Translation
from *Soviet Statutes and Decisions*, Fall 1979, no. 1.

3. For women released from performing heavy work and work with dangerous conditions of labor in accordance with the Decree of the Council of Ministers of the USSR and the All-Union Central Council of Trade Unions of April 25, 1978, No. 320, the following shall be preserved:

a) an uninterrupted period of work in the awarding of benefits under state social insurance, calculation of supplements to state pensions, payment of one-time compensation or supplements to wages for years of service, and compensation on the results of annual work, provision of privileges to persons working in districts of the Extreme North and localities equivalent to districts of the Extreme North, and also Archangelsk Region, the Karelian Autonomous Soviet Socialist Republic, and the Komi Autonomous Soviet Socialist Republic, and in other instances, when any rights, privileges, and preferences are connected with the uninterrupted nature of a period of work. The uninterrupted period of work shall be preserved if the interruption between the date of release from difficult work and work with dangerous conditions of labor and the date of starting other work or study does not exceed six months.

b) the average monthly wage at the previous place of work for the time of study or retraining, but not over six months. The average monthly wage shall be calculated from the total of the wage for the last two calendar months at the previous place of work in accordance with the procedure set forth in the decree of the People's Commissariat of Labor of the USSR of April 2, 1930, No. 142, "On the Average Wage and Payment for an Incomplete Month."

c) the right of use of organizational housing, and also children's preschool institutions at the previous place of work.

4) For women released on the basis of the decree of the Council of Ministers of the USSR and the All-Union Central Council of Trade Unions of April 25, 1978, from doing work giving the right to receipt of one-time compensation for years of service, payment for it shall be made upon final accounting in proportion to the time worked in the given calendar year. Payment on the totals of annual labor shall be paid by them during the period established for the enterprise or organization, on the basis of the wage actually received in the given calendar year.

5. To establish that the use of the labor of women in production operations, occupations, and jobs with difficult and dangerous conditions of labor provided in the List approved by the present decree shall be forbidden, regardless of the branches of the national economy at whose enterprises such production operations, occupations, and jobs exist.

6. For the state committees of the councils of ministers of the union republics on labor, the central committees, the republic, province, and regional councils of trade unions, to establish supervision of the release of women from difficult work and work with dangerous conditions of labor, their job placement and the organization of training in new occupations.

[Appendix not translated]

About the Editor

Gail Warshofsky Lapidus is Associate Professor of Political Science and Chair of the Center for Slavic and East European Studies at the University of California at Berkeley.

She received her Ph.D. from Harvard University. Professor Lapidus coedited Women in Russia with Dorothy Atkinson and Alexander Dallin, and she is the author of Women in Soviet Society, as well as numerous articles on Soviet society and politics.